W0037921

Fort Randall on the Missouri

Jerome A. Greene

Fort

Randall

on the Missouri 1856–1892

South Dakota State Historical Society Press PIERRE, SOUTH DAKOTA

© 2005

South Dakota State Historical Society Press

All rights reserved. This book or portions thereof in any form whatsoever may not
be reproduced without the expressed written approval of the South Dakota State
Historical Society Press, 900 Governors Drive, Pierre, SD 57501.

The activity that is the subject of this book has been funded, in part, with financial
assistance from the National Park Service through the South Dakota Historic
Preservation Office (SHPO), a program that receives federal financial assistance from
the National Park Service. Title VI of the Civil Rights Act of 1964, Section 504 of
the Rehabilitation Act of 1973, the Americans with Disabilities Act of 1990, South
Dakota law SDCL 20-13, the State of South Dakota, and U.S. Department of the
Interior prohibit discrimination on the basis of race, color, creed, religion, sex,
disability, ancestry, or national origin. If you believe you have been discriminated
against in any program, activity, or facility as described above, or if you desire
more information, please write to: South Dakota Division of Human Rights, State
Capitol, Pierre, SD 57501, or the Office of Equal Opportunity, National Park Service,
201 I Street NW, Washington, D.C. 20240.

This publication is funded, in part, by the Great Plains Education Foundation, Inc.,
Aberdeen S.Dak.

Library of Congress
Cataloging-in-Publication data
Greene, Jerome A.
Fort Randall on the Missouri, 1856–1892 / by Jerome A. Greene.
p. cm.
Includes bibliographical references and index.
ISBN 0-9777955-0-0
1. Fort Randall Region (S.D.)—History. 2. Fort Randall Historical Site (S.D.)
3. Frontier and pioneer life—South Dakota—Fort Randall Region. 4. Frontier
and pioneer life—Missouri River Valley. 5. United States. Army—Military life—
History—19th century. 6. Indians of North America—Wars—South Dakota.
7. Indians of North America—Wars—1866–1895. I. Title.
F659.F678G74 2005
978.3'59—dc22
2005017911

Printed in the United States of America

12 11 10 09 08 07 06   8 7 6 5 4 3 2

Contents

List of Illustrations

Acknowledgments

This study of Fort Randall has benefited from the assistance of numerous individuals and offices. I wish to thank the staff at Missouri National Recreational River, O'Neill, Nebraska, especially Superintendent Paul L. Hedren, Management Assistant Phil Campbell, Interpretive Specialist George Berndt, Administrative Officer Laurie Wise, and Administrative Assistant Jo Harkins. At the Harpers Ferry Center, I must thank my supervisor, John Brucksch, Deputy Associate Manager for Planning and Research, for permitting me to undertake the project, and Brenda D. Hooper, Administrative Assistant, for her assistance in the clerical and budget-keeping aspects of the assignment. Other individuals and institutions that provided materials or otherwise helped in the completion of the study include: Nancy Tystad Koupal, Director of Research and Publishing; Ken R. Stewart, Archivist; Marvene Riis, Acting State Archivist; and Carol Jennings, Research Assistant, South Dakota State Historical Society, Pierre; Douglas P. Sall, Director, Dakota Territorial Museum, Yankton, South Dakota; Thomas R. Buecker, Curator, Fort Robinson Museum, Fort Robinson State Park, Crawford, Nebraska, James E. Potter, Historian, Nebraska State Historical Society, Lincoln, Nebraska; R. Eli Paul, Overland Park, Kansas; Ephriam Dickson, Utah Museum of Natural History, Salt Lake City, Utah; Taran Schindler, Beinecke Rare Book and Manuscript Library, Yale University, New Haven, Connecticut; Virgil Dean and Nancy Sherbert, Kansas State Historical Society, Topeka; Larry Ness, Yankton, South Dakota; Craig Kenkel, Ron Cockrell, and Rachel Weekley, National Park Service Midwest Regional Office, Omaha, Nebraska; Thomas D. Thiessen and Douglas D. Scott, National Park Service Midwest Archeological Center, Lincoln, Nebraska; Gayla Koerting, Special Collections Librarian, and Anne Hinseth, Archives Assistant, I. D. Weeks Library, University of South Dakota, Vermillion; David Mook, Sioux City Public Library, Sioux City, Iowa; Elaine Gnirk, Burke, South Dakota; John F. Dunn, Hollis, New Hampshire; Ralph G. Porris, Williamsburg, Virginia; James May, Little Rock, Arkansas; Jack Broome, Burke, South Dakota; William A. Dobak, Office of the Chief of Military History, Washington, D.C.; John D. McDermott, Rapid City, South Dakota; Bob Rea, Fort Supply Historic Site, Fort Supply, Oklahoma; Andrew R. Supplee, North Sutton,

New Hampshire; Charles Mulhair, Niobrara, Nebraska; and Wayne F. McCray, Baton Rouge, Louisiana. I must particularly thank Richard J. Sommers, Director, Library and Manuscripts Division; Kathy Olson, Librarian and Archivist; and Randy Hackenburg, Photo Archivist, U.S. Army Military History Institute, Army War College, Carlisle Barracks, Pennsylvania.

In addition, I acknowledge the help of the following repositories and their staffs: National Archives, Washington, D.C.; U.S. Army Military History Institute, Army War College, Carlisle Barracks, Pennsylvania; South Dakota State Historical Society, Pierre; Nebraska State Historical Society, Lincoln; Sioux City Public Museum, Sioux City Public Library; Sioux City, Iowa; Special Collections, I. D. Weeks Library, University of South Dakota, Vermillion; Beinecke Rare Book and Manuscript Library, Yale University, New Haven, Connecticut; Norlin Library, University of Colorado, Boulder; Western History Department, Denver Public Library, Denver; and the Central Plains Region Branch, National Archives, Kansas City, Missouri.

To all of these people and institutions, I express my sincere gratitude.

New Post on the Upper Missouri

Fort Randall stood along the west bank of the Missouri River for thirty-six years and five months between June 1856 and November 1892. Strategically postured near the modern Nebraska boundary in what is present Gregory County, South Dakota, its tenure coincided with the opening by white Americans of much of the trans-Mississippi West, particularly that vast tract embracing the northern Great Plains and the country drained by the many tributaries of the Missouri and Mississippi rivers. Fort Randall began as a salient outpost on the American frontier—at the very demarcation of prairie and plains— and ended as a common garrison enveloped by settlement whose usefulness was superseded by other and later forts prolonging the tentacles of national expansion. It variously witnessed or played a central role in the military subjection, removal, and reconfiguration of Native populations in the region. Because the post stood as an icon of national policy, soldiers stationed at Fort Randall operated at the government's behest, with much of their time directed toward relations with American Indians and maintaining peace among white settlers and between them and the various tribes or in support of those enterprises throughout the northern plains. Indeed, these activities constituted Fort Randall's principal mission for most of its existence.

For several years in the 1850s, the Fort Randall garrison served federally sponsored exploring expeditions. When a major Indian outbreak erupted in Minnesota and Dakota during the Civil War, Fort Randall seasonally ushered men and supplies to the front and quartered troops involved in the campaigns. It also acted as a supply base for goods destined to other area forts and Indian agencies. During the steamboat era of the 1860s and 1870s, the post served as an arrival and departure point along the Missouri River as private and government-sponsored entrepreneurial interests proliferated up that water course as far away as western Montana Territory. During the latter decade, troops from Fort Randall escorted railroad surveyors into the Yellowstone-Powder river region of Montana. The post factored in the opening of the Black Hills, and its soldiers took an active part in the campaigns of the Great Sioux War. In the 1880s, Fort Randall hosted Indian prisoners of war and oversaw the final influx of white settlers into Dakota Territory. Throughout the course of its existence, the post witnessed pronounced changes in its environs, an experience registered during its own transition from a key frontier outpost on the northern plains to a tertiary, sedentary government station whose demise, predicted as early as the 1870s, was assured by the early 1890s. During its existence, Fort Randall stood as a beacon of government authority, a bastion of law and order to Indians and whites alike. Although long physically vanished, the post survives in the institutions that it introduced into the region, in the significant impacts that its garrison had on peoples and surrounding events, and in the burgeoning regional economy propagated by its historical presence. That is Fort Randall's legacy to the country.

The Missouri River and its bountiful resources had long invited human occupation. The stream's open, rolling, and well-watered adjoining lands offered abundant game for sustenance, as well as an area largely free from incursions by enemies. By the early years of the nineteenth century, several Indian tribes called it home, among them the Poncas, Omahas, Yanktons, and Santees. These Siouan-speaking peoples variously hunted and cultivated the region of modern southeastern South Dakota, northeastern Nebraska, southwestern Minnesota, and northwestern Iowa, trading with neighboring groups while occasionally fending off each other and erstwhile Pawnee, Cheyenne, and Lakota (Teton Sioux) intruders from the west and south. Many of the people lived most of the year in earth and grass semipermanent dwellings but moved about utilizing buffalo-hide tipis during the warmer months. These four tribes later became closely associated with Fort Randall, and during the post's existence they constituted the major Indian groups with whom the troops routinely related.

Decades before the establishment of Fort Randall, British and American traders and trappers passed by its future location seeking furs from lands bordering the more northern reaches of the Missouri River. In November 1794, an exploring party of Frenchmen under Jean Baptiste Truteau, intent on evaluating the fur resources of the upper Missouri for St. Louis Spanish interests, passed the winter surrounded by Omahas across the river from and slightly above the future site of Fort Randall. Subsequently, other parties passed by the site on their way north along the Missouri. Following the Louisiana Purchase of 1803, the first United States–sponsored expedition to penetrate the acquisition was headed by Captains Meriwether Lewis and William Clark, who ascended and descended the river in 1804–6 during their journey to and from the Pacific coast. After counciling with the Yankton Sioux in early September 1804, they passed near the future Fort Randall tract, referencing in their journal the place where Truteau had wintered and studying the prairie dogs that abounded there. On the return two years later, near the same site, they encountered a band of Lakotas who tried to intimidate them before the explorers boated downstream to St. Louis.[1]

The Lewis and Clark Expedition at once established American sovereignty in the upper Missouri country, commenced relations with the native peoples who lived there, and otherwise cemented the nation's future commercial hegemony in the region. It also ushered in a period of competition with Great Britain over fur resources and a consequent struggle with that nation over area tribal loyalties that only ended with the conclusion of the War of 1812 and American ascendancy in the fur trade. Much of the reasoning that ultimately affected decisions respecting the establishment of Fort Randall in 1856 was rooted in the fur trade that evolved during the first half of the nineteenth century. That commerce, and the relations with the tribes that became requisite for its existence, lay grounded in the trapping of beaver along the various affluents of the Missouri but more especially in the trade for buffalo hides and tongues with Indians of the upper Missouri basin. Tribes such as the Arikaras and Lakotas played an integral role in the expansion of the fur trade, particularly in the buffalo robe trade, and came to prosper enormously during the height of the enterprise between 1815 and 1850.[2]

During that heyday, a great many trading posts dotted the upper Missouri landscape, with more than one hundred estimated in the area of present South Dakota alone. These spanned the country between the Big Sioux River and the Black Hills, but most were concentrated along the Missouri where major populations of the Lakotas resided. Two posts, Fort Union, at the junction of the Missouri and Yellowstone rivers, and Fort Pierre, above the confluence of the Teton

River with the Missouri, eventually competed for the Indian trade and represented the nuclei of activity among all the fur posts. The trade peaked in the 1830s, and in the first year of that decade shipments to St. Louis from the upper Missouri embraced 26,000 buffalo robes, 25,000 pounds of beaver skins, 150,000 deer skins, 37,500 muskrat skins, and 4,000 otter skins. While many of these products came from trappers and hunters employed by the fur companies, most came from trade with the Sioux tribes who inhabited the region.[3]

The principal fur companies that operated in the upper Missouri were the Missouri Fur Company, the Rocky Mountain Fur Company, and the Western Department of the American Fur Company. By the 1830s, the latter two firms transcended all others, and by the mid-1830s the American Fur Company had consolidated with other firms to dominate the regional trade. In the middle of the decade, however, the Western Department of the American Fur Company was sold to a St. Louis business subsequently known as Pierre Chouteau, Jr., and Company. Pierre Chouteau combined his long-established ties to the trade with his innate business acumen to revolutionize the industry, especially following his introduction of steamboats to the upper Missouri. Steamboats permitted larger cargos to travel faster from the trade region to St. Louis. In 1832, Chouteau rebuilt an earlier post, Fort Tecumseh, near the mouth of the Teton on the Missouri, and it was soon renamed Fort Pierre.[4]

In Fort Pierre lay the antecedents of Fort Randall. Following the success of the American Fur Company's trade in the north country, the enterprise fell on hard times owing to depletion of beaver and other fur sources. Although buffalo robes still dominated the trade, overall decline in production coincided with a depressed European market due to changes in fashion. By 1850, the fur trade was waning, and the impact of the decline created repercussions among the tribes that had become increasingly dependent on it. Through the years, meanwhile, federal Indian policy had attempted to facilitate the trade by promoting friendship between whites and Indians and by discouraging intertribal warfare. The federal government founded a licensing process replete with regulations to monitor the trade and the traders, restricted liquor from the commerce, appointed Indian agents when appropriate, and provided the traders with military protection when necessary. Fear of foreign intrigue following the War of 1812 led Secretary of War John C. Calhoun to introduce a plan calculated to promote and protect the trade while thwarting British influence in the upper Missouri country.

Calhoun's design called for three military posts to occupy the limits of the region—originally one at the confluence of the Yellowstone with the Missouri, another at either Council Bluffs or the Great Bend of the Missouri, and a third along the upper Mississippi River in Minnesota. Because of Congress's refusal to appropriate the required funding, only a post opposite Council Bluffs was ever established on the Missouri under the Calhoun plan—Fort Atkinson on the Nebraska side of the Missouri, built in 1819 and named for Colonel Henry Atkinson, who commanded the expedition to establish the post. Another post, Fort Snelling, was erected on the Mississippi at the mouth of the Minnesota River. The establishment of these stations significantly advanced the military frontier into the fur region, introduced a permanent government presence, daunted the Indians, and provided a modicum of security for the trade. Yet despite the introduction of troops in the country, Indian unrest, exacerbated by age-old inter-tribal animosities, became an ongoing concern. In June 1823, Arikara tribesmen attacked a party of the Rocky Mountain Fur Company, killing fourteen and wounding eleven, which prompted the organization of a punitive campaign against the tribesmen. Led by Colonel Henry Leavenworth, the expedition of some 300 troops and civilians recruited liberally among the Teton Sioux, traditional enemies of the Arikaras, in its advance on the Arikara villages near Grand River (in present North Dakota). Confronted by the large force, the Arikaras at first parleyed with Leavenworth, then fled the scene before traders with the army set their villages afire.[5]

Hopeful of allaying fears among other tribes in the aftermath of the Arikara campaign and of impressing them with its power, the U.S. government settled on a policy that fostered peace with the Indians through treaties. In 1825, Henry Atkinson, now a brigadier general, joined with Benjamin O'Fallon, agent for the Indians along the Missouri, in an expedition promoted by Congress for the purpose of extending an official American presence in the Indians' lands. The Atkinson-O'Fallon Expedition ascended the river from St. Louis in keelboats loaded with artillery and with presents of guns, tobacco, and blankets. In a manner contrived to cow the tribesmen, the soldiers paraded with the ordnance. Distribution of the goods followed the councils. Twelve treaties were thus negotiated and signed, all conceding the preeminence of the United States in the region and in the fur trade while assuring the people of the federal government's amity toward them. The Atkinson-O'Fallon Expedition thus yielded the first such formalized accords between the upper Missouri tribes and the United States.

The expedition was also intended to determine a need for the establishment of additional forts to counter British influence among the tribes, but following examination of the country, that prospect was deemed unnecessary. As a result, Fort Atkinson closed in 1827, its function supplanted farther downstream with construction of Fort Leavenworth on the west bank of the Missouri. That post and Fort Snelling and collateral outposts along the Mississippi sufficed to monitor and protect the northern frontier. Moreover, the tribes in the region appeared settled and peaceful; beyond sporadic raids against distant rivals, they contented themselves with hunting buffalo and trading at the river posts. The tribes were administered by the Indian superintendent at St. Louis, who was assisted by a general agent assigned to Council Bluffs. Subagents helped with certain bands of tribes when required. These personnel also monitored the traders, who otherwise smuggled liquor among the tribes, and oversaw an equitable annual distribution of goods to help keep the people peaceful and amenable to the government's interests. Over the years, however, as the trade proceeded and regressed, the tribesmen both benefited and suffered. While introduction of new articles made their lives easier, it also brought a dependence on white goods that came to permeate tribal societies. The infusion of whiskey and its demoralizing effects, furthermore, often produced devastating results for families and whole bands of native peoples. By 1850, the fur trade was stagnant, and the Indians, ever dependent on the trade, were in a process of cultural metamorphosis.[6]

By 1850, the seven subtribes of the Lakotas, along with the Yanktons and Yanktonais, impelled by intertribal turmoil ultimately influenced by whites farther east, were completing a migration west that had started in the Great Lakes region during the eighteenth century. Because of the dispersed nature of their bands, along with timely government vaccination programs, these people had not been as susceptible to the devastating epidemics that struck the sedentary and more distant Arikaras, Mandans, and Hidatsas in the Missouri corridor, and the progress of the fur trade had corresponded with the increasingly dominant presence of these Sioux in that land. By the 1840s, as the trade abated, the Lakotas posed an increasingly intimidating presence to both whites and neighboring tribes in the region. At the same time, competition among the various peoples for the buffalo remained high, as the great herds, in fact, declined. Warfare driven by economic incentive emerged more and more in the intertribal forays for horses conducted by the Sioux and their enemies. Similarly, the Yanktons, representing the middle group of Sioux, lorded over the Arikara earth-lodge villages, alternately attacking or trading with the Arikaras as occasion demanded, until these people, with but a vestige of their former influence, moved away forever. In sum, the expansion of the Lakotas and Yanktons into the upper Missouri during the opening decades of the nineteenth century represented a counterpoint to the simultaneous appearance there of Euro-Americans.[7]

This convergence of regional interests between Indians and whites led directly to the establishment of Fort Randall on the Missouri River. During the 1840s, with the promise of rich land in the Oregon country and later with the discovery of gold in California, thousands of American citizens undertook the journey west via several overland routes. One of those was the Great Platte River Road, or Oregon Trail, which followed the Platte River and its affluents west into present Wyoming and continued beyond the Rocky Mountains through what is now Idaho to Utah, Oregon, or California, depending on the objective of the particular emigrants. This massive population movement for the first time opened the West and exposed its qualities and resources to multitudes of prospective settlers. The concept of a permanent Indian frontier earlier espoused by the government, wherein eastern tribes were resettled on lands west and south of the lower Missouri River, soon succumbed to the reality of the emigration, with treaties now opening lands west of the states of Iowa and Missouri. New territories of Kansas and Nebraska, created in 1854, joined that of Minnesota, which had become a territory in 1849. Already, settlement proceeded up either side of the Missouri River from the Platte, especially in the river valleys that fed into the Missouri. Sioux City, Iowa, which would become an anchor community for upriver settlement, was established in 1855.[8]

Military authority accompanied the advance west, with new stations appointed at Fort Kearny, Nebraska, in 1848 and Fort Laramie, in present southeastern Wyoming, purchased by the government from the American Fur Company in 1849. These posts oversaw the passage of emigrants on the Oregon Trail while providing important points for government maintenance of relations with the tribes. In 1851, a treaty concluded near Fort Laramie by representatives of the U.S. government and leaders of the Lakotas, Cheyennes, Arapahos, and other tribes sought to segregate the people into fixed regions removed from the major arteries of white emigration. A flaw in the rationale of dealing with the Indians was that Lakota leaders who signed the convention often possessed no authority to speak for those in assorted bands who either did not attend the treaty council or refused to endorse its proceedings.

The penetration by whites of Indian hunting lands along the Oregon Trail created discomfiture among the tribes, particularly among those of the dominant Lakotas and their neighbors, for the emigrant trains destroyed game, game habitat, timber, and grass in their course. The increased proximity of whites and Indians inevitably caused friction, and in 1853 relations between the Indians and the soldiers grew strained following a confrontation in which several Sioux were killed by troops from Fort Laramie. Tensions mounted, and on August 14, 1854, following the complaint of a Mormon emigrant to the post commander that an Indian in a nearby camp had killed his cow, a squad of twenty-nine soldiers of the Sixth Infantry headed by Brevet Second Lieutenant John L. Grattan marched out to the Brulé Sioux camp to confront the perpetrator. An argument ensued between Grattan and Conquering Bear, the Sioux chief, and the lieutenant directed his men to open fire on the Sioux. As the chief fell mortally wounded, the Sioux retaliated, killing all but one of the soldiers who escaped to the post before dying.

The deaths of Grattan and his men became a catalyst for the tenor of Lakota-government relations for much of the balance of the nineteenth century. A punitive expedition against the offending Sioux followed, headed by Colonel (Brevet Brigadier General) William S. Harney, designed to retaliate not only for the Grattan affair but also for mounting depredations against citizens along the overland roads. Forts Kearny and Laramie were to serve as depots for troops and supplies, along with the derelict former fur post of Fort Pierre on the west bank of the Missouri (near present Pierre, South Dakota), purchased by the government (over Harney's objection) for $45,000 in the spring of 1855. In August 1855, Harney entered the Sioux country of western Nebraska with close to 600 officers and men of the Second Dragoons, Sixth and Tenth infantry regiments, and the Fourth Artillery. On September 3, along Blue Water Creek, a few miles north of the emigrant rendezvous at Ash Hollow near the North Platte River, Harney's column struck camps of Brulés, Minneconjous, and Oglalas that sheltered warriors responsible for the recent depredations, delivering the tribes a devastating and demoralizing blow that yielded eighty-five dead compared to but four fatalities among the troops. Many women and children also were captured and the Indian camps destroyed. Harney then proceeded west to Fort Laramie before pushing his men north and east along the White and Cheyenne rivers to the Bad (Teton) River, directly through the Sioux country, intimidating other bands of those people en route to the Missouri.[9]

On October 19, 1855, Harney's forces settled for the winter at Fort Pierre, refurbished earlier in the year to accommodate two companies of infantry and four of cavalry. Fort Pierre's first army garrison consisted of a force of nearly 300 Second infantrymen under Captain Henry W. Wessels sent via steamboat to overhaul the place in early July, while Second Lieutenant Gouverneur K. Warren, of the Topographical Engineers, laid out a military reservation. (Of six companies of the Second Infantry assigned to Fort Pierre, four were shortly transferred to Harney's command near Ash Hollow.) Wessels and Warren found Fort Pierre in deplorable condition. Constructed of split logs planted side by side in the ground to create a square stockade twenty feet in height, it stood about a quarter mile back from the bank of the Missouri. Bastions at each corner permitted an unobstructed view of the surrounding open landscape. A large gate faced the river, while others were located at the sides and rear. Inside the stockade stood buildings suitable to accommodate a trading enterprise, including log storehouses and houses for trappers and traders. During the refurbishment of 1855, thirty-seven dark red-painted prefabricated buildings—"portable cottages"—devised by Captain Parmenas Turnley of the Quartermaster Department, a member of Harney's command, were manufactured in Cincinnati and transported up the river and placed near the stockade as accommodation for officers and men. Some of these amounted to flimsy company quarters capable of housing thirty men and were thrown up around a parade ground, while "knocked-down" storehouses were raised along the river. Government occupation of Fort Pierre, 1,525 miles upriver from St. Louis, made it the farthest advanced army post on the upper Missouri to that time.[10]

With Harney's arrival, Fort Pierre, now headquarters of the Sioux Expedition, increased its garrison to almost 900 officers and men, most of whom had to be quartered outside the post. The troops consisted of Companies D, E, H, and K, Second Dragoons; Companies A, B, C, D, G, and I, Second Infantry (which had arrived earlier); Companies A, E, H, and K, Sixth Infantry; one company of the Tenth Infantry; and Light Battery G, Fourth Artillery. Notwithstanding the occupation, Harney was displeased with conditions at Fort Pierre and registered his disappointment with the refurbishing troops for not passing on the dilapidated post and finding a spot with better grass and wood. By winter, his troops were scattered about in outlying cantonments. Food was insufficient and of poor quality, and some of Harney's soldiers died of scurvy. Many cavalry horses starved during the winter. Remembered infantryman Augustus Meyers: "Officers and soldiers suffered alike. The miserable huts in which we lived during the winter were unfit for stables. We almost froze in them, and when the spring came, the mud roofs leaked like sieves."[11] Worse, the post had but two latrines, both located only 250 yards from the fort's structures and constituting a morass of human filth.[12] "It is unfortunate," Harney complained, "that my orders were disobeyed in . . . [its] purchase; it is unfortunate the troops did not arrive in this country earlier; it is unfortunate they were stopped here; and most unfortunate of all was the absence of a commander of energy, experience, and industry."[13]

General Harney determined to find another site for a post. During the winter of 1855–56, he reconnoitered the Missouri River banks to locate one, traveling as far south as the mouth of the Niobrara River. In March 1856, Fort Pierre's fate was sealed when Harney learned that freight could not be landed within three miles below or five miles above that station. He therefore decided to remove his command from Fort Pierre to a wooded west-bank site twelve miles below the Missouri's Big Bend and formerly occupied by the Columbia Fur Company as Fort Lookout. In June, Companies B and D of the Second Infantry under Captain Nathaniel Lyon occupied Fort Lookout, and by August nearly 300 officers and men camped there, accepting freight delivered to that point by steamer. In early October, more troops of the same regiment arrived under Lieutenant Colonel John J. Abercrombie. Quarters were erected for three companies, along with houses for officers, kitchens, a bakery, and a hospital.[14]

Fort Lookout proved but a temporary expedient, and in early May 1856 Harney directed its dismantling. On June 30, 1856, he apprised the adjutant general in Washington, D.C., that to guarantee arrival of supplies for his men he had located yet a third site. "Should the Secretary [of War] accord with me the position I have selected, I desire to suggest the name of Fort Randall as its designation—it being a token of respect to the memory of a deceased officer of our Army—the highly esteemed Colonel Daniel Randall, late Deputy Paymaster General."[15] While several factors influenced Harney's selection of the new site, certainly river frontage accessibility for supplies coming upriver was paramount. The site also offered open approaches and a commanding view in all directions, and essential local resources of timber, grass, and water were abundantly available. The projected post was to be located on the west bank of the Missouri at a point thirty miles north of its confluence with the Niobrara River and a short distance north of the modern Nebraska–South Dakota boundary. Anticipating a renewal of operations against the Sioux, the general also proposed that troops garrison a post in the vicinity of Long Lake, "the most important point to be occupied on the river, in my opinion."[16]

By this time, however, Harney had met the Sioux in council and forged a treaty with them (March 1856) in which the Sioux had promised to keep the peace. The Sioux Expedition, consequently, was terminated, and orders from Washington directed Harney to proceed only with building the lower post—Fort Randall—as a permanent station on the Missouri. Harney shortly was ordered back to Fort Leavenworth, and the new post continued construction without his presence. When navigation opened on the Missouri in the spring of 1857, a steamboat from St. Louis reached Fort Pierre to load up transferable property, including the prefabricated cottages, and remove them downriver to Fort Randall, which, in effect, consolidated the military presence in the region. Fort Randall now comprised the direct legacy of the Sioux Expedition of 1855–56. As such, its mission was to keep the peace among the Indians and between the Indians and whites on the upper Missouri, while providing an unimpeded route between Fort Laramie, 300 miles to the west, and Fort Ridgely, 100 miles to the east. It would also protect emigrants and serve as a supply base and a prospective command center for any future operations against the tribes that might be required. The post, which effectively provided the concluding link in a chain of forts enclosing the northwestern frontier and previously composed of Forts Ridgely, Leavenworth, Riley, Kearny, and Laramie, would moreover prove to be the first link in a chain of military posts to be raised on the upper Missouri River.[17]

The first military presence at Fort Randall began with arrival by steamboat at the designated site on June 26, 1856, of eighty-four soldiers of the Second Infantry in the charge of First Lieutenant David S. Stanley, First Cavalry, and accompanied by First Lieutenant George H. Paige, regimental quartermaster of the Second Infantry. These troops went to work laying out the post. As conceived, the fort would replicate in arrangement and architectural character others in the West, to include the clustering of structures around a parade ground with no encircling stockade, thereby effectually if not purposefully introducing a semblance of order to a wilderness setting.[18]

To that end, in August Companies C and I, Second Infantry, along with Companies C, D, H, and K, Second Dragoons, commanded by Colonel Francis Lee, Second Infantry, reached the post as its first garrison, numbering 365 soldiers. These troops lived in tents while they ranged for timber for building and hay for the animals. Within two months, the Second Infantry field and staff arrived, along with the regimental band. Mounting desertions, especially from among the dragoon companies, complicated progress, and as winter drew nigh officers feared a repeat of the Fort Pierre experience. Nonetheless, Lee stifled criticism in correspondence to his Fort Leavenworth headquarters, citing satisfaction and contentedness at the post. In preparation for winter, 700 cattle, purchased from contractors, arrived in October. Captain Turnley served as quartermaster on site. Using extra duty men, he established camps several miles north and opposite from the post to cut wood and hay and built a large flatboat with which to transport materials from the east bank. Steamboats bore supplies of vegetables and clothing to the post. Two companies occupied Fort Pierre, while three stayed at Fort Lookout, through the ensuing winter. The remaining stores from both places arrived in the spring of 1857, as those posts were turned over to a St. Louis trading company.[19] An American Fur Company employee, Charles E. Galpin, contracted with the government to dismantle and remove the portable buildings to Fort Randall. An enlisted man at Fort Lookout described the work accomplished there in readiness for the move to Fort Randall:

Orders were received to abandon Fort Lookout, where we had worked so hard to build quarters, and to proceed to Fort Randall. ... We ... began to tear down the company quarters, for they were built of hewn timber which it was desirable to save. We also took down the officers' houses. All this material was hauled down to the river bank to be made into a raft and floated down to Fort Randall. We left all of the log cabins and the brick chimneys standing but removed the doors and sashes. ... A steamboat ... arrived at Fort Lookout and took on board the three companies and all of the commissary and quartermaster stores and other moveable property. The wagons and mules were sent overland in charge of an officer and escort.[20]

As established, Fort Randall stood within a quadrangle on the west bank, along the second terrace, perhaps a quarter mile from the Missouri. Ringed by rolling hills to the west that formed yet a third terrace as it yielded to the open prairie beyond, the location was "beautifully situated" with more than adequate wood for fuel and grass for forage derived from a fertile bottomland alluvial plain. Situated at a place where the river ran nearly 1,000 yards wide and was fully navigable for steamboats, the post occupied a broad sloping tip called Handy's Point, which possessed a suitable landing for steamboats. Here in its descent, the Missouri turned sharply east and then south along an otherwise high shoreline, affording Fort Randall a two-sided defensible waterfront to the north and east, respectively.[21] During the remainder of the summer of 1856, the troops continued raising the post, virtually reconstructing some of the buildings from upstream. When the raft from Fort Lookout arrived, "the re-erection of our quarters and officers' houses commenced," wrote Private Meyers.[22] Cabins of cottonwood for married soldiers, along with those for a dozen civilian workers, were constructed in a bottomland location designated "The Hollow." Civilian carpenters added ceilings to the buildings. When high winds blew away some of the portable structures, more durable and comfortable ones were erected of logs. New mess halls and a spacious hewn-log guardhouse were also constructed, and the troops moved into their quarters in late August.[23]

A penciled map prepared to accompany Captain Turnley's October 1856 report undoubtedly portrays the post layout as it then existed. It shows two clusters of buildings separated by approximately 1,200 yards, one relating to the Second Infantry and the other to the Second Dragoons. That for the Second Infantry stood on what was evidently the primary post location and consisted of the infantry soldier and officer quarters, about 800 yards west of the "Good steamboat Landing" at the river. These structures appear to have had kitchens/mess halls either attached or detached in their rear. East of the infantry quarters stood two storehouses and the sutler's store, both logically closest to the landing and just above the lower plateau. Slightly southeast of the officer quarters stood the hospital. The dragoon building cluster, seemingly subordinated to the infantry station, was situated across a large dry creek running toward the Missouri and consisted of four soldier quarters facing four officer quarters.[24]

One of the earliest detailed descriptions of Fort Randall appeared in a letter dated September 6, 1858, from a correspondent to the *Missouri Republican*: "The first bench was covered with cottonwood and other timber which [on approach from downstream] hides the fort, except the flag, from the boat. The buildings are twenty-four one-story log cabins, double lengthwise. There is one frame building, the only painted one, occupied by [the sutler] . . . of the post. The garrison comprises A, B, D, G, H and I, of the Second Infantry, 500 men, and a 'fine band of music.'"[25] Work on the buildings proceeded more or less continuously over the first several years. A refined description given years later described five barracks, four of hewn logs retrieved from Fort Lookout and one of unhewn timber. Each barrack measured 93 feet long by 22$\frac{1}{2}$ feet wide by 10$\frac{1}{2}$ feet high and was intended to house fifty soldiers. One-story officer quarters—three of frame and six of log construction—had paneled ceilings and walls. There were two storehouses for commissary and quartermaster supplies, along with a guardhouse and, by 1857, a hewn-log, winged hospital building measuring at least 100 feet in length.[26]

The first years in the new post afforded a consolidation period following its establishment, a time for Fort Randall to cast for itself a regional identity vis-à-vis other military and civilian enterprises. Mail for the post (as it had for Fort Pierre and Fort Lookout) traveled by carrier back and forth from Sioux City, approximately 140 miles away. The post continued its physical evolution after the initial work of 1856, as buildings were modified and construction of appropriate garrison support facilities continued. A traveler in early September 1858 noticed that logs for building houses at the post were still being hauled from upriver by raft and steamer. The fort "is composed of one story houses," the finest of which (and privately built) was the frame painted structure occupied by the post sutler, John B. S. Todd, a former captain in Harney's command who opportunistically resigned his commission in the Sixth Infantry to acquire the sutlership.[27] Todd's spacious store, erected of lumber imported from St. Louis, dispensed low-priced goods to the soldiers.[28] A visiting physician in June of the following year reported on the progress of the post:

> We looked about the Fort, which is no fort at all [meaning no stockade], only barracks, log cabins occupied by the soldiers, and better ones by the officers, all facing an open square, in the center of which is a [sun]dial and flagstaff, with a stand for the musicians. I afterwards saw a new hospital that is not quite completed. It is built of cedar boards and divided into seven rooms, each about 18 feet by 10, and 8 feet high, with about three windows and a door in each, and other rooms for a surgery and storehouse, which form wings.[29]

By that time, civilian carpenters and mechanics had been discharged, and most of the labor yet to be completed was accomplished by soldiers.[30] By then, too, provisions were under way for establishing a suitable reservation to buffer the post, particularly in view of the mounting presence of white squatters on Indian lands in the proximity of the fort who, it was feared, might cause unrest among the tribesmen. In August 1857, Colonel Joseph K. F. Mansfield, the inspector general, visited and recommended such, and in May 1858 Major Hannibal Day dispatched Second Infantry troops from Fort Randall to remove the intruders and demolish their buildings and equipment. But the soldiers were recalled, and the interlopers remained pending clarification of the applicable provisions of the 1834 Indian Trade and Intercourse Act. The issue of squatters continued intermittently thereafter. For a time, consideration was given to creating a quartermaster supply depot at Fort Randall to accommodate posts in Nebraska and Minnesota, but this never happened.[31]

During the first years of the post, the maintenance of good health of the garrison was a constant concern. The fort's isolated location made it imperative that its troops remain physically strong and free of disease. To that end, a post garden had been planted in the spring of 1856 a mile west of the fort, and well into the fall the troops enjoyed very large tomatoes, potatoes, and onions. In 1857, however, grasshoppers wreaked havoc in the garden. Partly as a result, during the winter of 1856–57 the post surgeon feared inroads of scurvy among the command and persisted in efforts to provide appropriate antiscorbutics for the men. At one point, the arrival of frozen potatoes by wagon prevented the outbreak of serious illness. In the spring of 1857, the men consumed wild artichokes, lime juice, molasses, and dried fruits to ward off sickness. Of course, in many instances proper accommodations were still lacking. The winter of 1856–57 was one of blizzards and freezing temperatures. Earth piled onto the roofs furnished some warmth, but the troops awaited the arrival of a sawmill to cut planks from the surrounding cottonwood growth to substantially improve the complex.[32]

A routine but critical operation of the Fort Randall garrison during the early years, besides construction-related activities, was to ensure sufficient and appropriate food and supplies for the maintenance of a healthy command. As the province of the post commissary of subsistence, that officer was responsible for seeking out and acquiring victuals from every possible area source—most notably the young metropolis of Sioux City. While irregular steamboats brought certain fare, the road between that community and Fort Randall during the unnavigable season saw recurrent wagon traffic, as the commissary sought out sources for such staples as potatoes. Occasionally, government purchases resulted in overabundance, and certain surplus commodities went on the auction block at the fort. A notice for such a sale in January 1858 imparted some knowledge of the diet of Fort Randall soldiers at that time: 188 barrels of pork, 155 pounds of bacon, 10,006 pounds of flour, 1,780 pounds of hard bread, 44 bushels of beans, 260 pounds of Rio coffee, 750 pounds of Java coffee, 1,175 pounds of brown sugar, and 20 bushels of dried apples. Contracts were advertised for freshly butchered beef to be delivered to the post "in quarters, an equal proportion of fore and hind—necks and shanks excluded—at such times and in such quantities as the A.A.C.S. [acting assistant commissary of subsistence] for the time being shall require."[33] Similarly, the post quartermaster officer was responsible for clothing (produced at government arsenals) and everything else. Bidders (covered by bondsmen) were also solicited by the quartermaster for "Cutting, Salting, Curing and Stacking of Hay," between 300 and 1,000 tons of which proved a mandatory consideration for the maintenance of garrison animals.[34]

At Fort Randall, as at any other mid-nineteenth-century American fort, oversight of post functions regarding the commissary, quarter-master, and sutler positions lay with the Post Council of Administration. This body, composed of representative officers from the garrison, met periodically to assess and recommend to the commanding officer the proper and most efficient means of accomplishing the fort's internal business. For example, in August 1856 the council recommended to the secretary of war that John B. S. Todd be appointed post sutler. In December 1858, it convened to audit the post treasurer's books governing the post fund and to levy an eight-cent-per-man tax on the sutler, based on the number of officers and men present during the two previous months (in this case, an average of 521). Early in 1859, a nonunanimous council urged the establishment of a post school and recommended that Fort Randall be designated a "chaplain post."[35]

Soldiers at Fort Randall during this formative period of its occupancy dressed in the regulation uniform pattern of 1855, although components of the previous pattern probably also carried over. By the late 1850s, however, each enlisted foot soldier wore or kept attire that consisted basically of a deep blue wool fatigue blouse, a pair of sky blue wool trousers, a forage cap, a dress blouse, a dress hat, a gray or blue flannel shirt, a pair of canton flannel drawers, wool stockings, a wool greatcoat, and a pair of leather shoes. On campaign, the men carried a canteen, haversack, blanket, and knapsack. The mounted soldiers (dragoons) with Harney dressed similarly but wore dark blue chasseur-style jackets trimmed in orange, boots instead of shoes, and on campaign carried their spare clothing and rations in saddlebags on their animals. They also wore saber belts, cross-straps, and slings to attach their rifles. Officers' uniforms, purchased privately by individuals, were to an extent similar but were fashioned of more refined materials. Small arms consisted of an 1847-pattern musketoon or an 1855-pattern rifled musket carried by each soldier and a saber and Model 1851 Colt's Navy revolver (carried on the saddle), besides, by the horsemen.[36]

Thus outfitted, the soldiers generally followed a prescribed daily routine that saw them rise at an early hour, perform fatigue and guard duty, drill, variously escort supply trains and mail wagons en route to and from Sioux City and other points, and respond to keep the peace between and among the neighboring Yanktons and Poncas and other tribes. Every Sunday had its dress parade and skirmish drill. Entertainment was sparse, although the small regimental band provided lively fare in the evenings and on weekends. Colonel Lee even sought the return of one deserter, a persistent alcoholic, because of his instrumental talent, noting, "I am informed that he probably is the *very best* Clarionet player in the Army."[37] On one occasion, apparently in 1857, an enlisted man's discovery of "gold" near the post set off a mild stampede among his fellows until the ore finally was assayed as pyrite.

Other avenues for entertainment of the men included the bottle, and at Fort Randall, as at other western posts, liquor did not go wanting for attention. Sutler Todd dispensed wine and beer to the men under guidelines of the Post Council of Administration. When Todd exceeded the prescription, he was restricted by the post commander, and when this happened, the wife of an enlisted man set up a small still in her home and produced corn liquor, which she furtively sold to the troops until she was discovered and her equipment destroyed. As well, whiskey smuggled from Sioux City made an appearance and helped swell the numbers in the guardhouse. Besides incarceration, infractions of military discipline at Fort Randall brought punishment by loss of pay, confinement at hard labor on a diet of bread and water, and flogging with a rawhide whip.[38]

Sometime during the first year's occupation of Fort Randall, the wives and families of officers and senior-ranking enlisted men arrived. "It was quite a novelty," recalled one soldier, "to see white ladies again and to see their children playing on the parade ground."[39] The wives of both officers and senior enlisted personnel who served at Fort Randall accompanied their husbands to stations on the frontier primarily out of a sense of devotion as well as duty to them. Army regulations made no provision for dependents, although their importance was recognized institutionally. The women and children, transported to posts at private expense, provided sources of comfort in an environment of deprivation largely devoid of social amenities. On the frontier, women who were often socialite daughters or immigrants shared the burden of living in tents and huts and made do with what resources were available locally through the post sutlers' offices and the Quartermaster Department. Women who tired of the experience headed east after a time, but those who stayed employed creativity in their spirits and daily routines to sustain a home life. The mortality rate for infants was high. Children who survived generally enjoyed good health, despite the usual childhood diseases, and experienced things like hunting, fishing, and Indian cultures that youth in the more settled regions could not. One deficiency was education. Although the army eventually required schools for children as well as enlisted men, many parents enrolled their offspring in boarding schools in the East. Because the army kept no tally of civilian dependents, there is no institutional record of actual numbers of women and children at Fort Randall at a given time. In fact, laundresses, who served the companies and who formally occupied housing on the post, were the only women to receive official recognition by the army (since 1802). They received pay for washing the soldiers' clothing, as well as fuel, a daily ration, and the post surgeon's care when required. Generally, laundresses were married to the senior noncommissioned officers on the post. They also variously functioned as nurses and assisted officers' families as cooks and midwives when required, in addition to performing their normal duties.[40]

Six companies—A, B, D, G, H, and I—along with the headquarters, staff, and band of the Second Infantry, under Colonel Lee, continued to occupy the post through the midsummer of 1857 following dismantling of Forts Pierre and Lookout. At that time, there were twenty-two officers and 365 men at Fort Randall. Two companies of Second Dragoons had transferred to Fort Kearny in the fall of 1856, and the remaining two departed for Fort Leavenworth in June, ostensibly to take part in anticipated operations against the Mormons in Utah. Four companies of the Second Infantry traveled temporarily to Forts Ridgely and Snelling to relieve Tenth Infantry troops to join in that campaign. In May 1858, four companies of the Second Infantry received orders transferring them downriver to Fort Leavenworth. This left Companies C, G, and I at the post, although two of the departing four returned in September and recruits joined. Companies of the Second Infantry composed the garrison at Fort Randall until mid-1859. (Colonel Lee, meantime, died in St. Louis in January 1859.) In May of that year, two companies transferred to Lake Preston, Minnesota, and in July four companies (E, I, L, and M) and the field and staff and regimental band of the Fourth Artillery, under Lieutenant Colonel John Munroe, arrived from Fort Laramie, relieving the Second Infantry units, which dispersed to Forts Riley, Laramie, and Ripley. Company H, Fourth Artillery (acting as infantry) arrived in September 1859, and the more than 500 men of that regiment thereafter garrisoned Fort Randall until the outbreak of the Civil War.[41]

During the first few years of its establishment and occupation by the Second Infantry, Fort Randall hosted a number of regional operations. In May 1857, for example, responding to reported depredations by Indians along the Little Sioux River and at Spirit Lake, Iowa, Major Day led a combined force of dragoons and infantry from Fort Randall. The force arrived too late to be of service, however, and terminated with orders directing the dragoons to Fort Leavenworth and the infantry companies to Forts Snelling and Ridgely. In January 1858, troops were dispatched to attend to disorders among the Poncas, while during the following spring Captain Lyon led troops on a march to Fort Scott, Kansas, and back for the purpose of "quelling Indian disturbances." Yet another mission proceeded in June 1858, when Captain Henry W. Wessells traveled with an escort of forty soldiers from Company C to Fort Union trading post, at the mouth of the Yellowstone River, to assist in the distribution of Indian annuities. In May 1859, an escort accompanied the mapping expedition of Major William F. Raynolds, Corps of Engineers, to the Yellowstone country.[42]

Perhaps most significantly for its regional implications, the post served as anchor and departure point for the explorations of Second Lieutenant Gouverneur K. Warren, of the Topographical Engineers, who had served on previous survey and mapping expeditions in the West. As noted, as a member of the Sioux Expedition in 1855 he laid out the military reservation at Fort Pierre for General Harney and in the following year reconnoitered the upper Missouri from above the Yellowstone to Nebraska City. Escorted by troops from Fort Randall, Warren in 1857 explored the Black Hills with Dr. Ferdinand V. Hayden and named Harney Peak for his mentor. Warren later scouted a road from Fort Laramie to Fort Randall via the Niobrara River, then journeyed afoot from Fort Randall to Sioux City recording topographical, natural, and meteorological data. Reaching the post from Fort Laramie on November 1, Warren met Major Day and the other officers of the Second Infantry. He took occasion "to acknowledge my indebtedness to this regiment for the aid and protection they have afforded me."[43] As a result of his surveys, which considered the practicability of routes and the economy of their relative costs, Warren recommended that Nebraska City rather than Fort Randall be used as the principal point of departure from the Missouri River for supplies earmarked for Fort Laramie.[44] More significantly, Warren's peregrinations in the Black Hills legitimized federal interest there and provided a catalyst for future relations with the Lakotas.

Indian Neighbors

2. A visitor to Fort Randall in September 1858 remarked on the presence of native people. "There are many Indians around the fort," he noted. "The teepees show off, and the papooses are many, bearing striking likenesses to the officers and men of the army, who are proud of the issue of their loins. One-half of the little ones hovering around the squaws are offsprings [*sic*] of white men."[1] Beyond the obvious matter of progeny, the statement pointed up the reality of the larger impact the post (to say nothing of its soldiers) would have on its Indian neighbors, for throughout its existence, Fort Randall would be involved in Indian affairs as they related to numerous tribes inhabiting the region. These tribes included the large body of buffalo-hunting Lakotas, or Teton Sioux, whose seven groups (Hunkpapas, Oglalas, Brulés, Minneconjous, Blackfeet Sioux, Sans Arcs, and Two Kettles) ranged over a vast area embracing the Black Hills and the Powder-Yellowstone river country; of these, the Brulés, Oglalas, Minneconjous, and Hunkpapas would assume roles in Fort Randall's history. The Santees, or Eastern Sioux (Dakotas), comprised of the Mdewakanton, Wahpekute, Sisseton, and Wahpeton (particularly the two first-mentioned groups), most of whom lived in Minnesota, also had a significant impact on the course of events at the fort. The Northern Cheyennes would have a more limited involvement with Fort Randall. Above all these, however, two omnipresent neighboring tribes dominated the fort's Indian relations from its beginnings in 1856 through much of its occupation—the linguistically affiliated Yanktons and Poncas. The histories of both of these peoples helped shape that of Fort Randall, and vice versa, for a considerable period, and the net results for the lifeways of both tribes were at best mixed.[2]

The Yanktons, along with their closely associated Yanktonai kin, represented the middle Sioux group of speakers of the Nakota Siouan dialect (versus the Eastern Sioux Dakota and the Western Sioux Lakota dialects) and were people who historically occupied lands near the headwaters of the Mississippi River in Minnesota. By the mid-nineteenth century, the Yanktons lived along the Missouri River south of Fort Pierre and generally ranged over what is now southeastern South Dakota. Originally, there were seven bands of Yanktons, but by the time of white presence along the Missouri these had coalesced into Upper and Lower groups. Like other prairie/eastern plains peoples, the Yanktons lived in buffalo-skin lodges, hunted buffalo and other game, and practiced some horticulture. Although generally restricted to that area, they nonetheless had representation at Fort Laramie in 1851, when the Yankton leader Smutty Bear signed a treaty with the United States (evidently as an adjunct to the Dakota tribes) specifying the lands on which each tribe would reside. Two years later, the Yanktons received annuity goods in accordance with an amendment to the treaty. Their numbers hovered at around 3,700 people, based upon an 1853 estimate given by their agent, who reported them inhabiting either side of the Missouri between the mouth of the White River up to Fort Pierre and hunting in the area from the Missouri east to the James River. In that year, the Yanktons suffered an outbreak of cholera introduced by the ongoing overland migration of whites through the central plains. After his arrival at Fort Pierre, Harney negotiated with the various Sioux tribes, including the Yanktons, and in the typical manner of white accommodation appointed Struck by the Ree as head chief of the tribe. Thereafter, the bands settled tenuously on rivers and tributaries bordering the east bank of the Missouri as they faced an uncertain future of poor game, insufficient annuities from the government, and an increasing white intrusion into their lands.[3]

The Yanktons had been party to the treaty system before, beginning in 1815, when William Clark, Ninian Edwards, and Auguste Choteau elicited an accord of peace and amity following the War of 1812. Other treaties affecting trade and land relinquishment followed between 1815 and 1837 in which the Yanktons assumed major or minor consideration.[4] (Harney's treaty with the tribes in 1856, while promoting peace among them and providing for continued emigrant travel, made promises that the government refused to deliver and was never ratified by Congress.)[5] During the late 1850s, as white intrusions increased, the Yanktons began to assert themselves, producing friction and incidents of violence. In 1857, some of Smutty Bear's people resisted settlers near modern Brookings, South Dakota, driving them away and burning their homes. Inevitably, land speculation organizations, including the newly formed Dakota Land Company of St. Paul, Minnesota, along with Fort Randall sutler John B. S. Todd and his partner, Daniel M. Frost, who owned trading posts above Sioux City and whose interests pervaded virtually all avenues of commercial and political endeavors, pushed for a treaty delegation to free up the land once and for all. In 1857, the Indian bureau appointed Todd to pursue a treaty. Late that year, a party of Yankton chiefs visited Washington, D.C., and next year signed another treaty that surrendered all of the Yanktons' lands in return for a reservation and annuities for the next fifty years. Considered a sellout by most of the Yankton people, the treaty wrought division within the tribe, most of whose members believed that it had been arranged by Struck by the Ree and an interpreter, Charles Picotte. John Todd, certainly one of its principal benefactors, signed the document as a witness.[6]

The Yankton Treaty of 1858, which concentrated the Yanktons on a reservation directly across the Missouri River from Fort Randall, carried implications that affected the garrison from that time until the post was abandoned. For one thing, it freed up more than 12,000,000 acres of land for settlement. The reservation, which encompassed 400,000 acres, fronted the Missouri for thirty miles from the mouth of Chouteau Creek to just above Fort Randall. Beyond opening up former Indian land for white settlement, which in itself would occupy the soldiers' attention, the treaty provided payments totaling $1,600,000 in cash and annuities to the tribe over the next fifty years (disbursed in a manner largely at the government's determination) and allowed for the construction of military posts, roads, and Indian agencies on the reservation, as appropriate. The Yanktons pledged to remain peaceful, not to engage in hostilities with other tribes, to resolve peacefully all such disputes through their agent, and to "acknowledge their dependence on the Government of the United States."[7] Furthermore, the imbibing of intoxicating liquor by any of the Indians would result in proportional decreases in their annuities. The Yankton Treaty was ratified by the Senate on February 16, 1859.[8]

Following establishment of the reservation in 1859, the government constructed a sawmill and agency buildings at a site later named Greenwood, opposite and downriver a dozen miles from Fort Randall.

Some 2,000 Yanktons occupied the tract. In 1860, the Lower Yankton people successfully raised nearly 400 acres of corn on the reservation. Almost half of this, as well as the yield of potatoes and turnips, was carried off by those Lower Yanktons who themselves refused to plant but raided the agency garden. Both Upper and Lower groups continued to hunt buffalo off the reservation in accordance with the treaty. Some of the people, however, raised white-style houses of logs or sod, complete with shingle roofs, and reconciled themselves to their new life. After late 1861, new fields were designated, livestock distributed, and band chiefs provided with modern homes as an incentive to keep tribesmen within the reserve boundary. But despite increased acreage dedicated to farming, losses through drought and grasshopper infestation in the mid-1860s tempered any success in transforming the people from free hunters to farmers.[9]

In many respects, the Yanktons were similar to the other local tribe that interfaced consistently with the Fort Randall garrison. Like the Yanktons, the Poncas spoke a dialect related to the Siouan language stock, but the Poncas were most closely related to the Omahas, with whom they were one time closely affiliated. Following separation from the Omahas early in the eighteenth century in the area of modern northeastern Nebraska, the Poncas occupied the Ponca Creek valley near the mouth of the Niobrara River, about thirty miles downriver from Fort Randall. Historically, the Poncas subsisted on hunted game, principally buffalo; planted crops of corn, beans, and squash; and gathered wild plants. Never numerous, they totaled approximately 800 between 1842 and 1871. They lived in earthen lodges and in less substantial rounded structures of sapling frames and skins, while leadership was vested in hereditary chiefs whose deliberations in council guided the people. The Poncas were usually defensively oriented in warfare, although they took the offensive against neighboring tribes who dared intrude on their lands.

As competition over game lands intensified during the mid-nineteenth century, the Poncas engaged enemy Sioux and Pawnees on the north and south of their range, respectively, to ensure themselves access to the buffalo country. A major confrontation erupted in 1855 in which the Poncas wiped out an entire Pawnee war party. Later attempts by the Poncas to farm their lands brought constant disruption from the Sioux, and troops dispatched from Fort Randall often helped the Poncas ward off these attacks. These assaults by the Sioux were devastating, and as a result the Poncas lost more than a quarter of their population. Early treaties between the Poncas and the United States in 1817 and 1825 sought to assure peace, and the latter accord located the Poncas' trading center at the mouth of the Niobrara River. Such problems as inroads by land-seeking whites and the Poncas' relationship with the Sioux led them to embrace the United States for protection, and on March 12, 1858, they signed a treaty with the government in which they relinquished their hunting grounds and accepted a reservation on the Niobrara. Ratified on March 8, 1859, the treaty set aside lands extending approximately twenty miles along the Niobrara and between that stream and Ponca Creek, starting some twenty-five miles from the mouth of the Niobrara. The treaty promised an agency, a school, farming equipment and training, and the obligatory annuities. It also included a provision that the United States would "protect the Poncas in the possession of the tract of land reserved for their future homes, and their persons and property thereon, during good behavior on their part."[10] Other provisions in the treaty mirrored those in the Yankton agreement, including those affecting the use of liquor on the reservation.

The proviso respecting protection was of critical importance in the relationship between the Poncas and the Fort Randall garrison. Their reservation stood but fifteen miles south of the post. Despite the accord—and the proximity of the fort—attacks by the Sioux continued, and in the summer of 1859 thirteen Poncas were slain and three children captured while hunting in western Nebraska. Several more Poncas died at the hands of Oglala and Brulé Lakotas and Cheyennes early in 1860, and in November of that year a Santee Sioux raid netted nearly a hundred of their horses. Such repeated losses became critical, as the Ponca chiefs explained during a council at Fort Randall that same month. Ponca agent J. Shaw Gregory requested muskets and cannon from the post without success. Post commandant Lieutenant Colonel John Munroe offered only consolation to the tribesmen, along with promises that the horse thieves would be tracked down and the horses returned. This did not happen immediately, however (in 1863 the Poncas received compensation from the government for the loss of the horses), and the Sioux attacks continued intermittently for years. Fear of the Lakotas, in fact, caused the Poncas to renew their alliance with the Omahas and forge a new one with their former enemies, the Pawnees. Because the Poncas could not hunt freely, they became increasingly dependent on government annuities for their existence.[11]

Throughout the period of treaty making with the Yanktons and Poncas in the 1850s, the new post of Fort Randall took an active role in monitoring Indian affairs in the region. Previous to those conventions, Indian title to lands east of the Big Sioux River, separating Iowa and modern South Dakota and continuing north through present eastern South Dakota, had been extinguished by treaty in 1851. After the establishment of Fort Randall, troops from the post often visited the Sisseton agency in Minnesota to oversee the distribution of rations at that place. In the case of the Yankton lands, troubles with squatters increased after the treaty was signed and before the tribe could move. Their agent, Alexander H. Redfield, posted notices and advised Major Day at Fort Randall, who threatened to arrest the trespassers, and troops under Captain Charles S. Lovell ranged to the mouth of the Big Sioux River evicting sooners and destroying their property. In February 1859, Frost, Todd, and Company organized the Upper Missouri Land Company and advantaged themselves of a Todd-influenced provision in the Yankton accord (permitting current white residents 160 acres at $1.25 per acre) to open a trading post eventually at the town of Yankton. Following ratification of the treaty, the land between the Big Sioux and Missouri rivers, north to an imaginary line running approximately from Fort Pierre to modern Watertown, was opened to white settlement. On July 10, 1859, settlers entered along the Missouri from Sioux City to Fort Randall, and the towns of Bon Homme, Yankton, Vermillion, and Elk Point were established. Of these, Yankton would become the leading settlement related to the occupation of Fort Randall. Meantime, residents of the tiny community of Sioux Falls cobbled together a provisional territorial government that lasted until Dakota Territory was created in 1861.[12]

Relations between whites and the Yanktons, as well as other Sioux tribes, worsened following the treaty, largely because the Upper Yanktons believed that their lands had been surrendered by their Lower kin. As mentioned, in the spring of 1858 Captain Henry Wessells and troops from the post accompanied the steamboat *Twilight* upstream to the Upper Yankton village at Fort Lookout, as well as to the camps of Lakotas and Arikaras and Assiniboins as far north as Fort Union. Disdain among the tribes over treaties and roads and the ever-increasing presence of whites in their midst was unyielding, and it only intensified in 1859 as more emigrants passed west seeking land and gold. Yet the reservation Yanktons, in whom the rudiments of farming were being instilled, were also becoming dependent on their new existence and, like the Poncas, now hunted relatively little. During the first annual disbursement of $10,000 as specified in the treaty (about $5.00 per individual), Agent Redfield called for Fort Randall's commanding officer and several junior officers to be present, for it created a "salutary" effect on the people.[13]

Throughout the early years of Fort Randall, there was almost always a representation of Yanktons and Poncas just outside the post. In 1857, Agent Redfield found forty lodges of Yanktons under Smutty Bear readying for a hunt. Most of these people, however—hangers-on whose lives were in one way or another dedicated to the sutler's store and the troops of the garrison—sought drinks, handouts, and whatever. The women evidently often fraternized with the men, and the impression is strong that sexual favors predominated from their mutual proximity.[14] Private August Meyers claimed that the Indian camp was "of easy access to the garrison, [and it] always proved interesting. I spent much of my time with the Indians."[15] A traveler commented on the number of tribesmen about, "and [we] visited one of their lodges. They did not have much to sell or trade" beyond moccasins and bows and arrows.[16]

The routine daily Indian presence about Fort Randall likely aggravated post officers, who needed no such temptations for their men, and possibly an opportunity to curb such a constant in the vicinity of the fort came in 1860. In an effort to assure sufficient area resources for Fort Randall, as well as to provide an adequate buffer zone in the face of encroaching land-hungry whites, the army established a military reservation around Fort Randall. Laid down in 1859–60 by First Lieutenant Joseph C. Clark Jr., Fourth Artillery, the boundary was approved by President James Buchanan on June 14, 1860. The new reservation assumed a rectangular shape, ten miles wide by twenty-four miles long, thereby encompassing approximately 96,000 acres. It extended along either side of the Missouri for a distance of eight miles above Fort Randall to a point sixteen miles below the post and, aligning with the course of the river, took a northwest-to-southeast-tilted configuration. About 25,000 acres were located on the east, or left, bank of the Missouri, where the boundary intersected a portion of the Yankton Reservation. Benefits accruing to the post with authorization of the military reservation included grass and timber, both from along the streams entering the Missouri on its west bank and from the various islands that the reservation incorporated. An agreement with Agent Redfield, finalized on March 27, 1861, assured that the Fort Randall garrison could cut 300–600 tons of hay on the Yankton Reservation at a payment of $1.00 per ton.[17]

Securing the immediate environs of Fort Randall with establishment of the military reservation helped consolidate the army presence after four years. During that period, as the government forged relationships with the surrounding Indian tribes, it also expanded its regional interest with creation of requisite roads and trails that embodied an incipient infrastructure on the north-central plains. One of the earliest roads in the area ran 323 miles along the Niobrara, Bad, and White rivers between Fort Laramie and Fort Pierre when they were both fur-trading posts. The army used the route in the late 1840s, and in 1855 a caravan of wagons preceded Harney's own march over it from Laramie to Pierre. Lieutenant Warren rendered drawings of the route and prepared a detailed mileage chart.[18] Following the general's decision to relocate south to Fort Lookout, and then farther south to Fort Randall, in the spring and summer of 1856, wagons passed along the east bank of the Missouri as they followed old Indian trails to the vicinity where the latter post was raised.

As Fort Randall developed, more and more trails and roads connected it to other outlying posts for the purposes of shuttling men and supplies, as needed. The major local highway became the Fort Randall Military Road, or Fort Randall–Sioux City Trail, laid out in 1856 to complement Missouri River traffic and to augment and replace it when the river was in a low stage or icebound. From the ferry landing (where a current-driven cable ferry system connected with the landing on the opposite shore north of the fort), the road paralleled the east bank of the river north and south of the post, but its main leg ran southeast, passing near or through what became Yankton, Vermillion, and Elk Point en route to the government warehouse on the levee at Sioux City. Ferries operated at the crossings of the James, Vermillion, and Big Sioux rivers. Mail was conveyed at irregular times (perhaps once or twice weekly) by an army ambulance bound for that purpose from Sioux City to Fort Randall, at which point mail earmarked for posts and agencies farther north was transferred into wagons brought from those upriver stations. Refinement of the Fort Randall Military

Road was on the agenda of territorial delegate candidate John B. S. Todd, who in 1861 noted that it would complement those "bustling, thriving towns." In 1864, Congress granted money for rebuilding the road and for bridging the Vermillion and Big Sioux rivers. By 1865, use of this highway was routine, and businessman A. H. Graber operated a "Sioux City and Fort Randall Express" stagecoach that made the round trip in five days.[19]

On a broader scale, Warren's surveys in 1857, some of which related to his Black Hills explorations, endeavored to locate the best supply routes across the plains between Fort Snelling and the mouth of the Big Sioux River (Sioux City) and between Sioux City and Fort Laramie. His expeditions made possible links between Fort Randall and Fort Laramie via the Niobrara and between Sioux City and Fort Laramie via the Loup and Niobrara rivers, both of which links utilized parts of the heavily favored route along the Platte, already traced by emigrants passing through Nebraska Territory. Although Warren favored the Niobrara route, he decided that "the neighborhood of Fort Randall . . . in a comparatively barren country destitute of inhabitants, and where the necessary store-houses can only be constructed at an expense not less than $100,000," together with "the great difficulties of the route from Fort Randall west," militated against its use.[20] Nonetheless, in 1859 the companies of the Fourth Artillery transferring from Fort Laramie to Fort Randall traversed the Niobrara route with twenty-three accompanying wagons.[21]

Warren's expeditions were timely, coming as they did during and following Harney's campaign against the Lakotas. As a military man, he saw the results in military terms: "There are so many inevitable causes at work to produce a war with the Dakotas [meaning all of the various tribes of Sioux] before many years, that I regard as the greatest fruit of the explorations I have conducted to be the knowledge of the proper routes by which to invade their country and conquer them." He recommended where to build posts for best effect in the event of war with the Indians, and he reported that those tribesmen "who may take refuge in the ravines and fastnesses along the Niobrara, or in the sand hills, could be operated against from forts Randall, Kearney [sic], and Laramie. Should the Isanties [Santees] and Ihanktonwans [Yanktons] be hostile at the same time as the Titonwans [Tetons], they should be operated against from Fort Ridgeley [sic]."[22]

Besides the government's interest, during the early 1860s, as part of early boosterism, civilian advocacy mounted for an emigrant route passing west through Dakota as an alternative to that through Nebraska, although the favored prospective route, via the "Fort Randall and Fort Laramie Road" of Warren's surveys, actually passed along the "Niobrarah route" through much of Nebraska. Another course, this a "new and short route" to the Black Hills following reports of gold in that locality, promised to lead miners and emigrants through Sioux City and Yankton "thence in nearly a direct line through fertile river valleys to the Black Hills and the mines of Montana and Idaho." This route extended west from Fort Randall "up the divide between the Niobrara and White Earth rivers to the Black Hills."[23] By the mid-1860s, the speculative climate among Sioux City promoters led them to seek and garner congressional authorization for a private road-building mission from there to the goldfields around Virginia City, Montana, largely by that route. The James A. Sawyers Expedition of 1865 paralleled the Niobrara River west and crossed through Wyoming and into Montana, but the route it blazed failed in due course for lack of funding. Continued interest in the gold country, however, prompted the Dakota legislature to urge that a post be raised in the Black Hills, that its governing district headquarters "be established at Yankton or Fort Randall," and that the "Sioux City and Big Cheyenne Wagon Road" be completed all the way to Montana.[24]

In addition to the major arteries among the regional military stations over which troops and supplies might move efficiently, other evolving roads crisscrossed the landscape between and among the budding communities, including that of Fort Randall. Besides the aforementioned wagon road from Sioux City to Fort Randall and on north, which constantly needed bridge improvements and grading maintenance, lesser roads either created, authorized, or recommended by the newly formed Dakota territorial legislature during the early 1860s with direct bearing on the military traffic to and from the post included one from Mankato, Minnesota, through Sioux Falls, Yankton, and Greenwood (on the Yankton Reservation) to a point downstream and opposite the fort, and another from Fort Ridgely, via Sioux Falls and Yankton, to the same place. These were sparked by the Santee Sioux outbreak against the settlements in 1862. Another laid out in the following year ran from Yankton via Bon Homme, Springfield, and Greenwood directly to White Swan (named for a Yankton chief), which stood across the Missouri from the fort. (Part of the labor entailed carving through some chalk bluffs between the agency and the fort along the east bank of the Missouri, a narrow cut known as the "Dug Way," a project accomplished by troops from the post late in 1863; the work shortened by several miles the trip between Greenwood and the Fort Randall ferry landing.) A road west of the Missouri ran from the mouth of the Niobrara via Ponca Creek to Fort Randall and provided the basis for another mail route to and from the post. These byways, along with a myriad of lesser trails among the communities and the ever present course of the Missouri, completed the early transportation network.[25]

By mid-1861—scarcely five years after Fort Randall had been established in the Nebraska wilderness—manifold changes had occurred both at the post and in the surrounding country. A correspondent in June registered the fort's pastoral appearance and remarked on the orderly disposition of its environs:

> It is situated . . . on a beautiful plateau descending gradually to the river. The most important buildings are those of the Commissary department and the Hospital. The officers all have good and commodious quarters, and the barracks are sufficient for several hundred soldiers. The Fort is located about 15 miles above the Yancton Indian Agency, and about 25 [sic] miles above the Ponca Reserve. The country between the Ponca Reserve and the Fort is open for settlement, and presents many eligible locations for good farms. The Yancton Reserve on the east side of the Missouri extends about five miles above the Fort, and is not subject to settlement—but above this for many miles up the river, the country is open for settlement.[26]

By its role in the clearing of Indian land title and establishment of reservations for the Yanktons and Poncas, besides its passive monitoring (except for John B. S. Todd) of the land boom and collateral infrastructural development of the early 1860s, and by its presence, Fort Randall enabled an incipient advance of Euro-American civilization into the country of the upper Missouri. The transformation occurred rapidly, within but a few years and likely faster than the same settlement trend occurred around other military posts elsewhere in the West, partly because the fort stood somewhat close to the already existing line of white settlement in Iowa and Missouri. But surely a powerful incentive was the Missouri River itself, that great phenomenon of nature whose ever-churning waters promoted the union of government, people, and commerce at an opportune place and moment, presenting advantages in the vicinity—as well as upriver—for prospective land and business successes. It was a dynamic of power and circumstance that vitally transformed the Dakota-Nebraska frontier for all time. Conversely, however, the coming of a new order to the upper Missouri tragically disrupted the lives and culture of the Yanktons, Poncas, and other native peoples who had previously inhabited the land. For the Indians, Fort Randall and what it represented brought changes of profound magnitude forever.[27]

Wartime

3 Fort Randall's tenure as part of the newly created Dakota Territory began on March 2, 1861, when enabling legislation was signed by outgoing President James Buchanan.[1] By then, Companies E, G, H, I, and M, Fourth Artillery; the field and staff and regimental band; and numerous families occupied the post. Company L had transferred east to Fort Monroe, Virginia, in May 1860, and Lieutenant Colonel Munroe had departed in January 1861—he would die in April—leaving Captain John P. McCown commanding the post. The soldiers barely had time to contemplate this new jurisdiction before—like those at all military establishments across the country—they were caught up in the national emergency of the Civil War, which erupted on April 16 in South Carolina. The conflict would have an immediate if indirect impact on personnel stationed at Fort Randall, and the post would eventually play a substantial role in events related to and following the Santee Sioux outbreak in Minnesota, which had become a state in 1858. Most urgently, the national crisis brought a need to transfer large numbers of soldiers from the West to the East to fill the ranks of Union troops destined to fight the rapidly mustering Confederate forces. As a contingency, the territorial government undertook to recruit home guards, with some likelihood that they might replace the federal troops at Fort Randall.

Since its establishment, Fort Randall had administratively belonged to the Department of the West, headquartered at Fort Leavenworth. In July 1861, in wartime realignment, the post fell briefly under the Western Department at St. Louis but in November went into the newly designated Department of Kansas, headquartered at Fort Leavenworth. In September 1862, Fort Randall would come under the Department of the Northwest, commanded by Major General John Pope, with headquarters in St. Paul, Minnesota. Meantime, in April 1861 three of the five companies (E, G, and I) of the Fourth Artillery stationed at the fort, along with the regimental band, headed downriver aboard the *Omaha*. The two remaining units (Companies H and M) were commanded by Captain John A. Brown, a Maryland native who disappeared without proper leave in July 1861 and presently joined the Confederacy. Soon thereafter, four other officers followed suit, leaving a garrison aggregating 110 men in the charge of First Lieutenant Thomas R. Tannat. Because of the war, no other troops were assigned until December 5, when three companies (A, B, and C) of the Fourteenth Iowa Volunteer Infantry arrived. The two regular artillery companies thereupon departed for Kentucky.[2]

The Fourteenth Iowa Volunteer Infantry, consisting of Companies A, B, and C, had been mustered during October 1861 in Iowa City. By and large, the men who made up the regiment were farmers, laborers, and shop workers with little prior military service. Captain John Pattee, Canadian born and a former Iowa state auditor, commanded the 300 men serving at Fort Randall. The troops marched 540 miles via Des Moines, Council Bluffs, and Sioux City to gain the post, and many were exhausted and in poor condition by the time they arrived. At Fort Randall, however, they found mostly light duty awaiting them, and Pattee worked to keep morale high by providing incentive pay beyond the soldiers' normal scale. By their labor, they initially obviated the need for letting hay contracts, and the supply remained high. Within a year, too, soldiers working the post sawmill created all the lumber and firewood required by the garrison.[3]

Two months after the Fourteenth Iowa settled in so comfortably, the first disruption occurred. It came with the sudden arrival at the post on February 4, 1862, of a group that included William P. Lyman, who commanded the Yankton Home Guards. An intimate of John B. S. Todd's, Lyman claimed to have been commissioned major in the Dakota Volunteer Cavalry and assigned to command Fort Randall. Since the Dakota Volunteer Cavalry at that date comprised but one unmustered company, and because the credentials that Lyman presented to Captain Pattee appeared dubious, Pattee denied them and declined to turn over his command of the fort. Some of his officers, however, concluded that Lyman's authority was genuine, and at that juncture the captain acquiesced, whereupon Major Lyman placed him under arrest. The Pattee-Lyman imbroglio was described at its height in a letter of a private of the Fourteenth Iowa: "When we came here first, Capt. Pattee took command and held it until about a month ago when Major Lyman was sent here from Dacota to take command of the post. Capt. Pattee was not for to giving up command to the Major, so the Major arrested [sic] him . . . Pattee still continues under arrest and will probably be discharged from the service. Lyman looks like a smart man and is well thought of, although he is called a 'Dacota Rat.'"[4]

Over the next few months, Pattee pleaded his case to the governor of Iowa and a senator from that state, who consulted with the the War Department. Ultimately, Lyman's commission was determined to be unauthorized in the federal forces, and he quit Fort Randall, leaving Captain Bradley Mahana in charge; with concurrence of the War Department, the competent Captain Pattee shortly relieved Mahana and regained command. In May, the Fort Randall garrison was augmented by the arrival of Company A, First Dakota Cavalry, under Captain Nelson Miner. Miner occasionally commanded the fort when Pattee traveled to the Yankton Agency to oversee distribution of annuities. Other troops likewise often visited the Ponca reserve, while some journeyed west of the fort to Hamilton Settlement to contend with irate Brulé tribesmen.[5]

On another front, Captain Pattee warred against Post Sutler George B. Hoffman, who had replaced his uncle, John B. S. Todd, following the latter's appointment as brigadier general of volunteers and almost simultaneous election as Dakota's first territorial delegate to Congress. (Todd left for army headquarters in St. Louis but shortly moved on to Washington.) Pattee believed that Hoffman's prices violated those set by the Post Council of Administration, and he accused Hoffman of dispensing liquor to the men, doubting his "business capacity and moral honesty" and believing that he was simply serving as a stooge for the absent Todd. Pattee further indicted Hoffman for keeping a card parlor and brothel in a tiny room behind the post office that attached to the sutler's store. Referencing the Indians near the post, Pattee claimed that although he had "never seen whoring at the office, . . . I am certain that it was a regular habit to take Squaws into the post office, the store room, and the bed room for that purpose."[6] When Pattee suspended Hoffman's appointment, Todd, as delegate, managed its restoration. Pattee, in fact, charged Todd with creating the Lyman imbroglio to ensure that the command of Fort Randall fell to someone he might control. Lyman had spent all of his time at the post, complained the captain, "in the Sutler's store drinking whiskey, playing billiards at the billiard room, or poker at his quarters, instead of laboring to improve the condition and discipline of the men over whom he was illegally appointed."[7]

The debate unfortunately spread into the ranks, and in December 1862 several enlisted men purportedly petitioned the adjutant general to condemn Pattee as a thief and a swindler. (This petition was eventually pronounced a forgery.) Todd, among other things, made accusations that Pattee had engaged in an operation with his brother, a commissary sergeant, looking to purchase furs with commissary provisions and move them to Iowa via government ambulance to be sold. Pattee denied the charges, and they were never proved. As well, Todd's attempts to oust Yankton Indian Agent Walter A. Burleigh in favor of a crony went awry when Pattee sent troops to arrest Theophile Bruguier and detain him at Fort Randall. Further, Dakota's new governor, William Jayne, worked with Todd to remove Pattee by writing the secretary of war for authorization to raise two companies of Dakota troops to replace those Iowans at Fort Randall. Although in May 1862 Company A of the First Dakota Cavalry had joined the garrison at the post, its tenure was brief, and the unit departed by the end of July.[8]

Pattee's contest with Todd and his cronies coincided with the beginning of events that would make Fort Randall an ingredient in the Santee Sioux outbreak of 1862. Prior to that event, Fort Randall's role in regional Indian affairs lay in monitoring activities around the Yankton and Ponca reservations and providing military support wherever required to ensure the protection of the white settlements. In September 1861, for example, Company M, Fourth Artillery, trekked to the Yankton Agency to subdue a disturbance. In the following months, such attendance continued. Captain Pattee and his successors regularly visited Greenwood with troops from the post to oversee distribution of cash and annuities in accordance with treaty provisions. When the Yanktons departed on a hunt, Agent Burleigh had a two-story octagonal blockhouse constructed at Greenwood to help protect his wards. Yet there were other signs that things were amiss among the Indians in the region, despite the Yanktons' pledge to "stand by" the government. In anticipation of a general Indian disturbance, the First Dakota Cavalry was recalled from Fort Randall and distributed around the southeastern part of the territory.[9]

Trouble among the Eastern Sioux had simmered for years following the incursions of whites and the concentration of the tribe on a strip of land along the Minnesota River. Despite agreements between the government, settlers, and tribesmen, the encroachment continued and was compounded by dishonest traders and creditors who routinely cheated the people on their annuities. Warfare erupted on August 18, 1862, and lasted more than a month, with fighting raging at Fort Ridgely and the German settlement of New Ulm. Within a week, 800 white settlers had perished at the hands of the Indians, with hundreds of others captured by the Mdewakanton leader Little Crow and his followers until relief arrived. Troops under Colonel Henry H. Sibley helped break the initial resistance and finally defeated the Indians at Wood Lake, halting the local violence. Eventually, Little Crow was killed. Some 300 of the Santees were tried and condemned to death; President Abraham Lincoln commuted the sentences of all but thirty-nine, who were hanged.[10]

During the outbreak, Santees had attacked and murdered whites near Sioux Falls. Throughout and following the Minnesota uprising, many of the Sioux participants fled west into Dakota, and their accounts of the warfare further fired the spirits of the Lakotas. A correspondent calling himself "Ajax" wrote from Fort Randall that the arriving Santees "are forming coalitions with the upper bands of the Sioux nation, with the intention of inaugurating a wholesale system of aggression and violence upon the Whites next spring." "Ajax" hoped that General Pope would "imitate the example of Gen. Harney, viz: a complete annihilation of the Indians. . . . By a war of extermination only, can safety to settlers be established on the frontier."[11]

As expected, the movement west of these Santees created certain consternation among the Yanktons, who were pressed to join their cousins in the uprising, as well as among the Poncas, who were terrorized by the Minnesota events and who believed that they represented "the lull before the storm" and that "movements will be made by all [the tribes] simultaneously against the whites and treaty Indians on both sides of the Missouri River." In September, rumor circulated that the Yankton Agency was under attack, and the Poncas believed that they would be next. They were still without their horses, they complained. Jittery, they first sent much of their ammunition for safekeeping at Fort Randall "to prevent its waste" if the Sioux attacked, an indication that they did not intend to defend their agency. But they later asked for the munitions back to fight the Sioux, and to indulge his wards the Ponca agent erected a blockhouse and mounted a cannon as a sign of the government's commitment to protect the Poncas.[12]

Despite the brevity of the Minnesota outbreak, its impact resonated in Dakota for many years thereafter and contributed to the mounting distrust between whites and Indians throughout the West that would last decades. Most immediately for Fort Randall, the outbreak marked an intensity in the use and visibility of the post as troops arrived, passed through, or joined one or more of several campaigns launched in the weeks and months following the initial shock of the Indian attacks on the settlements. Yet in the first month after the uprising in Minnesota, there was an attitude of watchful waiting among the garrison. A correspondent noted that "things are all quiet here, and no Indian disturbances apprehended, although the uninitiated who could see the numerous lodges surrounding the Fort would imagine that it was besieged. A band of Brulés are encamped in close proximity, besides quite a number of Yankton tepees are scattered here and there." He further described the presence of one hundred Yankton lodges immediately across the Missouri River from the fort. Obviously, the establishment of the military reservation had not curtailed the frequent assembly of tribesmen around the post, and the commentator questioned the "doubtful policy" of permitting "Indians, although they may be friendly, to hang around and spy out the land and then report during their migrations to other bands, who may perhaps be hostile to the whites." Despite that statement, the same reporter implausibly remarked that the recently promoted Major Pattee "has taken every precaution to guard against Indian treachery or surprise." In the same missive, the reporter commented on the presence near Fort Pierre (now owned by the American Fur Company) of 200 Santee participants in the Minnesota trouble, en route most likely to the upper Missouri.[13]

While laxity existed within the garrison, much of the soldiers' time was nonetheless dedicated to drill, and the troops had attained a modicum of discipline and proficiency in that training. Simultaneous with Pattee's advancement was his transfer to the Forty-first Iowa Infantry and the incorporation of the companies of the Fourteenth Iowa at Fort Randall into that regiment. Soon after, "'a gay and festive time'— celebrated the Major's inauguration to his new position."[14] Visitors to Fort Randall included "Governor Jayne and lady"; Newton Edmunds, who would succeed Jayne as governor; a Miss Foulk; and Sallie Burleigh, all of whom were "tendered the hospitalities of the Garrison by Major Pattee, at whose quarters they were entertained."[15] Other occasional guests numbered delegate Todd and U.S. Marshal George M. Pinney, who periodically reserved rooms at the post for upcoming sessions of the Third U.S. District Court. Also present was the registrar of the land office in Dakota City, traveling north at Governor Jayne's behest to determine the number of Nebraska volunteers that might be required to protect the upcountry.[16] The news from Minnesota, however, was such as to frighten many settlers in southeastern Dakota who feared that the Yanktons would be enticed to join in attacking whites. Occasionally, some Indians appeared seeking food and horses. They burned Sioux Falls following its evacuation by residents. Many settlers fled their homes to find safety in Sioux City, Vermillion, and Elk Point, even though Dakota cavalry and local militia called out by the governor and armed with weapons and ammunition requisitioned from Fort Randall ranged the country along the Missouri between September and November. Residents of Yankton, the new territorial capital of Dakota, raised a six-foot-high sod stockade in their community.[17]

On November 28, three months after the Santee Sioux outbreak, Major Pattee led Companies A and B of the Forty-first Iowa, along with Company A, First Dakota Cavalry, in search of two white women and some children reportedly held by the Indians in the vicinity of Fort Pierre. En route, the troops encountered two mixed-bloods together with the captives, who had been freed by the intercession of Sans Arc Lakotas. The Fort Randall soldiers contributed money ($256.50) to the victims, then proceeded to Fort Pierre, there leaving Captain Mahana and Company B while Pattee with Company A and the Dakota troops returned to Fort Randall (as of November, the Dakota company was again assigned to the post). Over the ensuing weeks, a detachment of the Dakotans under Lieutenant James Bacon surrounded and captured thirty-one reportedly starving Santee men, women, and children on Platte Creek, thirty miles upstream. The prisoners were taken to Fort Randall and the women and children quartered in various facilities, where they subsisted on army rations through the winter. Eight men were locked in the guardhouse. In one instance, the leader of the tribesmen attempted to escape, and the guard fired shots at him. He ran into Pattee's office for refuge but was there cornered and returned to the guardhouse. Within weeks, however, the eight Indians imprisoned in the guardhouse managed to cut through the floor planking, dig a hole through the wall, and escape, likely swimming the Missouri. Although the First Dakota Cavalry searched the area, the Indians were gone.[18]

Early in 1863, the War Department directed the moving of nearly 1,500 Santee men, women, and children still remaining in Minnesota, along with their horses, cattle, and wagons, via steamboat to a location near Crow Creek, some forty-five miles above Fort Randall on the Missouri River. Nearly 2,000 innocent Winnebagoes were also moved to a reservation just above the Santee tract. Part of the Dakota troops at Fort Randall joined in overseeing the arrival of the various tribesmen and helped erect agency buildings and a cottonwood stockade (soon thereafter named Fort Thompson after Indian Agent Clark W. Thompson) to protect supplies. On June 13, after the troops, while they rode upstream, were fired upon by Indians, Lieutenant Colonel Samuel N. Pollock of the Sixth Iowa Cavalry, who had assumed command of Fort Randall, directed forth a detachment of Iowa and Dakota soldiers under Captain Abraham B. Moreland. These troops located a small camp near Ponca Creek and attacked it, killing seven Indians in a manner that frightened tribesmen on the Yankton Reservation and otherwise became a locally debated affair. A sergeant with the Sixth Iowa allowed that the seven tribesmen had, in fact, been apprehended as prisoners and left with several guards, who claimed to have shot them attempting to escape. Major Pattee, however, who continued operating with troops among the Missouri River posts, maintained that the Indians had been captured while Moreland was looking about for stray horses and had been shot in the back as they walked ahead of the soldiers toward the fort. Most unfortunately, the killed tribesmen proved to be friendly Yanktons and Two Kettle Lakotas.

Other tragedies occurred intermittently throughout the year. In May 1863, two freighters were attacked by warriors near Greenway's Ferry east of Yankton; one died, and the other was wounded. Near the Missouri in Nebraska, seven children belonging to a family named Wiseman were murdered in July in a particularly heinous outrage committed by Indians reportedly from Minnesota under the leadership of the son of a noted Wahpekute named Inkpaduta. Lieutenant Bacon and his detachment trailed the Sioux but failed to overtake them. In early September, a stagecoach en route to Fort Randall came under attack at Tackett Station near Choteau Creek. The Indians killed Sergeant Eugene F. Trask, Company B, Forty-first Iowa Infantry, before stealing horses and making their escape. As a precaution, detachments of Dakota troops took station until the following spring at Greenwood, at the Yankton Agency, at White Swan, and at a home on Platte Creek.[19]

With the increased Indian activity, the First Dakota Cavalry had been bolstered early in 1863 with the mustering of Company B at Sioux City. Fort Randall and the Iowa troops by then had been assigned to the new First Military District of the Northwest (Dakota Territory and northwestern Iowa), headquartered in Sioux City under Brigadier General John Cook.[20] Security around Fort Randall increased, and in June, as preparations ensued for a major regional campaign against the tribes, an important edict at last went forth forbidding Indians and others not formally sanctioned from entering the military reservation:

> Headquarters 1st Battalion 6th Iowa Cavalry,
> Fort Randall, D.T.
> June 6th, 1863
> To whom it may concern:—
> 1. No Indians will be allowed to remain on this Military Reservation.
> 11. All Indians found on this reservation will be regarded as hostile, and treated as such.
> 111. Any person not connected with the army, who shall correspond with, or who shall in any manner harbor or conceal any Indian or Indians on this military reservation, without special permission from these Headquarters, shall be sent beyond the boundary of this reservation, and not permitted to return; and soldiers or persons connected with the army so offending, will be severely punished according to the nature of the offense.
> iv. This not being a trading post, all trade and traffic with Indians on this reservation is forbidden. The property of any one so offending shall be confiscated, and the person so offending sent beyond the boundaries of the reservation.
> v. Indian Agents are ordered to keep their Indians within the boundaries of their respective reservations, and all friendly Indians are ordered to remain within said boundaries, as such friendly

Indians cannot, by military officers and soldiers in the service of the Government, be distinguished from the hostile roving bands that infest the country.

By Order of

Lt.-Col. S. M. Pollock

Comd'g F'cs.

W. A. Heath, A.A.

1st Bat. 6th Iowa Cavalry[21]

A letter in Yankton's *Weekly Dakotian* related how "the 'natives' didn't relish the idea at first, but finding resistance and parley fruitless, they 'took up their beds and walked,' and are now across the river . . . where they will be compelled to stay, or take the awful consequences. The only copper faces about the garrison now, are our old standbys—the seven Santee prisoners—who have been in close confinement in the guard-house for several months."[22]

The order respecting Indians on the military reservation presaged the beginning of the Sioux Expedition of 1863. Although General Pope had decreed the Minnesota war at an end, he intended to punish the offending Santees. The campaign would involve armies under Colonel Sibley and Brigadier General Alfred Sully. Sully, who had been an army captain with the Second Infantry at Forts Pierre and Randall in 1856, fielded a command eventually totaling 2,500 men that included units of the Forty-first Iowa Volunteer Infantry (mounted), eight companies of the Second Nebraska Cavalry, a battalion of the Sixth Iowa Cavalry, besides elements of the Seventh Iowa Volunteer Cavalry and the Thirtieth Wisconsin Volunteer Infantry, complete with requisite horses, cattle, and wagons. Ideally, Sully would work in concert with Sibley's force of 2,000 infantry and cavalry, which would ostensibly pursue the Santees west from Minnesota while Sully ascended the Missouri and positioned his forces to halt their flight and destroy them. Sibley indeed met the Santees in July at Big Mound and Dead Buffalo Lake in present eastern North Dakota.[23]

Sully's column, however, was delayed, at least partly by low water on the Missouri River, which halted him for a week at Fort Randall, much to the chagrin of Department Commander Pope. On June 28, twenty officers greeted Sully at the landing and escorted him to the parade ground, where the troops were arrayed. "The band gave three rousing cheers; the glorious old Star-Gemmed Banner drooped its proud crest, and the soldiers gave the usual salutation, 'Present—arms.'"²⁴ On July 4, American independence was observed as follows:

> A salute of 34 guns was fired at noon, and in the evening a large assemblage of officers and soldiers convened at the hall. The ladies of the garrison also turned out in goodly number, which gave to the occasion a social and "civilized" appearance. Lieut. Ryan was called to the chair; when the exercises commenced with Martial music, furnished by Morton's excellent band, which was followed by an eloquent prayer from Dr. Peebles and a National Song by the Choir. Mr. McKinstry of the 6th Iowa, was then called to the stand, and gave us a soul-thrilling and patriotic oration, which was well received. Gen'l Sully followed in a short and affecting speech, in which he reviewed the events of the past seven years, alluding to the period when Fort Randall was founded, and to his old regiment, the 2nd Infantry (Regulars), who built this post, many of whom now "sleep their last sleep" on the banks of the Potomac and Rappahannock, sacrificed upon the altar of the Union. The General's remarks were enthusiastically received, and he closed amid a tumult of cheers. . . . Loyalty, patriotism, and strict decorum were the marked features of the evening. Copperheads dwell not in Fort Randall.²⁵

The layover provided the expedition an opportunity to make ready for its advance. Tasks accomplished before departure included the re-alignment of wagon wheels, the shoeing of horses and mules, the loading of wagons, and "a thousand nameless things." "The numerous camps, the herds of cattle, squads of cavalry riding to and fro, presents [sic] a lively aspect to those uninitiated in the art of war, while long trains of wagons, with six mule teams, are constantly on the move from the ferry to the camps."²⁶ On Sully's direction, contingencies in the delivery of supplies called for storage of corn (some simply piled on the shoreline opposite the post) and other commodities in support of the expedition at Fort Randall. Provisions would be loaded on available steamboats for the push upriver. Throughout the campaign, an express rider with horse would remain posted on the east side of the Missouri.²⁷

Sully departed with his command on July 5, leaving a company of the Thirtieth Wisconsin Volunteer Infantry at the post pending its movement up to Fort Pierre. Ultimately, many supplies had to be transported by wagon from Fort Randall. The steamboat bearing the expedition's stores reached the soldiers on August 19. Thus provisioned, Sully proceeded north and west, engaging a large assembly of Santees and Tetons at Whitestone Hill in the James River valley of present North Dakota. He inflicted heavy casualties and captured 156 prisoners while sustaining losses of twenty men killed and thirty-eight wounded, then returned to Fort Pierre in mid-September. East of that old post, Sully established another, eventually named Fort Sully (and henceforth replacing Fort Randall as the farthest north active federal outpost on the Missouri), from which sorties intermittently went forth to find and attack the Indians. Companies A and D of the Sixth Iowa Cavalry were sent upstream from Fort Randall to garrison Fort Sully, while Company K of the Sixth Iowa replaced Company A, First Dakota Cavalry, at Crow Creek's Fort Thompson. The Dakota troops took up a station opposite Fort Randall, while soldiers of the Seventh Iowa Cavalry and Thirtieth Wisconsin Infantry (two companies) would garrison that post through the winter.[28]

Downriver, troops from Fort Randall and the temporary stations, as well as Company B, First Dakota Cavalry, continued ranging through the southeastern Dakota countryside. While these movements helped secure the region from Indian attack and helped restore a semblance of stability, all was not well. Over the preceding few years, the Poncas had been repeatedly terrorized by the Lakotas, and Ponca children had been taken prisoner. Moreover, they remained displeased with their reservation boundary, which did not include the mouth of the Niobrara River. At one point, the tribesmen forcibly detained their agent and refused to allow delivery of annuities, necessitating his request for troops from Fort Randall. Most sinister of all, in December 1863 a party of soldiers of the Seventh Iowa Volunteer Cavalry operating out of Niobrara, Nebraska, encountered fifteen Poncas—men, women, and children—returning to their agency from the Omaha reservation. The troops, probably drunk, attempted to rape the women, then destroyed the Poncas' lodges and provisions, and finally killed several of them. The murderers were never punished, although the government in time awarded monetary compensation to the tribe. But the incident compounded the already frayed composure of the Poncas on the heels of the Sioux outbreak and a year of poor crop production and did nothing to improve their relationship with federal troops.[29] Unfortunately for the Poncas, government attention remained focused on the Sioux, and the outbreak prompted calls for an increase of troops in the region, including recommendations for "at least a regiment of Infantry and a battalion of Cavalry" at Fort Randall.

Throughout the early 1860s, in spite of the activities affecting area Indians, the soldiers at the fort maintained their routine, accomplishing drill and fatigue duty when in garrison. The post commissary officer periodically sent out requests for bids for supplying beef cattle to the post, and in September 1862 a large number of the beasts were purchased at Yankton. Similarly, corn and potatoes comprised dietary staples always in demand. Contracts were repeatedly let for the cutting and delivery of wood. The district court that convened at Fort Randall on October 22, 1862, Judge Joseph L. Williams presiding, heard the case of a man indicted for bringing "spirituous liquors" on to the Yankton Reservation, for which he was duly ordered jailed for thirty days and fined a sum (including court costs) of $522.76. Mail service to Fort Randall was often slow, and the territorial legislature asked for more speedy delivery between Sioux City and the post. Meanwhile, Major Pattee, who was promoted lieutenant colonel of the Seventh Iowa Cavalry in June 1863 and reassigned to district headquarters at Sioux City, shortly devised a system for escorting the mail stage on the route as protection against roving bands of Indians. Mail service on the west side of the Missouri, between Fort Randall and Niobrara, was briefly interrupted by flooding late in 1863, while the establishment of Fort Sully up the Missouri temporarily prompted a private mail delivery service to that point.[30]

While the various military campaigns proceeded in response to the Sioux outbreak, the Fort Randall garrison otherwise followed a daily regimen without notable exception, especially after the departure of Sully's command. Steamboats still docked frequently at its landing, discharging supplies from downstream for the use of troops there and afield. Several noteworthy events related to the garrison of Fort Randall took place while events swirled in the months following the Sioux outbreak. On May 24, for example, while four companies of the arriving Sixth Iowa Cavalry ferried the Missouri River to the post, a soldier of Company H was pushed overboard by a horse, which fell after him into the river. As a rescue attempt proceeded, another mount tumbled over, landing atop the flailing trooper and forcing him under. In late July 1863, General Pope ordered the evacuation of "the large number" of women (excepting laundresses) and children from Fort Randall. It reportedly caused "quite a commotion within the *crinoline circle*."[31]

Garrison routine during the period of Sully's campaign continued largely as before, with typical daily military orders going to detachment commanders to "load the train now waiting on the other side of the river with the rations required . . . for the troops at 'Fort Antietam' [Fort Sully]"; to individual officers to "purchase a Stack of Hay . . . of [citizen] G. L. Tackett at Choteau Creek . . . for the use of Escorts and troops Stationed at that Point"; to "march from this Post on the morning of Thursday the 8th day of Oct. 1863 for Vermillion D.T. there to relieve a Detachment of Co. 'A' Dak Cav."; to "detail one company of 2nd Neb Cavlry now at this Post to escort the Supply Train, now Loading on the other Side of the River, from this point to Crow Creek Agency"; and to "detail 1st Lieut. Bacon Co. A, Dacota Cav'y and twenty men of same Co to proceed to the Yankton Indian Agency and relieve the detachment of C & E, 6th Iowa Vol. Cavalry." Post councils of administration were routinely appointed to "attend to all duties devolving on them." It also became critical for troops to constantly guard the landing and flatboat at the river: "Commander of Co A will detail a Corporal and Eight men to act as Boatsguard for the ensuing week. They will report at the QMrs at Bell Ringing tomorrow morning."[32]

One policy locally enacted at Fort Randall (and likely at other regional posts, too) during the period of the 1862–65 Indian war concerned the distribution to area tribesmen of bad foodstuffs. For example, in November 1863 Colonel Pollock directed the issue to Winnebagoes of twenty-five pounds of "condemed [sic] or Spoiled meat" and fifteen pounds of "condemed or Spoiled Rice." Pollock also ordered the distribution "to Big Indian and his band [of] Two hundred pounds of Condemned pork and one hundred pounds of Spoiled Rice." Similar disbursements were made to Wekuthke, Little Thunder, Wau-kam-how-kah, and their people of meat and rice "which is unfit to be issued to Soldiers."[33] Quite likely, the policy presented the double benefit of relieving the commands of putrid, or marginally putrid, food stocks while at the same time fostering among the Indians an appearance of government generosity.

While Indian activity generally appeared fleeting in the vicinity of Fort Randall at the beginning of 1864, there occurred occasional reports that required military response. During the late winter, following the murder by "Hostile Indians" of a Sixth Iowa soldier near the post and amid concerns that Indians lurked in nearby woods and ravines, detachments canvassed the countryside. They were instructed not to harm "friendly Indians" and to take prisoners only those "of a doubtful character." Known "Hostile Indians," on the other hand, were to be killed outright.[34] In a regional sense, however, as a result of Sully's campaign, Indian trouble had spread farther up the Missouri, and the seeds of conflict had swept well beyond the Santees to embrace tribes like the Yanktonais, Northern Cheyennes, and Lakota Sioux, and among the latter in particular the Hunkpapas, Blackfeet Sioux, Sans Arcs, and Minneconjous. (The contagious nature of the Minnesota outbreak had been apparent as early as October 1862, with an attack by Yanktonais from Fort Berthold on a mackinaw containing eleven men from the far upriver port of Fort Benton. One man, seriously wounded in the thigh, had been left at Fort Randall to recuperate.)[35] In order to check and control these upstream peoples and keep them from disrupting the land and river arteries in the West, General Pope planned yet another offensive that would punish the remnant involved in the Minnesota outbreak while admonishing through chastisement all others.

The establishment of new posts would facilitate Pope's policy. In eastern Dakota, General Sibley would build and garrison Fort Wadsworth and provide 1,500 cavalry, infantry, and artillery troops from the Minnesota volunteer regiments for General Sully, who would reorganize at Fort Sully on the Missouri and then strike west. Sully would take with him the two First Dakota Cavalry companies, eleven companies of Lieutenant Colonel Pollock's Sixth Iowa Infantry, three companies of the Seventh Iowa Volunteer Cavalry commanded by Lieutenant Colonel John Pattee (most of these troops had variously formed elements of the Fort Randall garrison), a battalion of Minnesota cavalry, and a battalion of Wisconsin infantry. The troops garnered from Sibley comprised a regiment of Minnesota mounted infantry, a battalion of Minnesota cavalry, and two sections of a Minnesota artillery battery. Steamboats would transport Sully's campaign supplies, while his troops, including most of the Iowa battalion at Fort Randall, ascended the east bank of the Missouri. At the post, Colonel Pollack was charged with sending upstream via steamer all remaining serviceable saddles and bridles and with moving swiftly forward all troops, supplies, and teamsters.[36]

Late in June, the expedition—more than 2,200 men strong—got under way from Fort Sully, marching up the east bank of the Missouri, meeting and absorbing the Minnesota contingent, and continuing upstream to near Long Lake, where Fort Rice was established and Wisconsin troops were stationed. From there, Sully moved west to Heart River, then on toward a concentration of several thousand Hunkpapas, Blackfeet Sioux, Sans Arcs, Minneconjous, Santees, and Yanktonais known to be at Killdeer Mountains in present western North Dakota. On July 28, 1864, Sully's command attacked the Indian position with artillery fire supported by cavalry and infantry, inflicting heavy casualties and sustaining few of their own. By evening, the engagement was over. Sully returned briefly to Fort Rice, then headed his expedition west to the Yellowstone River, where supply problems eventually dictated his turnabout. Posting a company of Wisconsin infantry at the mouth of the Yellowstone, Sully marched down the Missouri, contacting the friendly Arikaras, Mandans, and Hidatsas and leaving a company of the Sixth Iowa at the fur post of Fort Berthold before moving on to Forts Rice and Sully and closing out the expedition.[37] Throughout the period of Sully's 1864 campaign, one company—G—of the Sixth Iowa Cavalry had remained in garrison at Fort Randall. Beyond the movement of troops from the post to serve on the expedition, General Sully had recruited there fifty-one Yanktons to accompany his command as scouts, which seems to have constituted the high point of Fort Randall's involvement in the expedition. It was expected, however, that chiefs of the defeated tribes would assemble during the winter at Fort Randall to meet with Sully and forge a peace treaty "on terms entirely satisfactory to the Government."[38]

By this time, in the wake of General Sully's 1864 campaign, Fort Randall was but one of several military posts on the upper Missouri River. Early in 1865, Sully wrote Major General Samuel R. Curtis, commander of the Department of the Northwest, offering a review of stations from north to south on the river and showing the following disposition of troops: at Fort Union he posted a single company of the Thirtieth Wisconsin Infantry, and at Fort Berthold he left one company (G) of the Sixth Iowa Cavalry. Downriver, at Fort Rice, were six companies of the First U.S. Volunteers ("Galvanized Yankees"—former Confederate prisoners who had been sent from the East), while at Fort Sully there were three companies (B, H, and K) of the Sixth Iowa Cavalry. Farther downriver, at the Santee/Winnebago reservation at Crow Creek, was the blockhouse and a detachment of Company K, Sixth Iowa Cavalry. Another blockhouse, with fifteen soldiers, stood about forty-five miles below Crow Creek, midway between that point and Fort Randall. Fort Randall was now garrisoned by four companies (A, C, L, and M) of the Sixth Iowa Cavalry under Colonel Pollock. Below Fort Randall, at the Yankton Agency, was Company B, First Dakota Cavalry, while on the James River six miles downriver from Yankton, Sully placed Company I, Sixth Iowa Cavalry. Stationed at Vermillion was part of Company A, First Dakota Cavalry, with the remainder located at the crossing of the Big Sioux River to the southeast.

Early in 1865, Sully proposed a military presence at several other points to protect settlers—one company at Sioux Falls, another at the James River, and a third at Crow Creek Agency, with the lines in between being constantly patrolled. (This plan, repeatedly advocated by territory officials, was instituted the following year.) He further advised that the Fort Randall garrison be reduced to one company of infantry and two of cavalry. Sully complained about the layout of the post and urged that it be changed: "It is not built like a post. The buildings are very much scattered. It takes a very great number of sentinels to guard it. . . . [I advise] pulling down part of the post and making it a fort instead of a village."[39]

In the spring of 1865, following rumors that the Lakota tribes wanted to talk, yet another expedition—Sully's third—moved out of Fort Sully via Fort Rice and Fort Berthold toward Devil's Lake, where a large force of Santees had reportedly gathered. The campaign, drastically modified in scope that redirected it east instead of west, proceeded despite Territorial Governor Newton Edmunds's determination against further warfare and to mollify the Indians with treaties instead. Edmunds believed that previous campaigning had focused too far beyond the white settlements and wanted more local protection. Moreover, the territory now faced drought and grasshopper infestation, which, together with warring Indians, combined to deter emigration. While Edmunds, who was also Indian superintendent in Dakota, sought through Interior Department authorities to organize a commission to meet with the tribesmen, General Pope resisted the plan with continued support for a military solution. Sully's expedition, meantime, by autumn had failed to find and engage large numbers of Sioux and therefore returned to the Missouri River. Yet his campaigning over the preceding two years had destroyed much of the Indians' supplies, causing hunger and forcing them to stay on the move seeking game, a factor that ironically contributed to Governor Edmunds's evolving peace strategy.[40] Through the summer of 1865, the Sixth Iowa Cavalry continued to garrison the upper Missouri posts, with two companies remaining at Fort Randall. By mid-October, however, the role of the Sixth Iowa in the regional proceedings was finished, the regiment's term expired, and the troops were mustered out at Sioux City. General Pope ordered replacements from Colonel Nelson Cole's recently concluded Indian expedition in what is present Montana and Wyoming, including one hundred men from that command to be stationed at Fort Randall.[41]

Brigadier General William S. Harney.
Source: South Dakota Historical Collections 1 (1902): 44–45.

The Fort Randall
Military Reservation as
established in 1860, as
rendered by First
Lieutenant Joseph C.
Clark Jr., Fourth
Artillery. Source:
National Archives,
Record Group 77,
Cartographic Archives
Division.

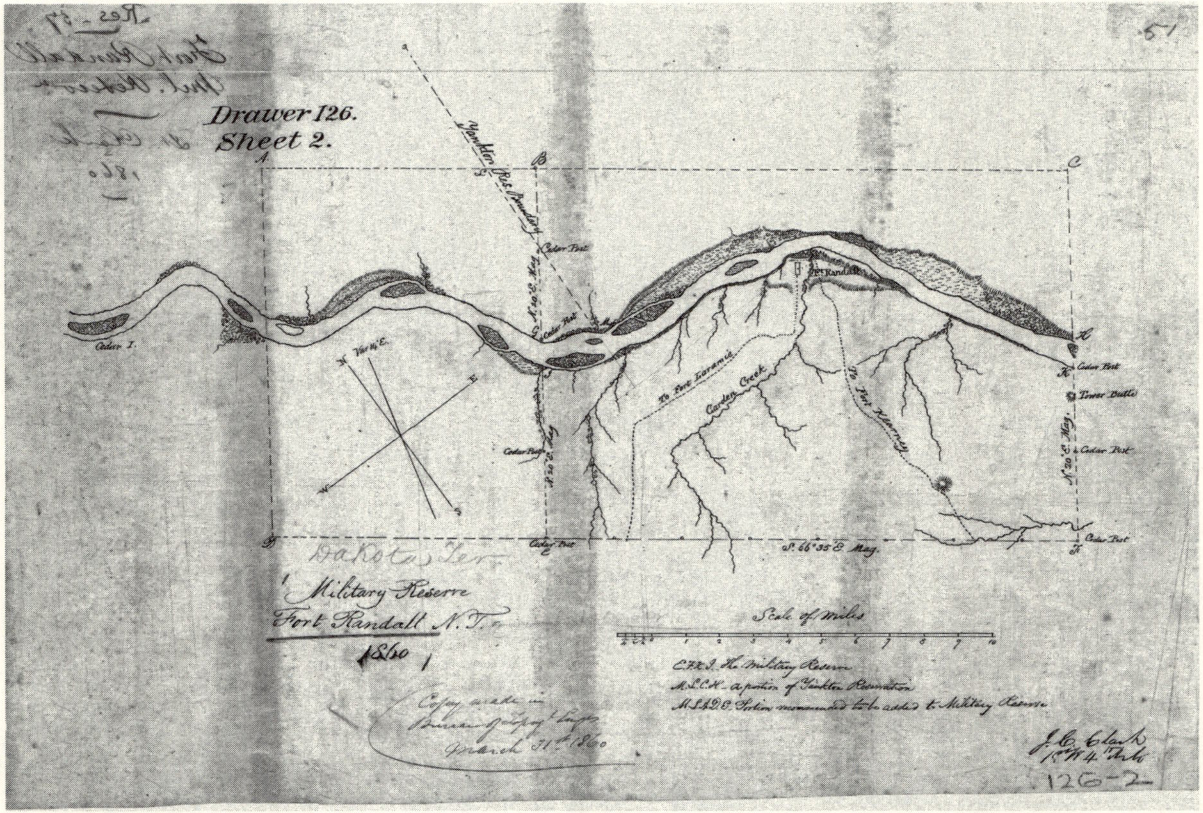

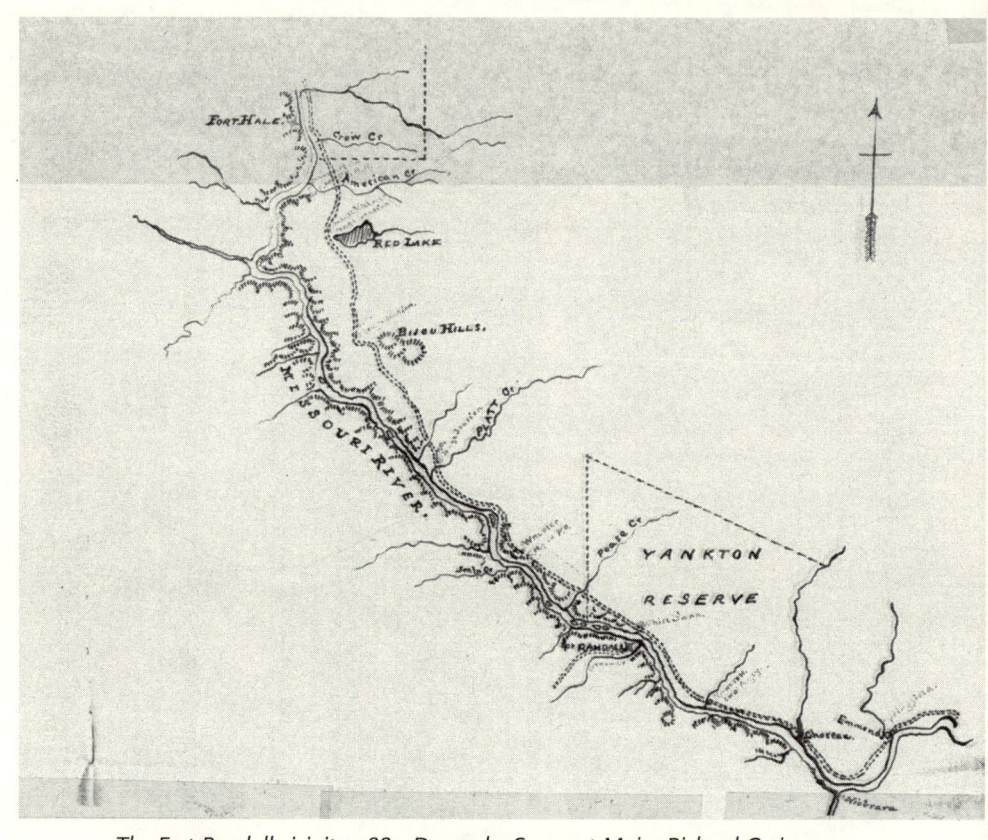

The Fort Randall vicinity, 1881. Drawn by Sergeant Major Richard Craig, Twenty-fifth Infantry. Source: National Archives, Record Group 393, Entry 6, Letters and Telegrams Received, Fort Randall, S.D., Box 6.

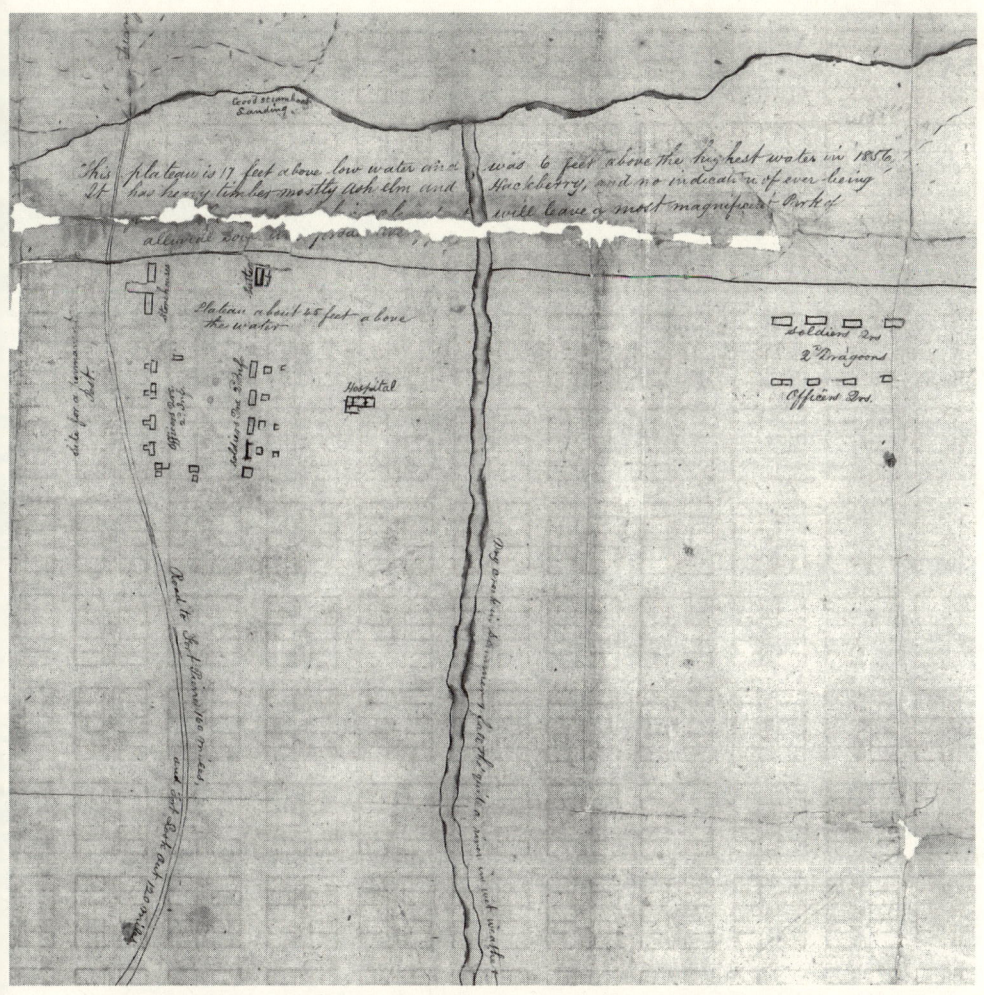

Earliest known plat of Fort Randall, ca. October 1856. Drawn by Captain Parmenas Taylor Turnley, acting quartermaster. Source: National Archives, Record Group 49, Cartographic Archives Division.

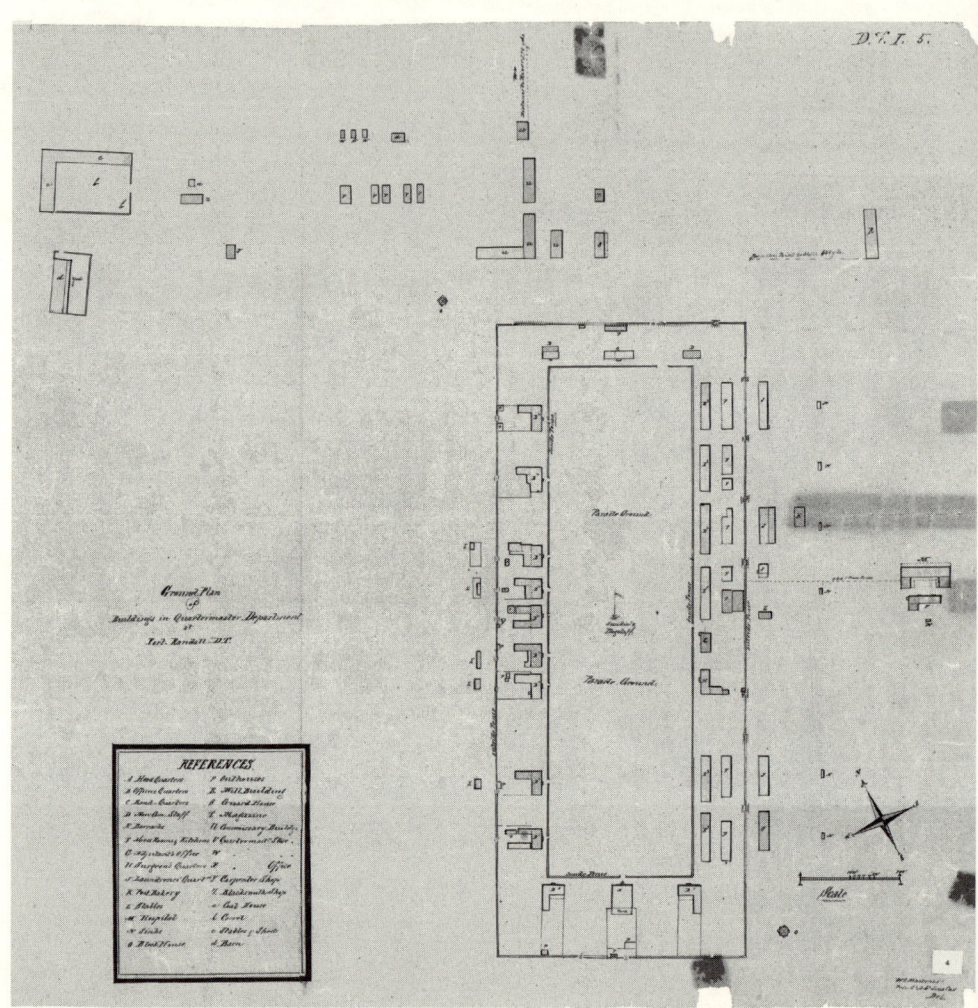

Plat of Fort Randall, ca. December 1865. Drawn by Private W. S. Mackenzie, Company A, Sixth Iowa Cavalry. Source: National Archives, Record Group 77, Cartographic Archives Division.

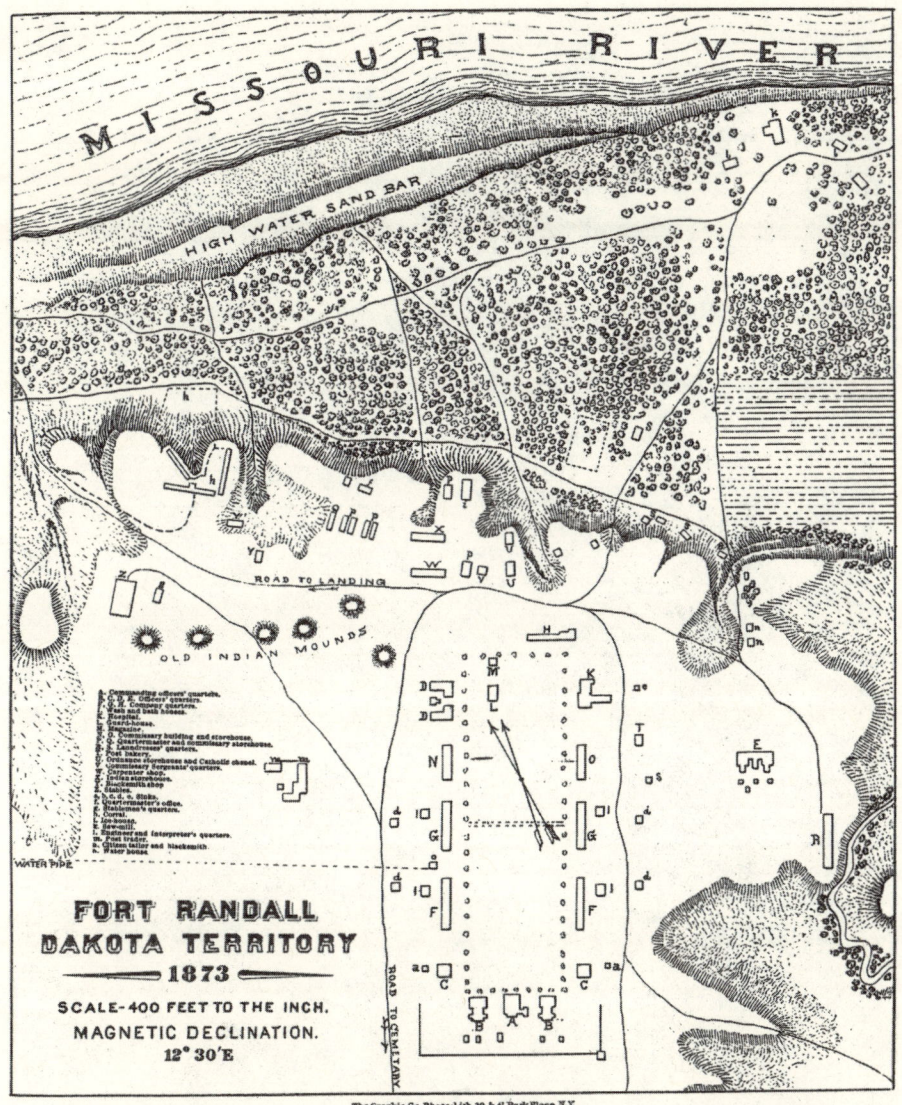

Plat of Fort Randall, 1873, showing area roads and trails. Source: John S. Billings, Report on Hygiene of the United States Army with Descriptions of Military Posts. Circular No. 8, War Department, Surgeon General's Office, May 1, 1875; reprint, New York: Sol Lewis, 1974.

FORT RANDALL, NEBRASKA TERRITORY.—FROM A SKETCH BY OUR OWN CORRESPONDENT.

Fort Randall, Nebraska Territory, 1858, with view generally to the north. This woodcut appeared in
Frank Leslie's Illustrated Weekly, July 3, 1858. Courtesy of the Nebraska State Historical Society, Lincoln.

Painting of Fort Randall, July 19, 1860, showing log barracks and quarters, looking generally west, with commanding officer's frame quarters at far end of the parade ground. This rendering, drawn by William Jacob Hays, was purportedly copied from a photograph. Courtesy of the Kansas State Historical Society, Topeka.

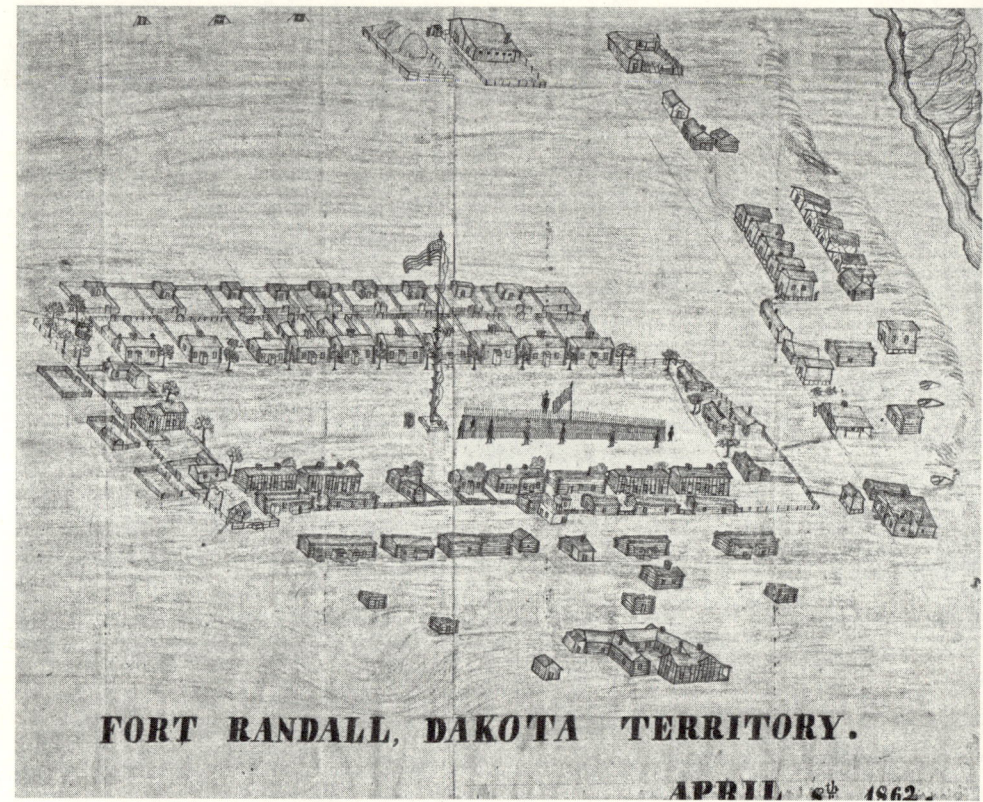

FORT RANDALL, DAKOTA TERRITORY.

APRIL 8th 1862.

Fort Randall, Dakota Territory, April 8, 1862, view to the northeast. Drawn by Corporal Lambert Martin, Fourteenth Iowa Volunteer Infantry. Note the log structures as well as what appear to be the portable cottages near the Missouri River. Infantrymen armed with bayoneted muskets parade near the flagpole, while to the right (east) appears an artillery piece with caisson. Lambert shows an apparent blockhouse at the upper left edge of the garrison. This was apparently short-lived, and blockhouses were raised at the approximate southwest and northeast corners by 1865. By the mid-1880s, however, both had evidently been leveled as nonessential. Courtesy of Yale Collection of Western Americana, Beinecke Rare Book and Manuscript Library, Yale University, New Haven, Conn.

Fort Randall in 1865. View generally west showing log structures bordering the parade ground, with storehouse in foreground. Photograph by Lieutenant William H. Blyton, Company M, Second Infantry. Courtesy of Larry Ness, Yankton, S.Dak.

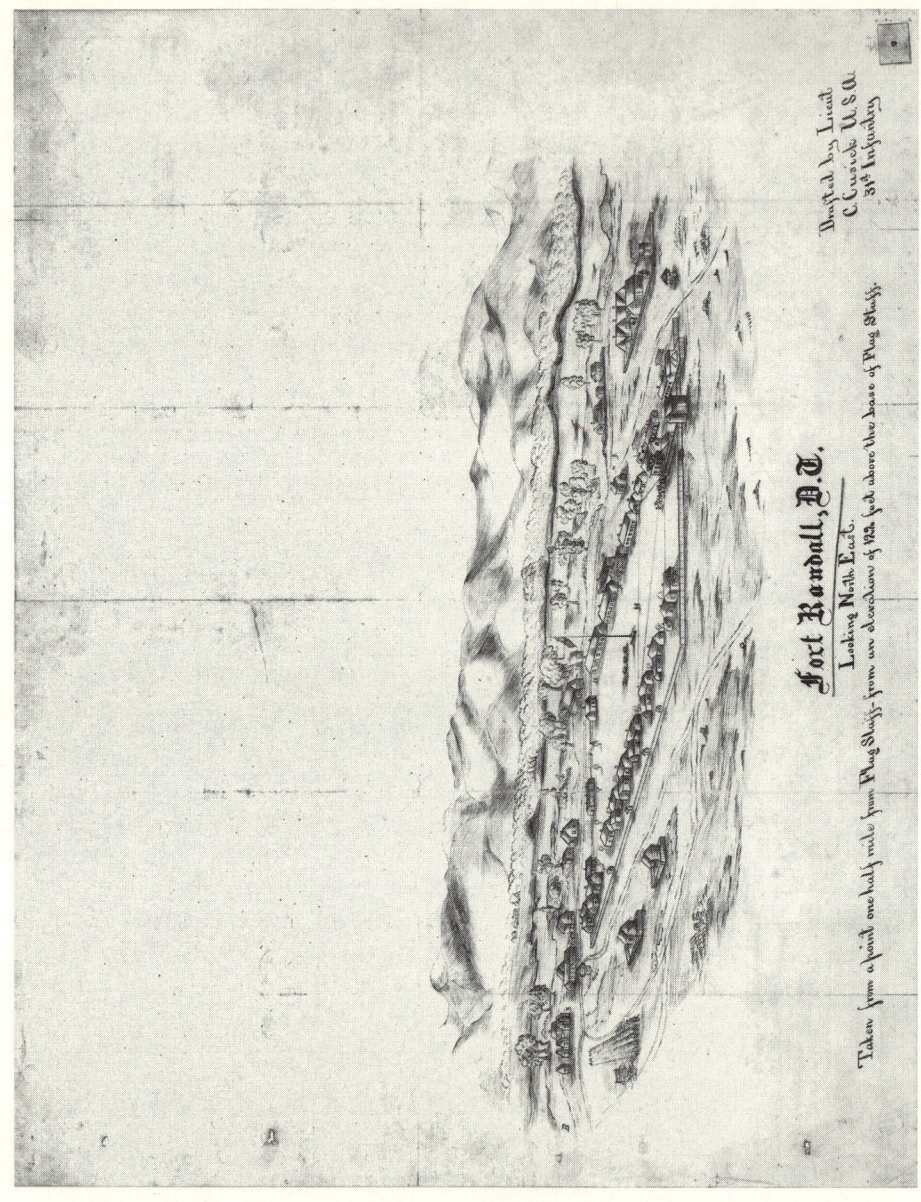

Fort Randall, D.T.
Looking North East.

Taken from a point one half mile from Flag Staff, from an elevation of 124 feet above the base of Flag Staff.

Drafted by Lieut. C. C. Cusick U.S.A. 31st Infantry

"Fort Randall, D.T.," as drafted in ca. 1867 by Second Lieutenant Cornelius C. Cusick, Thirty-first Infantry. View generally east, toward the river. Note the four pieces of artillery on the parade near the flagpole. Log buildings can be discerned among frame ones, while at the extreme left near the northeast corner stand the remaining portable cottages. Source: National Archives, Record Group 77, Cartographic Archives Division.

Fort Randall, ca. 1874, showing the two-story frame barracks constructed early in the decade and the new hospital at top center. Courtesy of South Dakota State Historical Society, Pierre.

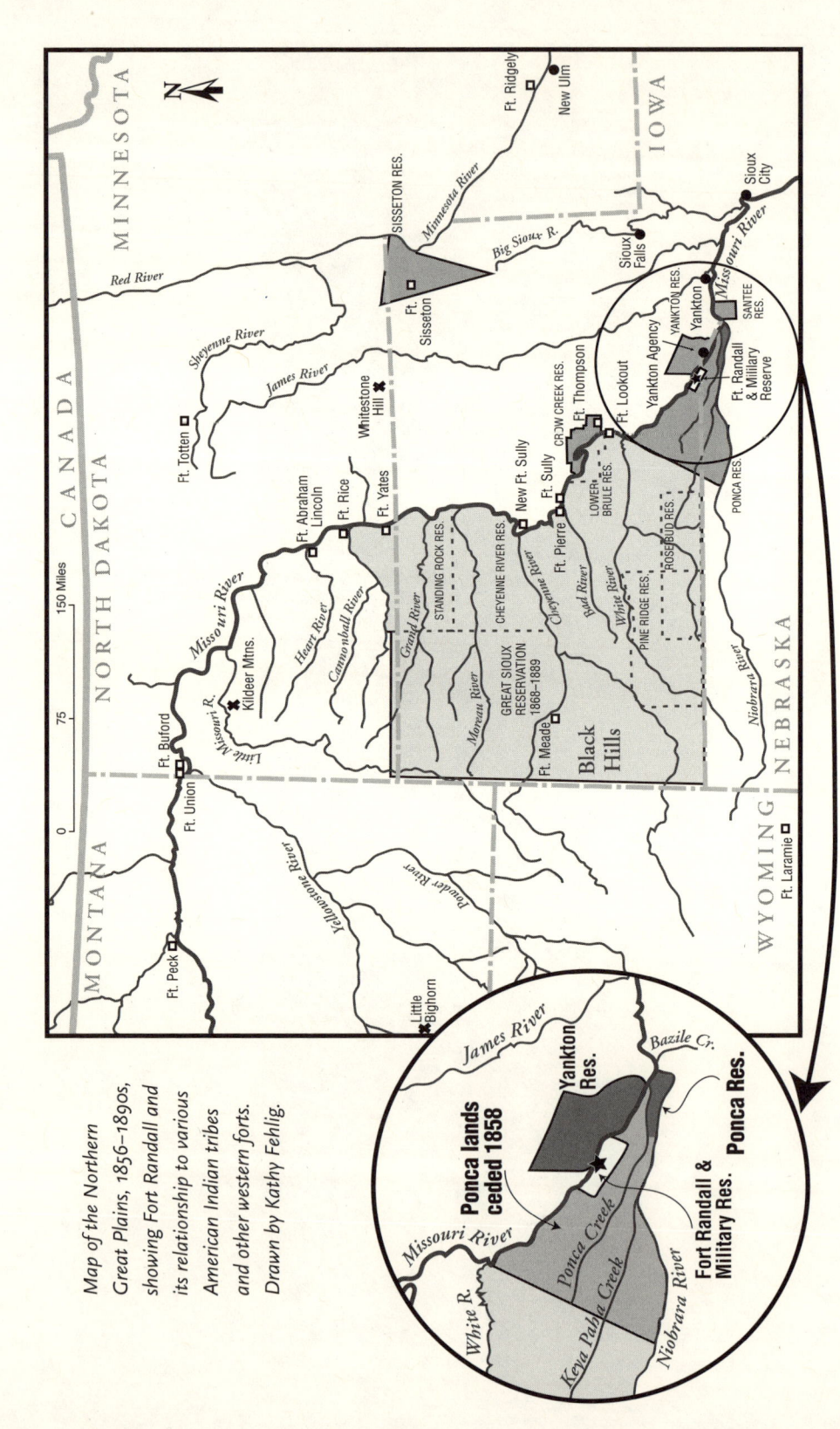

Map of the Northern
Great Plains, 1856–1890s,
showing Fort Randall and
its relationship to various
American Indian tribes
and other western forts.
Drawn by Kathy Fehlig.

Post quartermaster office, Fort Randall, 1865.
Photograph by Lieutenant William H. Blyton,
Company M, Second Infantry. Courtesy of Larry Ness,
Yankton, S.Dak.

Post quartermaster office, 1866, showing soldiers of the Fourth U.S.
Volunteer Infantry, with storehouses beyond. Photograph by C. L. Hamilton.
Courtesy of South Dakota State Historical Society, Pierre.

Log officer quarters along west perimeter of parade ground, 1866.
Photograph by C. L. Hamilton.
Courtesy of South Dakota State Historical Society, Pierre.

"Outside Guards' Qrs," Fort Randall, with Missouri River in the background, 1865. Photograph by Lieutenant William H. Blyton, Company M, Second Infantry. Courtesy of Larry Ness, Yankton, S.Dak.

Double officer quarters, 1882, perhaps located at the northwest end of the parade ground. Courtesy of South Dakota State Historical Society, Pierre.

View of the rear of a two-story barracks along the west side of the parade ground, ca. early 1890s, showing detached kitchen and privy (foreground). In the distance are the flagpole and the new hospital complex beyond. Source: Photograph album, ca. 1891–92, Fort Randall and Twenty-first Infantry. Courtesy of Larry Ness, Yankton, S. Dak.

*Soldier standing on the parade ground, with barracks and officer quarters
to the west, ca. early 1890s. Note substantial trees bordering the parade.
Source: Photograph album, ca. 1891–92, Fort Randall and Twenty-first Infantry.
Courtesy of Larry Ness, Yankton, S.Dak.*

*Fort Randall chapel, which functioned also as a library and Independent Order
of Odd Fellows lodge, as built in 1875 by soldiers of the First Infantry using funds
donated from various sources. Its ruins stand yet today overlooking the site of Fort
Randall. Date of photograph and photographer are unknown. Courtesy of South
Dakota State Historical Society, Pierre.*

Barracks at Fort Randall, ca. 1886. Man in foreground is airing his bunk mattress. Courtesy of South Dakota State Historical Society, Pierre.

Soldiers of Company B, Twenty-fifth Infantry, wearing dress uniforms with newly adopted helmets, stand at attention in front of barracks, in winter, ca. 1882 (note leafless vines on porch). Officer at far left is Captain Charles Bentzoni. Courtesy of South Dakota State Historical Society, Pierre.

Soldiers of Company A, Fifteenth Infantry, in front of barracks, summer, ca. 1886. Note full-foliaged vines on porch. Courtesy of South Dakota State Historical Society, Pierre.

Soldier members of Echo Lodge No. 2, Independent Order of Odd Fellows, Fort Randall, ca. early 1890s. Bearded man seated at left in center row is John H. McLaughlin, later caretaker of the abandoned post. Note shooting medals that adorn the collars and breasts of some of the men. Source: Photograph album, ca. 1891–92, Fort Randall and Twenty-first Infantry. Courtesy of Larry Ness, Yankton, S.Dak.

Fort Randall troops on maneuvers, ca. early 1890s.
Source: Photograph album, ca. 1891–92, Fort Randall and Twenty-first Infantry.
Courtesy of Larry Ness, Yankton, S.Dak.

Officers of the Fifteenth Infantry at Fort Randall, ca. early 1880s, left to right: front row, unidentified, Captain John W. Bean, First Lieutenant George H. Kinzie, Second Lieutenant Charles E. Garst; center row, unidentified, unidentified, Lieutenant Colonel Peter T. Swaine, Captain Henry R. Brinkerhoff; back row, First Lieutenant Samuel S. Pague, First Lieutenant David R. Burnham, Second Lieutenant William F. Blauvelt, First Lieutenant Thomas F. Davis, Second Lieutenant Andrew S. Rowan. Courtesy of U.S. Army Military History Institute, Carlisle, Pa.

Mrs. William J. Lyster, wife of Lieutenant Colonel William J. Lyster, commanding officer of Fort Randall, together with Second Lieutenant Samuel Seay Jr., Company F, Twenty-first Infantry, ca. 1891. The girl is identified as Leddie Schultz. Lieutenant Seay commanded the post when it was abandoned in 1892. Source: U.S. Army Military History Institute, Carlisle, Pa.

Life at Fort Randall

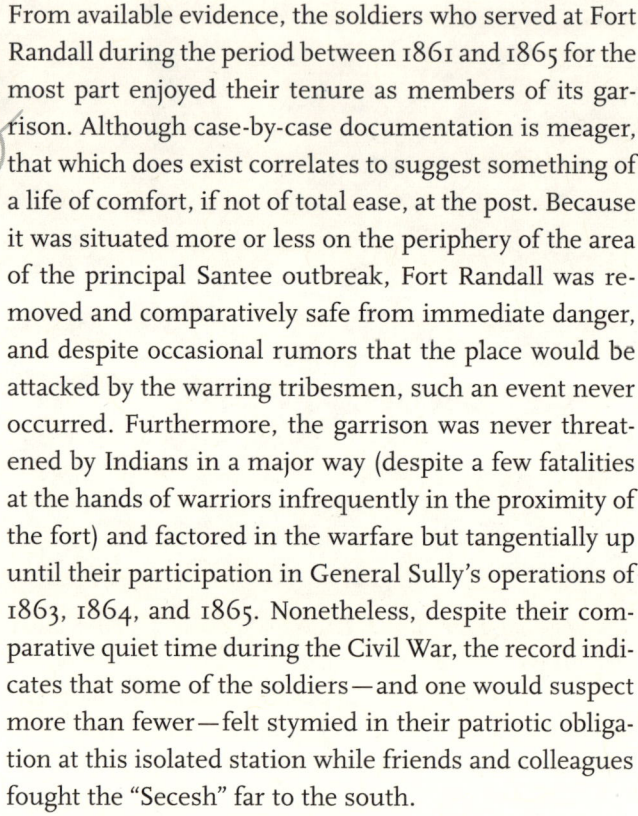

4 From available evidence, the soldiers who served at Fort Randall during the period between 1861 and 1865 for the most part enjoyed their tenure as members of its garrison. Although case-by-case documentation is meager, that which does exist correlates to suggest something of a life of comfort, if not of total ease, at the post. Because it was situated more or less on the periphery of the area of the principal Santee outbreak, Fort Randall was removed and comparatively safe from immediate danger, and despite occasional rumors that the place would be attacked by the warring tribesmen, such an event never occurred. Furthermore, the garrison was never threatened by Indians in a major way (despite a few fatalities at the hands of warriors infrequently in the proximity of the fort) and factored in the warfare but tangentially up until their participation in General Sully's operations of 1863, 1864, and 1865. Nonetheless, despite their comparative quiet time during the Civil War, the record indicates that some of the soldiers—and one would suspect more than fewer—felt stymied in their patriotic obligation at this isolated station while friends and colleagues fought the "Secesh" far to the south.

The quarters at Fort Randall had dramatically improved since its establishment. Captain Pattee recalled that "the buildings were constructed of logs mostly, some of round logs and some hewed logs, and were fairly comfortable. The magazine and guard house were of logs hewed both sides, and were good substantial buildings. The storehouses for commissary and quartermaster's property were frame buildings and very commodious."[1] Enlisted men barracked in stove-heated rooms measuring eighteen feet square that were insulated against the cold "with matched cedar which makes them as warm as if they was [sic] plastered," although it would seem that there might be some crowding with sixteen men assigned to each. Supplies were more than sufficient, with blankets, towels, buckets, and shovels abounding—even such toiletries as mirrors, brushes, and combs "to make ourselves look slick," wrote Sergeant Amos R. Cherry of Company B, Fourteenth Iowa Infantry. Food was abundant and varied, Sergeant Cherry exulting: "We get plenty to eat and more than we can eat. . . . We have beefe three days in the week and pork four days. When we have pork we have rice in our soupe; when we have Beefe we have Beans. . . . On sabath days we have warm buiscut roast Beefe and Pie and molasses."[2]

The comforts did not end there. As with the supplies, clothing seemed more than adequate, both in availability and quality. Sergeant Cherry's "sky blue" caped overcoat and socks kept him sufficiently warm, despite temperatures of −20 degrees during the winter of 1861–62. Leisure time allowed the men to pursue aesthetic interests, such as a theater and even a lyceum (complete with a two hundred–volume library), where such topics as woman's suffrage were vigorously debated. For the many soldiers who did not share those interests, there was a billiard room with two tables or the post sutler's store with numerous articles for sale for cash or by credit against a soldier's pay. Under these conditions, the men stationed at Fort Randall at the outset of the war years seemingly took pleasure in their service there compared to enlisted men elsewhere.[3]

As the months passed, the good times for the most part continued. One soldier of the Second Nebraska described the post in mid-1863 as having buildings "large & comfortable, adapted to the health & comfort of the men. Streets are decorated with trees," while the presence of "women and children . . . made the place look like a thriving eastern village." At this time, liquor sales by the sutler were carefully regulated if not altogether discontinued, and in December 1863 a directive required the search of all trains on the road opposite the fort and consequent seizure of any intoxicating spirits. Buildings in the area were likewise to be inspected if "there is any cause to believe liquor is kept for sale or furnished or to be furnished in any manner to any Soldier or other person." Any intoxicants found were to be confiscated and sent to Fort Randall.[4]

Of particular significance in keeping morale high at the post in the shadow of the ongoing regional warfare was inauguration of the *Fort Randall News*, which promised "to be a credit to the Territory." The post's Dramatic Association also maintained an active calendar, announcing upcoming performances of *Toodles* and *Off for the War*, while other diversions included a "tenpin alley, kept by a Jew down at the ferry boat landing" and, at least by late 1864, a chapter of the Order of Good Templars (of which eighteen men attended its first meeting).[5] In July 1863, reports of army successes at Vicksburg and Port Hudson, Mississippi, cheered the men. "This garrison has been in a perfect blaze of excitement and flooded with ecstatic joy for a whole week," wrote an observer. "The boys begin to entertain hopes of a speedy release from Uncle Sam's service and a return to the 'girls they left behind them.'"[6]

Direct insight into life in and around Fort Randall at the time of the Minnesota outbreak and its aftermath is revealed in selections from two extraordinary series of letters written by two soldiers whose total time there spanned the period from 1861 to 1863. Corporal Lambert A. Martin, who grew up in the area of Albany, New York, enlisted in Company B, Fourteenth Iowa Volunteer Infantry, and arrived at the post in December 1861. Martin was "messed off sixteen in a room" and described in detail the furnishings at hand as well as the troops' general appearance:

> Each mess has decorated their room as well as their limited means will allow, each person having a box or trunk which the Regulars left. . . . Our room, which is in the Aristocracy understand, has a table on one side of the room, a stand on the other. A large box stands in the centre of the room, a two-storried bed stead in each corner of the room, two windows to the front & between them sets our stand above which is one gilt-edged Mirror 18″ by 14. Two shelves below [are] filled with books & decorated with red fringe. At the right of the glass is a Roster. Above this is a case telling the month, days of the week. . . . On entering the room you will see before you on the opposite wall a notice which reads, No spitting on the floor. Our room has to be swept 3 times per day, & every thing has to be kept in the most perfect order. Every straw [must be] picked off our parade ground, which contains 5 acres. Every time we come out to drill, our boots shine black & our buttons must glisten like gold & not a dirty spot is allowed on any of the clothing. . . . Nothing to do but black our boots & receive $13.00 per month.[7]

At Fort Randall, Martin noted, "the boys in their rooms . . . are full of jokes & fun," and he described Christmas in garrison as "a jolly day," with "liberty" and whiskey given the men on that day and on New Year's Day. Every Sunday, Martin attended a Bible class and a prayer meeting at the post, while every Thursday evening saw a lecture or discussion group, known as lyceum, in which the commissioned officers participated. "Our Literary Societies are composed of members who are obliged to (like myself) meet & let the Gas escape to prevent an explosion, which would otherwise inevitably take place, causing, perhaps, the annihilation of the fort." (Evidently, the discussion groups deactivated during the warmer months and reactivated as winter approached.) Like Sergeant Cherry, Martin extolled the meals of "bread & biscuit, roast beef, soup, coffee, pork, etc.," later observing that his colleagues ate "beets, parsnips, carrots, potatoes, beef, bread, fried cakes & apple pie[—]a half a pie apiece." "Our victuals are well cooked [and] . . . our washing costs us 45 cents per dozen," he commented. Once, in April 1862, he complained about the pork. "[Our pork] is awful. It is bacon put up in barrels & . . . then marked B.C. You know B.C. means before Christ, but this signifies bacon . . . , & it is very wormy & the boys in our company will not eat it at all." But overall, he observed, "We are . . . doing well. Reason [is] because we have full bellies & nothing to do and $13.00 per month. Yes, & spend $20 per month at the Sutler's Store."[8]

Indeed, life at Fort Randall could not have been better. The weather that first winter was moderate, with snow seldom seen. "All enjoying good health & in fine spirits," wrote Martin in March 1862, within three months of his arrival. "[We are] living on the fat of the land at 'Uncle Sam's' expense." "After the war is done away with, we would as leave remain here as not, for we are having a gay time & have had ever since we came here." Garrison duty during the winter consisted of such fatigue as going for wood and cutting and hauling ice from the river. As temperatures rose in the late winter and spring, the soldiers trained on a more regular basis, although their time was not totally consumed by it. "Drill three hours per day is all the military we have to do," wrote Martin. "Some [of the men] are so lazy that it is like pulling eye teeth to them. Soldiering is a lazy occupation especially in a fort as we are now situated." Target practice, however, was almost nonexistent, at least during the first few months at Fort Randall, an omission possibly due in part to the condition of the available muskets. According to Martin, after being there five months, "we have not shot our guns save at the target, and that but two or three times." Although the Indian threat seems not to have been presently dominant, it nonetheless remained. "If you would like to know how my hair is cut," wrote Martin, "I will tell you it is Fort Randall style, close to the head. Most of the boys have theirs the same way. This is to prevent the Indians from taking scalps. I [also] found this to be an advantage [during] . . . hot weather."[9]

In the spring of 1862, natural events took their toll on Fort Randall. In late March, Martin reported that "the river broke up . . . & a steamboat that was at our wharf here was carried off with the ice. We are without a boat except a yawl which we can cross the river with after the ice goes down." In June, storms and high waters buffeted the post and shoreline. Martin noted winds so strong they knocked over trees as well as the flagpole, "breaking it in 3 or 4 pieces. . . . We will have a new one up in a few days. The river now is very high. The water fills the broad channel to the top of the bank & is still raising. . . . The bank is caving in sometimes, 2 to 8 feet at a lick." So fierce was the tempest that part of the steam mill, located close to the river, washed away downstream.[10]

Seasonal change brought other duties, including the cutting and gathering of hay. Amid soaring temperatures in the summer of 1862 —from 94 to 98 degrees during late June—Martin accompanied and frequently supervised haying parties some ten miles west of the post, where they often remained for weeks.[11] His account of this routine yet almost universal type of army labor affords a look at one constant of enlisted life on the upper Missouri during this formative period: "Yesterday 33 of us left the fort for the prairie to make hay. We came here & camped yesterday. Our men are divided into squads of 10 men & a corporal at a squad & detailed to workers, extra duty men drawing twenty-five cents extra per day & our [one?] whiskey. I have in my charge 10 men & can work or not, just as I see fit. I was out this morning & mowed a few swaths. . . . We will be out about a month. The amount of hay we will cut is 200 tons. . . . We mow by hand. I wish we had a mower." On August 3, Martin noted: "We have been out since the 13th of July & will return to the fort on Tuesday next, making 22 days outside the garrison. We have put up in cache a large quantity of hay & good hay too. Seven teams still drawing to the garrison & it will take them three weeks to finish hauling."[12]

More often than not, in spite of their easy living, the state soldiers at Fort Randall were consumed by the specter of the ongoing Civil War and relished whatever news they could gain of the unfolding martial events. Occasional garrison observances only fueled their interest. For example, following the April 1862 death of Major General Charles F. Smith in the South, Martin commented: "Tomorrow we will fire our cannon, three in number, thirteen guns in honor of General Smith who died at Savannah, and have a grand parade flag at half mast."[13] More than anything, however, the men were concerned about their own noninvolvement in the action. "I tell you we are greatly mortified and no mistake about it for all we have [is] a pleasant time," Martin penned his parents. "Yet we would throw all those pleasures aside & willingly go . . . into the field of action & stand by our brothers who are now there engaged. To be sure, we do not wish to hurry on to death, but we would like to gain for ourselves an honor & fame for something more than to sneak off to Fort Randall & let those suffer & die who are equally as good as ourselves."[14]

As scarce news of the early fighting in Virginia and the South reached the post, it was accompanied by an almost constant yearning by Fort Randall's men to do more, and they seemed always to have anticipated their transfer south. "We at this post expect to go south this summer as soon as the boat comes up the river and the Dakota Boys [First Dakota Cavalry] will garrison this place. We are anxious to take an active part & undoubtedly will." In April, Martin wrote his brother of his concern: "If we remain here on the fat of the land we will enjoy ourselves first rate. We could not ask for anything better for comfort but we do not feel that we are doing our country much good and therefore we will gladly go & quickly too, to the south." The following day, his hopes for transfer seemingly waning, he wrote, "We have received no more news of our being relieved & I think it useless for us to look for any such to take place concerning us but still we hope to be [sent] to the land of *Seceshia*."[15]

By late summer 1862, the First Battalion of the Fourteenth Iowa Volunteer Infantry had been detached from that regiment and designated the Forty-first Iowa Battalion Infantry.[16] Coincidentally with that reorganization, two events offered potential excitement for the garrison. One was the Santee outbreak in Minnesota and the ramifications that it might pose for the troops in Dakota. More immediate was circulating gossip of operations of Confederate guerrillas in the vicinity of Fort Randall, reportedly for the purpose of inciting the Indians against the federal troops there. Now, wrote Martin,

> We are not, in fact, so anxious to leave as we have been. No, we will not be driven away but [will] fight to maintain & preserve & defend this post. Guerillas [sic] infest our place but as yet no damage has been done. Capt. Gardner a Rebel officer formerly an officer in the U.S.A. at this post has been seen & recognized among the Guerillas by those that knew him & it is reported that the band of Guerillas in Nebraska intend to capture this post. They number five hundred & have done a great deal of damage along the Platte river, & near Omaha on the Mo [Missouri] River, captured a boat & now all business is suspended on the upper Mo. We have a picket guard out every night, scouting parties out by day [composed of] both Indians & soldiers. The Guerillas are on horses. They are armed with short rifles, revolvers, & Bowie knifes [sic]. We stand in readiness to give them a warm reception at any time by night or by day. Our defense is poor but we will make any number of the enemy pay dear for the place before we surrender. They are doubtless after the powder in the magazine knowing there is a good large quantity there. It would do us good to have a big fight for we are all *spoiling for one* and if we can't go south to fight, I hope some of them will gratify us by coming here.[17]

There is no record of any contest ensuing between guerrillas and the men of Fort Randall. Although guerrilla activity was of major interest in nearby areas like Missouri, it is likely that Martin's comments were motivated by rumor and exaggeration meant to impress his readers.

More genuine was the volatile Indian situation following the outbreak in Minnesota that spilled over into Dakota Territory during the fall of 1862. While that development was primarily restricted to the area upstream from Fort Randall, there were nevertheless corollaries for the post and its garrison. As early as January 1862, Indians had burned a haystack and stolen cattle feed from a settler's place on the east bank of the Missouri and within a half mile of the fort. Major Pattee had responded to the incident and with a detachment shortly captured a number of Santee warriors and incarcerated them. As a result of such incidents, regular patrols of troops through the country surrounding Fort Randall increased by June.[18]

For obvious reasons of security, Indian matters assumed increased attention following the outbreak. In a missive of September 27, 1862, Corporal Martin alluded to several councils as having occurred between the post commander and unspecified tribesmen. In reference to Sibley's battle at Wood Lake just days earlier, he exaggeratedly noted that "the whites north of here fought the Indians, killed 400 of them and frightened several to death, driving 500 more in the river where they were shot & even killed one another thinking their own tribe had betrayed them." News of the encounter "caused us to celebrate the evening & 'twas nearly 12 o'clock before the drums were silenced and the shrill voices of the boys. We had a general jolly occasion." A week later he recorded that "Fort Randall is all quiet. The excitement being almost, if not quite, over. The [Yankton] Indians are around in great numbers but are not hostile. The Agent has called them in to receive their annuities." Martin commented on the possibility of the Yanktons joining the Santees: "Whether the calculations of the Redfaces is to fight or to remain peaceable, I can't say. We have our rifles now, they came yesterday & we could fight now with a better grace than with our old condemned muskets, but I think, & we all think, that a stick will be all that we will need as long as we stay here. We didn't think so a month ago . . . , but now it is quite different. No anticipation of a molestation from any quarter unless it be to go south & that will suit us exactly."[19] Yet in November 1862, he passed on word that Fort Randall had indeed been targeted for attack. "A Santee friendly who deserted his band . . . reports that it was the intention of the Indians to attack this fort, but upon hearing of Little Crow's defeat by Col. Sibley & supposing General Harney was in Dakota with 4000 men, they abandoned the idea."[20]

General Sully's first expedition did not get under way until the summer of 1863. In the meantime, as explained, the troops at Fort Randall conducted scouts in the vicinity of the post with the intent of watching for Indians and protecting white citizens. The signal movement was Pattee's march north in November 1862 for the purpose of finding and rescuing the women and children reportedly held by tribesmen near Fort Pierre. This maneuver drew much attention from those garrisoned at Fort Randall, where little activity had preceded beyond normal fatigue and escort duty and patrol assignments. It was apparently hyped by certain of the men, including Martin, as a major enterprise leading far afield, as it indeed must have seemed to the jaded command, and Martin wrote his brother in somewhat melodramatic terms:

> We are on the point of leaving the post to commence a winter campaign with the Indians near the Black Hills, which are 300 miles "north west" of our present locality ("Fort Randall").... I'll explain our expedition. Viz: Maj Pattee was ordered by Gen Pope to take a detachment of men leaving but enough to garrison the post & proceed at once up the Mo River searching every Indian encampment until those white women ... were found & recovered. Also to take prisoners or annihilate the Santee bands who are domiciled in the vicinity of the Black Hills preparing for an aggressive war upon the whites in the spring. These were engaged in the late Minnesota war & are the aggressors & we will punish them if it lies in our power. They number 600 & are well armed. On the twenty-third of this month (Tuesday next) we bid adieu for the time being to Fort Randall. Then 200 able bodied men, 100 infantry (Company B) & one hundred cavalry (Company A Dakota) with revolvers, bowie knives, carbines, rifles, sabres & two pieces of artillery will leave here to march on to victory or a defeat.... We are going to fight & nothing else & we expect to have a tough time of it going at this time of the year when the cold piercing winds of the northwestern prairie will face us & bid defiance to our progress, yet we'll penetrate our way with firm step & bold heart to the rescue of those poor captives & the punishment of the captors. I should have called them infernal wretches or something worse. Yes, we are stimulated & every man will doubtless be as good as a veteran under the present circumstances. Fur coats, mittens, overshoes, caps, & mufflers are being made ... & ere we take up our line of march, each & every man will be in possession of the above named articles of his own make which will tend to make him more comfortable when the thermometer gets "a feet below Cisero." We will be provided with Sibley tents, with stoves.[21]

On December 1, Martin added:

> Today we met two teams driven by half breeds who were on their way to Fort Randall with [the sought after] two white women & two children who were bought by them for eight pencils & a quantity of gun powder & caps. They are now with us in camp and will pro-

ceed in the morning to Fort Randall where they will take the stage for their home. One of the women, a married lady about the age of twenty-five is comely & quite intelligent; she says that the Indians pride themselves on their spryness to dodge the union balls when they see them fired.[22]

As mentioned earlier, the troops, but recently paid, took up a collection for the former captives, who continued on to Fort Randall and then on to their homes. Martin proceeded to Fort Pierre and remained in its vicinity into the following spring.[23] His unit did not accompany Sully's campaign, and he stayed around Fort Pierre and at the Crow Creek and Winnebago agencies before moving to Fort Sully.

Martin never returned to Fort Randall. On July 4, 1863, he wrote his parents: "The boys are none of them feeling very well. Some sick in Hospital, some sick in quarters & others complaining a little, which ailment this Doctor attributes to soda biscuit, rusty bacon, coffee, & not enough exercise. Two of our boys have died. . . . These were the first deaths that occurred in our company since we enlisted. Coming so suddenly & taking two from our ranks in so short a time shocked us terribly, and we hope those sick may recover & the company not mourn the loss of any others."[24] On July 21, he told them that he had contracted "bilious diarrhea" but had recovered quickly. In August, he announced that he had dropped thirty pounds since leaving Fort Randall. On August 17, Martin reported that "I am not sick, but like two-thirds of the company I am reduced almost unfit for service. Cause—camp disentary [sic]."[25] In early October, however, the malady —perhaps amoebic dysentery—worsened. His condition quickly declined, and on the morning of October 15, Lambert Martin died.[26]

Another soldier who left substantive information about life at Fort Randall was Corporal Horace Austin from Michigan, a soldier in Company A, First Dakota Cavalry, who was stationed there in 1863 and 1864. In March 1863, in the aftermath of the Santee uprising in Minnesota, Corporal Austin remarked that "there has [been] many left this Teritory in feere [sic] of the Indians." At Fort Randall, he reported, "there is a little girl here that has been bought from the Indians. She was captured in Minnesota last year by the Indians who killed her father before her eyes. She was in the willderness [sic] 8 months & all the relatives she has in the world is one brother & she has the bitter intelegence [sic] of knowing that he is a prisoner with the savages she has just left. She speaks the Indians language [*sic*] well & seems like a bird let out of a cage."[27]

Like Lambert Martin before him, Austin described life at the post as relaxed and relatively free from worry about Indians, where he could purchase dried apples for eighteen cents per pound. As for the countryside, he wrote: "There is not many people live within 50 miles of here & what there is are mostly Frenchmen living with Squaws. Some of the Officers & soldiers have their wives here, & those are nearly all the white women there are within 70 miles or this side of Yankton. There are several white men living with Squaws here." Austin referenced the truism of military life being governed by bugle calls. "We do every thing by the sound of the bugle[—]get up, eat, answer roll call, drill, mount guard, take care of our horses, & go to bed, &c., &c., by the bugle." He spoke of an itinerant preacher having visited the garrison on Sunday and of having traveled to Yankton and back "after some government stores."[28]

In other missives, Austin mentioned saber drill for the cavalrymen and pulling guard duty, where he "walked back & forth on the porch in front of the guard house." He stated that the government permitted the men to furnish their own horses and equipment, if they wished, and paid them forty cents per day for the use. In April 1863, Austin wrote that "there is [*sic*] no prospects of any Indian troubles more than common." In May, regarding the upcoming Sully campaign, he noted that "we expect to start above after the Indians in the fore part of June, & we hope to get back in 4 or 5 months from that time. If we are not gone longer than that it will be a pleasant trip." As for the caliber of the cadre and his own daily routine, Austin offered the following: "My Captain is as good a man as the sun ever shone upon. The Lieutenants are not as good, but with a good Capt. we are all right. I have seen some officers abuse the men under them & I believe that there is many an . . . abuse laid up to be settled when Oficers [*sic*] and privets [*sic*] are again on eaquel [*sic*] footing. My duty is when I am detailed to take charge of wood parties, fatigue parties & police parties & when on guard to change the sentinels [*sic*] every 2 hours." Later that month, Austin took part in the establishment upriver of the Santee and Winnebago reserves, and in August he participated in a ten-day scout looking for Indians.[29] When he finally took an opportunity to leave Fort Randall on a short visit to Sioux City, he remarked, "I felt like one let out of a dungeon [*sic*]." Although Indians roamed about, they apparently had few run-ins with soldiers from the garrison and confined themselves mostly to stealing horses and other livestock. Austin described the shooting of the Iowa soldier:

The mail was going . . . with one soldier (Mr. Trask) & 2 citizens & the Indians stoped [sic] them & seeing the soldier shot him through the heart. The driver ran. They shot but he escaped. The other man they let go because he was half Indian. They then took the team and left. Mr. Trask was as fine a man as we had in this garrison. It is not safe to go out of sight of the Fort unarmed. They feere [sic] an armed Soldier & well they may. There is no one here that says ["]poor Indian["] nor never will any one that has become acquainted with the brutes. They are good when they have to be & they will shake hands & then shoot a man.[30]

On October 18, 1863, a severe winter storm struck the post. "It killed 40 government mules & horces [sic]," reported Private Austin. He noted that he would be leaving to garrison the new post, Fort Sully, for the winter, and he included in his letter home a membership certificate in a temperance society that he had joined at Fort Randall. Austin told his mother and sister that he had received a letter from an old girlfriend in Brooklyn, New York. "I would give fifteene [sic] cents to see her to night." He offered apologies for the brevity of his letter, stating that "there is loud talking & swearing in the room and it bothers me."[31]

By mid-November, he and his fellow soldiers had returned from Fort Sully to Fort Randall and were living in tents pending moving into quarters at the post.[32] The reportedly hard winter that set in late that year had, by January 1864, turned mild. "It has thawed some of late," wrote Austin, "and [my] poor boots has caused me to have wet feet, and by this I have caught some cold. But I expect to have some new boots soon." While at the fort, his diet was probably all that a soldier at that time and place could have asked: "We had a good dinner which consisted of rost [sic] beef, good gravy, good bred [sic], good butter, hominy [sic], which by putting sugar on it (as we have no milk), is very good." All in all, life at Fort Randall for Austin was far from disappointing. "I am well satisfied. Of course it is some [somewhat?] lothesome [sic] here but I am better of[f] than I would be [in the] South. Some times I think that I am not doing as much as I aught [sic] to for my country."[33] As Austin's reenlistment time approached, he pondered what to do, for if the Civil War continued, he might be subject to the draft, a development inimical to his strong sense of patriotism. "I will never be drafted into my Countries [sic] service. I will serve it voluntarely [sic] if at all. I will not clame [sic] a Country to be mine that I serve as a drafted man."[34] In the end, he reenlisted, for he accompanied Sully's 1864 expedition to the upper Missouri country.[35]

Unfortunately, none of Austin's later letters have been located (and possibly do not exist), so that the particulars of his subsequent career with the Dakota troops are not known. Nevertheless, those that have survived, along with those written by Corporal Martin, offer important testimony regarding the life and activities of the men of the Fort Randall garrison during its occupation by state and territorial forces during the Civil War. As such, they have helped to flesh out a previously little-known record of soldier life and duty there, accordingly adding a rich human dimension to the post's history.

Postwar Change

5 The close of the Civil War saw a transitioning of Fort Randall. Late in April 1865, in memory of the assassinated President Lincoln, the post, like others in the country, assumed a thirty-day period of mourning. The headquarters building was draped in black cloth, while officers wore "the badge of mourning" on their left arms and their swords.[1] The observance signified a sad yet stark demarcation from the past four years in which Fort Randall had at first stood as an effective arbiter between the Yankton and Ponca reservations, stemming all potential trouble from those fronts, as well as a bastion for the white settlements against possible Indian incursions from Minnesota, and later saw its status as the farthest advanced federal fortification subordinated to several new posts on the upper Missouri. Future years would see Fort Randall maintain its position in regional Indian affairs while emerging in more of a support capacity to the new upriver posts and to army operations farther west.

In the postwar era, as the nation continued the westward migration of the 1840s and 1850s that had abated during the conflict, many white Americans drawn by economic incentive sought lands on which to settle, cultivate, and raise stock; gold and the promise of other mineral wealth drew others. The federal government facilitated the migration via the Homestead Act and other stimulus legislation. Seeking to protect steamboat and overland routes, during the late 1860s and early 1870s in the region of the northern plains the army established appropriate defenses to protect the traffic west. On the upper Missouri, the rudimentary network established by General Sully in 1864 and 1865 saw improvement under Brigadier General Alfred H. Terry, commander of the newly created Department of Dakota (1866), which superseded previous administrative jurisdictions, with the additions of Fort Buford (1866) at the mouth of the Yellowstone River and Fort Stevenson (1867) above Knife

River. Both Dakota posts further strengthened the Missouri River corridor defenses that started with Fort Randall and included Forts Sully and Rice. (Fort Sully, in fact, was abandoned because of its unhealthful situation—it was there that Corporal Lambert Martin and others had died in 1863. A "new" Fort Sully was rebuilt in 1866 farther upstream, approximately midway between Forts Randall and Rice.) Similarly, the roads from Minnesota leading to Montana were additionally protected with the erection in 1867 of Forts Ransom and Totten in eastern Dakota to augment the earlier stations of Forts Abercrombie (1857) and Wadsworth (1864). These developments paralleled the construction of several new posts (Sidney Barracks and Forts D. A. Russell, Sanders, and Fred Steele) to guard overland routes in the Department of the Platte, commanded by Brigadier General Christopher C. Augur.[2]

In relation to these newer posts, Lieutenant General William T. Sherman, commanding the new Division of the Missouri, designated Fort Randall a supply depot, and goods targeted for the upstream forts were moved there from Sioux City. After nearly a decade, Fort Randall had by 1865 assumed something of a regal serenity that pointed up the ease and comfort of its accommodations. In 1866, it was still the largest post on the upper Missouri, and boats plying the river often stopped to purchase provisions. "They have an arsenal here, several large warehouses and 2 or 3 stores," noted one wayfarer.[3] An army wife named Sarah Canfield came up the Missouri and described Fort Randall as being on the edge of civilization. She saw a post with log blockhouses with loopholed walls bearing swivel guns and a lookout from which a soldier scanned the horizon with a telescope.

A penciled drawing prepared in late 1866 or early 1867 by Second Lieutenant Cornelius C. Cusick, Thirty-first Infantry (later reconstituted as the Twenty-second Infantry), suggests that substantial improvements had been accomplished on the post since the late 1850s. Cusick's depiction shows additional officer quarters, barracks, and supposed outbuildings and shops, all nicely appointed and graced with trees and shrubbery. The buildings obviously represent a mix of the old log structures together with new frame ones and perhaps include some of the old portable cottages left over from the founding days. The river appears closer in Cusick's drawing than in Captain Turnley's 1856 plat, an observation possibly explained by the viewing angle to the northeast in which it was rendered. Several tipis stand on the ferry landing across the river, but none appear on the post side. Three sides of the fort (north, east, and west) were surrounded by a fence that likely would double as a breastwork in case of attack. Blockhouses stood outside the fence, at the southeast and northwest corners of the complex. Later information indicates that on the east side of the post, a wooden bridge spanned the gorge of Garden Creek, which ran into the Missouri, and accessed a road leading south to Fort Kearny. Another wagon trail, the Fort Laramie Road, led west from the southwest end of the fenced area. This road traversed a valley running along hills near a promontory termed Mount Carrie, where fort residents could recreate and relax. "Friendly Indians and soldiers [and] officers of the Post and their ladies," noted post surgeon George P. Hackenburg, "often resort to this enchanted dale in summer evenings to enjoy the fresh, balmy breezes of the valley."[4] Occasionally, the Indians held pony races there, to the delight of garrison residents. The post cemetery was located at the base of the east side of Mount Carrie.[5]

Regardless of how pristine the fort looked in Cusick's drawing, appearances were deceiving. Although new buildings had risen during the interim, the post since 1856 had evolved and weathered until the quarters were deemed uninhabitable. The drafty log structures were failing, a perverse joke among the men citing their excellent ventilation. Kitchens were dirty, and vermin and rodent infestation was rampant. The latter condition elicited an order calling attention to the "filthy condition of grounds in rear of the quarters" and directing its cleanup.[6] Repairs were constant, and there were complaints that some of the troops were getting into unoccupied buildings and ripping out lumber, doors, and windows; an order threatened with courts-martial any men caught pilfering the structures. In May 1866, the army's inspector general, Colonel Delos B. Sackett, found the place derelict and reported that Fort Randall was beyond saving. He also complained about the state troops' bedraggled order and poor equipment as well as their officers' overall neglect of supplies and animals. Sackett cited Pattee, for example, for permitting 2,500 sacks of corn to stand exposed where rodents and Indians could access it at will. Despite repairs to the barracks in 1868 that placed them in "very good condition" according to the post surgeon, the condition of the post's physical plant continued to deteriorate through the last years of the decade. Following a visit by Major General Winfield S. Hancock in the summer of 1869, the commanding officer of Fort Randall received directions "to rebuild that post, making it more compact and better suited for the purposes of a frontier military post."[7] Late that year, a fire caused by a defective flue swept through the officer quarters. "The quarters of Dr. Gray and Captain Fisher were almost entirely consumed, and the quarters of Lieut. Woodson, were partially burned."[8] The fire offered further inducement for rebuilding.[9]

With disbandment of the state and territorial forces at the end of the war, Fort Randall and the other upriver posts would receive reconfigured garrisons of regular army troops. In the fall of 1865, however, after the Sixth and most of the Seventh Iowa volunteers departed, approximately 350 soldiers of the Fourth U.S. Volunteer Infantry (composed of "Galvanized Yankees"), a detachment of the Seventh Iowa, and a battalion of Minnesota troops garrisoned the fort. Most of these were mustered out in the spring of 1866, and in June the field and staff and Companies A and B of the Thirteenth Infantry arrived under command of Major Hiram Dryer. The November arrival of Companies F, I, and K boosted garrison strength to 325. Almost simultaneously, under a national reorganization of the army, the eight companies composing the second battalion of the Thirteenth Infantry were restructured as the Twenty-second Infantry.[10] The new regiment, commanded by Colonel David S. Stanley, made its headquarters at Fort Sully, where several companies were also posted. When in March 1867 Major Dryer died at Fort Randall, he was briefly succeeded as post commander by Lieutenant Colonel Elwell S. Otis. In May, Otis departed to occupy Fort Rice with all the units except the eighty men of Company F who remained at Fort Randall under Major Alexander Chambers. The major arrived on August 9 with his family, "a horse, and two magnificent greyhounds." For more than a year, this solitary company garrisoned the post until augmented by the arrival of Company C from Fort Sully, bringing the total number of soldiers present to about 140. In May 1869, in further reorganization, Companies C and F merged into a single Company C of the Twenty-second. Within weeks, Company D joined from upriver, and Captain Charles A. Webb took command. In June 1869, Webb was succeeded by Major Joseph N. B. Whistler as post commander. Meantime, in addition to the garrison fluctuations, Fort Randall had been designated as a rendezvous point for recruits in the new District of Southeastern Dakota; during the first half of 1867, eight detachments of recruits, each numbering ninety men, reported to Fort Randall and from there were distributed throughout the Department of Dakota.[11]

During the late 1860s, post routine continued much as before. Twice-monthly muster and inspection of companies and quarters by the commanding officer proceeded regularly. The Post Council of Administration continued its meetings of governance, while boards of surveys met to fix cause and responsibility for material losses among the garrison in all manner of goods, animals, and equipment. Courts-martial proceeded in the garrison. Fort Randall still drew its provisions from downstream, with contracts commonly let in Sioux City for fresh beef (ten cents per pound) and proposals solicited for 200 tons of hay and 400 cords of wood. In August 1866, the assistant quartermaster at the post visited Yankton to contract for 1,000 bushels of lime, likely used in construction repairs at the fort.[12] Post orders directed the men's daily activities: a school for noncommissioned officers in session as of early 1867; the placement of overshoes by the guard "on the shelf designated for their storage"; the prohibition of whiskey within the garrison; commencement of a course of "theoretical instruction in Infantry tactics" in the room used as the post chapel early in 1868. When available medical supplies proved inadequate for a surgical procedure on one soldier, he was ordered to Sioux City for treatment.[13] On March 10, 1867, following the death of post commandant Major Hiram Dryer from "Inflammation of the Lungs," the troops were directed to parade at 7 A.M. the next morning "for the purpose of escorting the remains . . . beyond the limits of the Post."[14]

In April 1867, Lieutenant Colonel Elwell S. Otis, for unknown specific reasons, was constrained to issue a strangely adamant yet acquiescent order affecting a perceived laxity in the deportment of his command:

> The Commanding Officer regrets to have discovered among the troops at the garrison the existence of disaffection and to witness daily the unmilitary bearing and appearance of many of the soldiers serving at this post. The duties of a soldier are not trifling, but on the contrary very responsible—arising from that mutual dependence which exists between the constituent parts of every military organization and the authority vested in men serving in certain capacities upon the prompt execution of which depends their

reputation for manhood and the welfare and safety of the troops with which they are serving.

A thorough knowledge of the duties absolutely required at the hands of every soldier, and of the position which he holds and should endeavor to properly maintain, should be sufficient to call out his energies and foster his pride. The Commanding Officer therefore hopes to see in [the] future more promptness and a stricter obedience on the part of non-commissioned officers and privates. And while he demands this, it shall be his study to make the duties as light as possible, consistent with the safety of the post, the health of the Garrison, the instruction of the men and the performance of the labors imposed by Government. It shall also be his study to secure for the men of the command their full share of allowances, to protect them in their rights and privileges as soldiers, [and] to encourage among them recreation and amusements and to use the authority with which he is clothed mildly yet firmly.

But willful disobedience in premeditated offenses shall be met with the extreme vigor of the law.[15]

Some idea of garrison life at Fort Randall during this period can be gained from the schedule of bugle calls that governed the soldiers' duties and daily regulated post functions:

Hereafter and until further orders the following hours of Service and Roll Calls will be observed by the command.

Reveille	Daybreak
Police Call	15 minutes after Reveille
Breakfast Call	6. A.M.
Fatigue Call	7.30 A.M.
Surgeon's Call	7.30 A.M.
Guard Mount, 1st Call	7.45 "
Guard Mount, 2nd Call	8. "
Fatigue Recall	11.30 "
1st Sergeants' Call	11.45 "
Dinner Call	12. M.
Fatigue Call	1. P.M.
Fatigue Recall	6. P.M.
Retreat	Sunset
Tattoo, 1st Call	8.50 P.M.

| Tattoo, 2nd Call | 9 | " |
| Taps | 9.15 | " |

Beyond this routine, which changed occasionally, there were Sunday morning inspection calls at 7:45 A.M. and 8 A.M., followed by church call at 10:30 A.M.[16]

Because of Fort Randall's location on the Missouri River, it was mandatory that a ferry be maintained to ensure deliveries of supplies and to allow passage of personnel back and forth for access to the roads leading upriver or down to the Yankton Agency and the settlements as far away as Sioux City. During times of potential Indian trouble, "Boat-Squad" duty entailed assignment of a noncommissioned officer, usually a corporal, and eight men to keep watch over the ferry operation. In 1865, the commanding officer directed the construction of a new ferry "large enough to carry over one Government wagon, loaded, and six mules; and, in addition, the men to row it." Within a year, however, the boat was considered "utterly worthless" and "unfit for further service," and a new one had to be built. Later, the boats were civilian owned and operated, were strictly monitored by the officer of the day, and were not allowed to cross "between Sundown & Reveille except for the purpose of crossing the mail." There is indication, too, that there were upper and lower landings at what was now dubbed "Fort Randall Point," with the former presumably located on the west bank north of the fort and the latter being the customary ferry landing.[17]

Meantime, in August 1865 the troops at the post had succeeded the now-defunct *Fort Randall News* with a new tabloid, the *Independent*, published weekly. The few surviving issues suggest that its readers consumed four pages on Indian affairs, national news, poetry, jokes, and some very short stories. A brief local news column reported on fort-related happenings:

The weather for the past week has been pleasant but changed last night, consequently it is very cold. The ice on the Missouri river remains firm; wagons cross and re-cross daily on the ice.

Private David Hill, Co. D, 4th U.S. Vol's, had his hands badly frozen last week while carrying the mail from this Post to Fort Thompson. Private C. M. Shelton, Jr., one of the same party, was taken with a fever on his return to this Post, and has been in the hospital ever since. The party got as far as Pratt Creek, and were obliged to turn back, the weather being so cold they could not proceed.

We are compelled for the first time during the winter to chronicle a death at our Post: Peter Erikson of Co. H, 30th Wis. Vols, died on the 8th inst., after a protracted illness, from Chronic Dysentery. He was a native of Norway, and an exemplary young man. Services appropriate to the occasion were held at the Chapel.

[March 29, 1866] Our old friend Mr. C. L. Hamilton, returned last week and is located at his old stand; he is prepared to take pictures of a size and quality, which cannot be surpassed in the States. We advise those who wish to procure Indian Photographs, to apply immediately.[18]

The editor complained of the dearth of local news. "Few persons are fully aware," he wrote, "how dull things are here until they try to find something in the way of news to publish."[19] In one portentous note appearing in the *Independent* in the spring of 1866, the editor referenced Indian depredations committed in the area of Fort Rice the previous summer under the leadership of a previously unknown individual. "From Lt. Eaton, stationed at Fort Berthold, we learn that the rascal was a warrior of the Unkpopa tribe, whose breast is full of hatred to the white man, and he goes by the euphonious title of 'Sitting Bull.'"[20] In view of events nearly fifteen years hence, when the Hunkpapa leader would play a momentous role in the history of Fort Randall, the reference was both portentous and ironic. Despite an appeal for funds to keep up the *Independent*, they were not forthcoming, and the paper ceased publication with the March 29, 1866, edition.[21]

Over the course of the last years of the decade, the troops at Fort Randall continued duty much as they had in the past. Holidays such as the Fourth of July occasioned the suspension of drill and fatigue and the observance of suitable commemoration activities. Besides daily garrison duties, the men performed their service in the Fort Randall neighborhood, responding to a host of local and regional needs as the primary available federal station. When steamboats sank in the Missouri, troops went to the relief of passengers and to help salvage government stores before (or after) scavengers beat them to the vessels. Area Indians needed constant attention, with detachments of troops going to and from the Ponca and Yankton agencies. Problems with trespassers on the military reservation continued, with squatters ignoring directives to leave and often inciting the Indians with illicit whiskey. Although in 1867 21,000 acres were relinquished by the government, the affected area was restored to the military reservation three years later, and an 1869 edict compelled squatters to leave or be forcibly removed. In 1874, however, Congress reversed itself, reopening that portion to settlers (and paying formerly ejected settlers an assessed value of their improvements) while relinquishing those parts of the reservation that had been settled on prior to its 1860 establishment. The problem with squatters would continue, however.[22]

A mainstay at Fort Randall, as well as at other posts around the country, was the post sutler's establishment, where officers, soldiers, and their families—as well as civilian transients and settlers and even Indians—could buy tobacco, clothing, a wide variety of personal and household articles, and, in accordance with the whim of the post commander or his superiors and during selected periods, liquor, generally in the form of beer and whiskey. Fresh fruits, vegetables, and eggs were purchased from area farmers for sale in the store. Obviously, because of potential sales, the appointive position of post sutler (post trader after March 1867) became a lucrative political plum that, despite half-hearted attempts to regulate, usually made its holders wealthy men. Since the 1850s, John B. S. Todd proved an able sutler, building a spacious home and store on the east edge of the garrison (toward the river landing, like the army storehouses) and, with the governance of the Post Council of Administration, keeping prices relatively low. Todd sold ale to the soldiers with certain controls. As mentioned, during his tenure Todd was often at odds with the post commander for various reasons.[23]

After Todd's departure for greener pastures (he evidently retained interests in the business as well as ownership of his home, however), George Hoffman succeeded to the position and won reappointment in October 1862. By late 1865, Charles E. Hedges, "an upright and efficient dealer," ran the operation, and in August 1869 the post photographer, Charles L. Hamilton, took over as post trader. These men saw greater attempts to control their operations, especially regarding the dispensing of alcohol. To better secure the military reservation, a directive in 1866 called for the strict removal of all Indian traders, Indians, and whites not otherwise employed by the Quartermaster Department and outlawed any Indian trade by the post sutler. Moreover, as of November 24, 1866, neither "whiskey, beer, [n]or other intoxi-cating liquor" could be sold, and an unsuccessful attempt to smuggle in whiskey four months later brought an order to inspect all incoming packages addressed to enlisted men. By September 1867, the prohi-bition had ended, and moderate amounts of beer (two glasses per man) were permitted. But the problem of availability remained. When steamboat owners started selling whiskey at the landing in 1869, dis-trict commander General Stanley not only threatened to arrest the bartenders and send them downriver but also decreed that all post traders' stores of "spirituous liquors" be confiscated by post com-manders.[24]

Miscellaneous incidents always occurred, directly involving sol-diers from Fort Randall or necessitating a response from the post. In August 1866, for example, Dr. Ferdinand V. Hayden, along with two teams, an Indian guide, and an escort of five soldiers, embarked from the post on a geological foray into the Badlands and Black Hills. He returned to welcoming throngs in Yankton in early October. During the fall of 1866, ten gold prospectors riding a mackinaw down the Missouri from Fort Benton camped near the mouth of Pratt Creek, above Fort Randall. While they slept, one of them, intending to plun-der his colleagues, killed a man with an ax and severely wounded an-other before the others awoke to chase him into the woods. The party managed to get the injured man into the boat and down to Fort Ran-dall, where they left him in the care of the post surgeon while a de-tachment started north to find the culprit and bury the dead victim. Apparently, the killer eluded capture. Similarly, when in September 1869 a felon shot the sheriff of Yankton County, soldiers from Fort Randall took part in the hunt to arrest him.[25]

The lure of potential mineral wealth in the Black Hills continued to intrigue citizens in eastern Dakota, and in 1866 the governor cham-pioned construction of a "Sioux City and Big Sheyenne Wagon Road" that would lead there and beyond. Talk about a civilian expedition to investigate the reports culminated in 1867 when a party of entre-preneurs organized in Yankton to push across the territory and into the Hills. In June, the commanding officer at Fort Randall received orders to furnish the party "two mountain howitzers and a hundred rounds of ammunition" from the post. But General Sherman resisted any such plan and urged General Terry to admonish citizens against such ventures. The proposed expedition never proceeded; in 1868, following the Fort Laramie Treaty with the Lakotas and other tribes that turned the Black Hills over to the Teton Sioux, General Sherman issued a directive forbidding the troupe from going forward.[26]

While these enterprises continued to occupy the post garrison, the matter of Indian affairs was of prime importance and constantly required the attention and commitment of officers and men. Although oversight of the Yankton and Ponca reserves remained a high priority, as the decade evolved the Western Sioux—Lakotas—began to emerge as an important element garnering increasing attention and affecting operations at Fort Randall and other regional stations. Likewise, the atmosphere introduced after 1868 by President Ulysses S. Grant's "Peace Policy" among the tribes, a curious coexistence of denominational religious advocacy with the military purposes of the War Department, brought confusion and turmoil on and off the reservations. The most immediate change, however, regarded the Winnebagoes, the small tribe that had moved to Crow Creek in 1863 rather than face Minnesotans angered in the wake of the Santee outbreak. Never happy with their circumstances vis-à-vis the Santees and beset with sickness and food shortages that threatened starvation, the Winnebagoes took matters into their own hands and in 1864 and 1865 began intermittently leaving the reservation to descend the river to live with their relatives, the Omahas, on that tribe's reservation below Sioux City. Soldiers at Fort Randall kept watch for those who escaped, capturing some and holding them in the guardhouse pending their return to Crow Creek. Some of the Winnebagoes attempted to canoe downstream; those who were stopped had to winter near the post under doubtful circumstances. Finally, early in March 1865, after the Omahas agreed to provide a parcel for their kinsmen and women, the government and the Winnebagoes reached an accord permitting their relocation south.[27]

During and following Sully's last campaign on the upper Missouri, Governor Edmunds, dissatisfied with the military results, continued to pursue peace treaties with the Sioux and other tribes. His arguments had impressed President Lincoln, who influenced a forthcoming congressional appropriation to establish a peace commission to negotiate with the Indians. Lincoln's successor, Andrew Johnson, appointed the Northwestern Indian Commission, composed of both military and civilian representatives. At a meeting in Yankton, Edmunds was selected chairman, and the commissioners and tribal leaders assembled at the site of the first Fort Sully in October 1865. The resulting Fort Sully treaties, involving the Yanktonais and parts of all seven tribes of Lakotas, did little beyond ratifying stipulations of the 1851 accord at Fort Laramie in which the tribes reconfirmed whites' use of overland routes both existing and contemplated through Indian lands. The commissioners reaffirmed Sioux ownership of the land north of the Platte. The Fort Sully treaties were ratified by Congress. In 1866, the commissioners reconvened upriver, negotiating treaties with other Tetons as well as the Northern Cheyennes at Forts Rice, Berthold, and Union. Because of events unfolding elsewhere among the Indians of the northern plains, however, the 1866 pacts were never ratified. While the completion of treaties by the Edmunds commission reduced the fears of settlers in southeastern Dakota, the fact that all elements of the concerned tribes had not been involved in the deliberations assured their ultimate ineffectiveness.[28]

Like the Winnebagoes, the Santees endured worsening conditions at Crow Creek. Early in 1866, their status deteriorated when several hundred starving Yanktonais, Brulés, and Sans Arcs pressed onto the reservation from eastern Dakota and from the vicinity of Old Fort Sully. Compounding matters, more Santees arrived, having been freed from prison in Minnesota, making unbearable the situation at Fort Thompson. To relieve their plight, the government in April 1866 removed the tribe to northern Nebraska, much against the wishes of Dakota politicians, who feared their proximity to "a portion of our most promising settlements." There they remained until 1868, when they were settled at an agency established for them along the Missouri below the mouth of the Niobrara River. Meantime, in 1867, by virtue of treaty, another agency was created for Santees who had not taken part in the 1862 warfare. These people from the Dakota-Minnesota border country—many of whom had not participated in that conflict but had nonetheless fled north—were placed on two reservations in northern Dakota, Lake Traverse and Fort Totten. Significantly, too, under the Fort Sully agreement, the Lower Brulés agreed to go on a reservation across from the Santee and old Winnebago tract at Crow Creek, and in 1868 an agency was established for them, administered from Fort Thompson.[29]

Other, more distant events also took place that would affect the Fort Randall garrison and, in fact, validate the post's continued existence. In 1868, following Chief Red Cloud's war against the invasion by emigrants of tribal hunting lands in eastern Wyoming and south-ern Montana, government representatives counciled with leaders of the Lakota Sioux and other tribes at Fort Laramie, Dakota (soon Wyoming) Territory. As part of the accord, federal authorities agreed to close three forts raised in the territory in 1866 to guard passage along the Bozeman Road to the Montana goldfields. Those Lakotas and Northern Cheyennes who attended the Fort Laramie sessions and who subscribed to the treaty promised to remove themselves to a reservation that effectively constituted that part of present South Dakota westward from the Missouri River, while retaining hunting rights in Wyoming and Montana.[30]

Among other things, the Fort Laramie Treaty of 1868 provided agencies for the Indians going onto the Great Sioux Reservation, with that for the Oglalas, Brulés, and other bands to be located for ease of supply on the west bank of the Missouri at the mouth of Whetstone Creek, just thirty miles northwest of Fort Randall. The retired General Harney, who helped negotiate the treaty, was placed in charge of the new northern reservation district, including the upriver agencies, for most of the following year and on September 7, 1868, stopped en route at Fort Randall, the post he had founded twelve years earlier. There the general met nearly 1,000 awaiting tribesmen in proceedings looking to the opening of the new agency. A witness described the scene as the Indians congregated about the post: "The hills to the North along the Missouri river, and near the fortifications, are covered with cattle, horses, mules, ox-wagons (each of these weigh [sic] a ton and carry three), tippees [sic], Sibley tents, the belongings of the Indians, or rather half breeds and Canadian French, and others that are here to receive the new reservation."[31] During their wait, representatives of the tribesmen met at least once at post headquarters with Major Chambers.

The stockaded Whetstone Agency was erected rapidly, but not many of the Indians appointed to settle on that part of the Great Sioux Reservation ever arrived. Instead, a large number of Sioux and Cheyennes, termed "Loafers," many of them mixed-bloods, congregated there. Regardless, the establishment of the Whetstone Agency resulted in the transfer of one company of the Twenty-second Infantry from Fort Sully to Fort Randall, which by association with the new agency took on added importance. By 1870, some 4,500 tribe members drew rations and annuities at Whetstone, but the facility was not fully addressing the needs of the majority of people for whom it was intended. Many of the people disliked the area along the Missouri River; Spotted Tail refused to locate there, remaining farther west on the White River, and Red Cloud stayed for a while in the Powder River country with the Sioux who had refused to sign the treaty. Following an 1870 visit to Washington, D.C., by Red Cloud, Spotted Tail, and other headmen, government officials decided to establish two agencies for the people — Red Cloud Agency and Spotted Tail Agency — as far as 250 miles west of the Missouri. Whetstone thereafter became a transportation depot for supplies bound for these two agencies. Significantly, the shift in attention from the formerly roaming tribes in eastern Dakota to those farther west brought a change in mission for Fort Randall. From a frontier garrison established to provide direct response in the midst of Indian country, the post factored henceforth in more of a support capacity, providing troops and supplies for stations founded and campaigns to be initiated on the northern plains.[32]

Nonetheless, minor incidents continued in the vicinity of Fort Randall that required the attention of the garrison. In the fall of 1865, a trading post on the Keya Paha River, sixty miles west of the fort, came under attack by Brulés, who killed a man. Troops from Fort Randall arrived too late to pursue the warriors successfully. In March 1866, a smallpox scare gripped the fort. The disease was reportedly borne by Indians "on their way down the river towards this Post," and personnel were accordingly vaccinated by medical staff. Similarly, in July 1868 Brulés attacked a party driving cattle bound from the Niobrara River to the post commissary, stealing the animals and inflicting casualties among the drovers. Again, troops went in pursuit from Fort Randall but failed to find the culprits. The incident resulted in the addition of an army escort for all such incoming cattle deliveries. On October 9, as droves of cattle ascended the trails from Kansas bound for the upriver posts, however, the Brulés struck again, this time circumventing the escort by setting fire to the surrounding grasslands. "By destroying our pasture," observed the post surgeon in a detailed report, "they expected to retain our droves and cut short our supplies."

> It has been ascertained that the country on both sides of the upper Missouri for two hundred miles has been burned out. These fires approached the fort from all directions accompanied by a terrific storm. The night scene . . . beggars description. Mountains, hills,

and plains were covered with a progressive sheet of flame. The air was densely filled with smoke. . . . Night before last the fire swept over the plateau on which are located the buildings of the fortifications, a tract of land one mile wide and about four miles long hemmed in by high hills on the south and the Missouri on the North. As the fire approached the Fort, the alarm was given, and the long roll called. Every man jumped from his bed. . . . The flames were rapidly approaching our stables and corrals where we had our winter stores for our horses, mules and cattle, including about 2,000 tons of hay. In close column the men met the enemy with bundles of brush, and bags tied to sticks with which to whip into submission this good servant but a very bad master. A line of men strung across the plateau perhaps a mile long were now in fierce hand to hand struggle with the advancing foe. For a long time, the men tried in vain to check the march of the fiery crawling fiend. His ally, the storm, made him now still more appalling. But now, the men gained a mastery over it, the bright flames here and there extinguished, and lost in a dense smoke. We were about to congratulate ourselves, when a cold, fierce Boreas came down the plateau, and with one breath defiantly . . . [started a fire] in the rear of the men. The bugle sounded the retreat; officers in excitement screamed out their commands and the men rushed back once more. . . . The next morning . . . the face of the earth was as black as soot. . . . As our pastures were thus destroyed, immediate measures were taken to disperse our herds. To-day I witnessed the operation of swimming several hundred head of Texan cattle across the Missouri. They are to be sent North on the East side of the river, where there are less hostile Indians to molest them.[33]

Citizens alarmed by the erstwhile Indian raids, along with Dakota Territory governor Andrew J. Faulk, urged the territorial legislature to call for the reinstatement of troops at Fort James, along the James River, and at Fort Dakota, near Sioux Falls. Both posts, previously abandoned, were regarrisoned for several more years with soldiers detached from Fort Randall.[34]

On June 3 and again on June 12, 1867, Fort Randall came under direct attack by mounted Indians, probably Brulé Lakotas. In the first instance, about fifty warriors tried to stampede the post herd and managed to wound a soldier and get away with twenty-one horses and mules. In the second instance, as a large body identified as Cheyennes approached the post, whose garrison numbered fewer than one hundred effectives, the discharge of howitzer fire sent them away. Later that summer, trying to gauge the Indian situation in the area, division commander Sherman journeyed up the Missouri, stopping briefly at Fort Randall while continuing on to district headquarters at Fort Sully. Meantime, in fulfilling its responsibility for oversight to the Yankton and Ponca reservations, the garrison monitored the distribution of food to the Yanktons, whose crops were beset by grasshopper infestations and drought conditions. Moreover, the commissary officer repeatedly was ordered to deliver food to hungry tribesmen coming to the post. When nearly the entire Ponca tribe, on the verge of starvation, appeared at Fort Randall, Major Chambers issued the people beef, flour, cornmeal, sugar, and coffee from government stores. In addition to their pitiable circumstances, both tribes were variously targeted during these years by territorial politicians for removal to free up lands for white settlement.[35]

In March 1869, Brulé and Two Kettle warriors struck a wood party a mile from Fort Randall, killing a wagoner and driving off several mules. Throughout the late 1860s, intermittent intertribal raiding occurred between Yanktons and Santees, on the one hand, and Pawnees in Nebraska, whose pony herds offered a ready attraction, on the other. At least one confrontation took place near the post; yet troops arrived at the scene too late to stem the fighting. A soldier reported in September 1869 that "the Indians had two fights close to this post this last month. We could hear them firing the first day, but none of the troops went out to see them. The Yankton Indians has [sic] got some of their [Pawnee?] scalps, and they have a dance every night over them at this post."[36] Evidently, the use of Indian scouts was wasted during these exercises, and their use was subsequently terminated as being "utterly worthless." The unlawful introduction of liquor to the Indians proved the genesis of many difficulties. In 1869, Captain DeWitt C. Poole, Twenty-second Infantry, was assigned Indian agent at Whetstone. He quickly learned of the presence of spirits smuggled in by disreputable whites. In one incident in October 1869, the resulting drunkenness brought on the killing of the Oglala Big Mouth by Spotted Tail of the Brulés. Directly after the murder, a detachment of twenty-one soldiers from Fort Randall in the charge of Captain Charles A. Webb, together with a howitzer, arrived to protect citizens and government property. Webb subsequently arrested one white man and two mixed-bloods for providing contraband whiskey. Fort Randall soldiers quelled potential disturbances at Whetstone over succeeding months and variously remained stationed at the agency until 1872. A similar incident involving the Yanktons resulted in troops from Fort Randall destroying at least fifteen gallons of whiskey at their reservation.[37]

Any account of the condition of Indian affairs as they related directly to the Fort Randall garrison must include the gruesome project of post surgeon George P. Hackenburg, who spent four months in 1868–69 collecting Indian skulls, mostly by robbing tribal cemeteries, for delivery to the Army Medical Museum. Hackenburg proudly described having accumulated specimens from "ten different tribes" through his "skull-hunting" expeditions, which took him by foot and horseback some 300 miles in seeking his quarry. Among the cemeteries he ravished was that at Ponca Agency, where he purloined "half a dozen skulls," then got a dozen more from bodies "simply boxed, lying in deep square holes," as yet unburied. Hackenburg also journeyed north of the post and on at least two occasions raided Sioux graves and scaffolds. In one instance, he disinterred "the mother of a noted chief who is now on the war path." In another, he targeted a scaffold: "I ran to the top of the hill, quickly climbed one of the poles, and was in the sacred presence of the dead. One sweep of the scalpel gashed the ceremonial blankets, and secured for me one of the most perfect and beautiful anatomical specimens I ever saw. The ants and worms had dissected every particle of flesh away, leaving the cranium with all the teeth in a perfect condition." When the surgeon learned that nearby Indians had been watching him, he proceeded to lie to them, feigning ignorance of what the scaffold contained while graciously accepting their invitation to dinner. The skull hidden in a bag under blankets on his horse, Hackenburg wrote, "I sat down on the ground and ate a hearty Indian meal without asking any questions. Sometimes 'ignorance is bliss.'"[38]

As a result of the Fort Laramie Treaty of 1868, the 96,000-acre Ponca reservation on the west side of the Missouri River—which had been reconfigured three years earlier to permit Ponca ownership of the mouth of the Niobrara—was inadvertently ceded to the Lakotas as part of the Great Sioux Reservation. The blunder corresponded with renewed attacks on the tribesmen by the Brulés, a situation not immediately rectified despite the almost continuous presence of troops from Fort Randall. With their crops suffering from repeated grass-hopper invasions, coupled with their disinclination to hunt buffalo farther west because of the Lakotas, the Poncas faced a potentially debilitating crisis. Over the immediately ensuing years, however, food relief for the afflicted Poncas arrived following congressional appropriations under the Peace Policy that provided subsistence for the reservation tribes.[39] But the growing tragedy for the Poncas was not over, and in the years ahead the soldiers at Fort Randall, just thirty miles away, would play an instrumental part in their evolving history as well as a peripheral role in an important chapter of American Indian history.

Turbulent Seventies

The arrival of the 1870s saw Fort Randall increasingly fulfill its destiny as a depot and support facility for stations located farther north and west on the frontier, while continuing to monitor area Indians and the progress of white settlement. Correspondingly, the 1870s also proved important in the history of the post because of its extended involvement in more distant Indian-military affairs and in the collateral events of national expansion that took place on the northern plains during that decade. These included the Yellowstone Expeditions of 1871, 1872, and 1873; the discovery of sizable gold deposits in the Black Hills in 1874 and the resulting gold rush; and army prosecution of the Great Sioux War in 1876–77, which finally wrested from the nontreaty Lakotas their coveted sacred grounds and hunting lands and incarcerated them on the Great Sioux Reservation. Fort Randall's role in these and related proceedings, especially in terms of its participating personnel, was significant.

The location of the Lakota agencies along the Missouri River following the 1868 Fort Laramie Treaty revitalized the purpose for Fort Randall's existence and probably ensured its immediate survival. By 1870, it seemed, civilization had fairly encompassed the post. Besides steamboat traffic that docked above the fort and daily stagecoach service between the post and Sioux City (and weekly service running beyond to Fort Sully), there was important commercial growth in the vicinity of the post. Directly across the river from Fort Randall, the town of White Swan had arisen, seeded both by the presence of the post and the Yankton Agency. At least two Missouri women were plying their assets among the troops. Their efforts were noted by a Sioux City paper that termed them "White Squaws" and suggested, according to one historian, "that settlement of the country had reached a state of refinement whereby the soldiers no longer were obliged to rely upon native talent for their after-hours recreation."[1]

Twenty-second Infantry troops continued to garrison Fort Randall through the late 1860s and into the 1870s. As regimental headquarters, the post received recruits in late December 1869, many of whom were distributed to other posts in the spring. In February 1870, Major Chambers transferred to the Fourth Infantry at Fort Fetterman, Wyoming. Three months later, the regular complement numbered four officers and 136 enlisted men when the fort welcomed the field and staff and ten companies of the Fourteenth Infantry, seven of which were destined for the upriver Indian agencies. In midsummer 1870, the remaining three companies occupied a bivouac outside the post until they, too, departed to police the agencies. Thereafter, until June 1874 Fort Randall's strength fluctuated minimally between 124 and 265, with the number of officers commensurately ranging between six and fifteen over the same period. The companies of the Twenty-second stationed at the post through these four years were variously B, C, D, G, H, and K, and Colonel Otis remained in essential command. In June 1874, however, the five companies of the Twenty-second then present (B, D, F, G, and H) transferred east to the Division of the Atlantic, relieved by the field, staff, band, and Companies C, D, G, I, and K, First Infantry, under Mexican War and Civil War veteran Colonel Thomas G. Pitcher, which arrived from the Department of the Lakes (the remaining five companies went to Fort Sully and the Lower Brulé Agency). Lieutenant Colonel Pinkney Lugenbeel replaced Pitcher as regimental commander and was posted at Fort Randall for most of the decade, until succeeded in October 1879 by Colonel William R. Shafter. Except for a five-month augmentation by three companies (A, E, and H) of the Seventh Cavalry between May and September 1875, Fort Randall remained garrisoned by the First Infantry through the end of the decade, with the number of enlisted men present ranging between 72 and 255 but averaging about 182. The number of officers present averaged about nine. The post served as headquarters of the Southern District of the Department of Dakota as well as regimental headquarters throughout the balance of the 1870s, with the First Infantry companies variously assigned there, at Fort Sully, and at the Lower Brulé Agency.[2]

By the close of the 1860s, Fort Randall required substantial physical improvements if the post was to continue. Modifications to the landscape during the tenure of the Twenty-second Infantry created a pastoral image to some visitors, one of whom in 1865 had described the fort as a village entered by walking from the river through a lovely cottonwood grove and replete with the sutler's residence, several private homes, a photo gallery, and the omnipresent blockhouses. Yet by 1870, many of the buildings survived in poor condition, some having been in service since the mid-1850s, while questions circulated as to whether Fort Randall was to be retained or abandoned. The presence of the new agencies settled the matter, and in 1870 post commander Otis directed its renovation.

Over the next two years, $20,000 was expended to replace the rustic log cabins with modern, gable-roofed, two-story frame barracks and to complete necessary refurbishment and repair of the post quartermaster and commissary warehouses and construction of cognate and other new structures. At the same time, functions of certain buildings also changed, and others were replaced by modern ones; by 1873, for example, a new hospital stood near the northeast corner of the post. Under the new arrangement, two modern two-story frame enlisted barracks and three of one story, mostly completed during the summer of 1871, now stood on either long side of the parade ground and at the north end. Most of the officer quarters, including two new ones, remained clustered near the home of the commanding officer, itself renovated and added to in 1871, at the southwest end of the quadrangle. Two others, new in 1871–72, stood near the north end of the parade ground, while another consisted of the refurbished and enlarged former hospital. A new laundresses' quarters stood some distance east of the post, but it proved too small, and some laundresses continued to occupy several of the old log structures. A storehouse for Indian goods stood near the new quartermaster/commissary complex northeast of the parade ground toward the river, while such refinements as a tailor shop were also located there. A new post trader's store and complex stood west of the main post, separated from it by the road leading south to the cemetery. Oddly, the magazine, at most posts normally positioned some distance away because of its volatile content, here stood along the northern edge of the parade ground, dangerously close to both officer and enlisted quarters. The guardhouse contained cells 8 feet high by $2^2/_3$ feet wide and $6^1/_2$ feet long, each with but a rectangular slit for ventilation and meant to confine "for short periods men who have become violent and unmanageable through intoxication." Perhaps oblivious to hygienic concerns, the new post bakery (1874) was positioned on the southeast edge of the garrison perilously in line with several barrack privies.[3]

A singular addition to the Fort Randall complex in 1875 was the stone interfaith chapel. Before that time, a post chapel, library, and reading room were located in the north barrack room of Company G of the First Infantry. Built from funds and labor donated by soldiers at the post, as well as from monies contributed by the Independent Order of Odd Fellows (IOOF) and otherwise solicited among settlers in the vicinity, the roughly cruciform-shaped new chapel stood on a solid stone foundation just beyond the north corner of the quadrangle. It had stone-fill walls two to three feet thick veneered with yellow chalk rock quarried from the river bluffs two miles below the post. Reportedly, Lieutenant Colonel Pinkney Lugenbeel, the post commander, conceived of the idea for the chapel, and its construction was executed under the direction of George Bush, former post carpenter at Fort Randall. Cottonwood sawed from Missouri River islands provided beams, while imported red and white pine served for trusses, trim, and shingles. Black walnut from the East was used for interior woodwork, including a choir loft and pews. An organ was installed. When finished, the attractive chapel, complete with working bell tower with spiral staircase, double-hung entrance door, pointed arch doors, stained-glass windows, and a rounded window with a painted angel in the gable above the entrance, was reportedly "the handsomest church in the Territory." (A circular broadcasted that "the Church bell will be rung at 10.30 A.M. for five minutes and then tolled for ten minutes. It will be rung again for five minutes and then cease, when the services will begin.")[4] Estimated cost stood at $20,000. Emblazoned at the entrance was an inscription, "Christ Church — Erected by First U.S. Inf. 1875." Besides church services (east wing), the building functioned as a library (west wing) and as quarters for post organizations, including Echo Lodge No. 2 of the IOOF of Dakota Territory (Yankton's was No. 1), which occupied the centermost room behind the chapel proper. On May 2, 1879, the first wedding took place in the chapel — that of Hattie Lugenbeel, the post commander's daughter, to S. H. Gruber — officiated by Episcopal bishop and missionary William H. Hare.[5]

These projects, but for some additions and modifications in subsequent years, represented the last large-scale development at Fort

Randall until its abandonment in 1892. In 1876–77, for example, the stable was repaired and enlarged with the addition of a shed, a new sawmill was erected, walks were built, and trees were planted. More officer quarters were recommended to "make this a very comfortable five-company post." Less intensive structural refinements consisted of a picket fence 900 feet long raised around the post cemetery; new walks were also constructed in the cemetery, trees planted, and eighty-seven new headboards placed over the graves. Another change involved improvement of the telegraph line between Fort Randall and Fort Sully in the early 1870s, along with authorization for completing another line from Yankton to Fort Sully via Fort Randall. By this time, the post's water system consisted of a concrete reservoir, situated atop a bluff, into which water was steam pumped through a pipe some 2,700 feet from the Missouri River. It was then force pumped into a water wagon for distribution throughout the fort.[6]

Within and around the garrison, post routine governed the activities of officers and soldiers much as before. Habitual duties included the conduct of boards of survey and courts-martial, completion of bills of lading, meetings of the Post Council of Administration to fix a surtax on the post trader and to monitor various post operations, the repair and construction of roads, the drilling of troops in the tactics of infantry and artillery, training (for example, "Estimating Distances"), repairs to buildings, inspection and repair of telegraph lines, providing escort duty, chasing deserters, assigning extra duty men and wood parties, and effecting bureaucratic paperwork relative to all of these matters as well as regarding the assignment and reassignment of enlisted men and officers. Post civilian employees included engineers, blacksmiths, teamsters, telegraph operators, and interpreters. Fort Randall, moreover, continued throughout this period as a consolidation and distribution point for recruits destined for the upriver posts.[7] For enlisted men in January 1872, drill took place twice a day, "Saturdays and Sundays excepted, and between the hours of ten and eleven A.M. & two & three P.M.," with instructions in the School of the Soldier according to *Upton's Infantry Tactics* (1867). In one instance, muster and monthly inspection of the troops "in great coats and light marching order" took place on February 29, 1872. When an officer of the Twenty-second Infantry, Captain George H. Cram, died unexpectedly at the Ponca Agency in August of that year, other post officers were directed to wear "the usual badge of mourning." Crimes rarely occurred within the garrison community, but in October 1871 unknown persons burglarized the home of an engineer who operated the post sawmill, stealing checks, cash, and clothing. Courts-martial also proceeded, some for serious charges but others for less severe offenses.[8] In April 1874, for example, Corporal James O'Hara of Company D, Twenty-Second Infantry, was reduced to the ranks. His sin? He had "blackened the face of Private Jeremiah Daily and other enlisted men . . . with Ink or Blackening while they were asleep in their bunks, to the ridicule of these men by the rest of the Company."[9]

Other routine procedures included the arrival in March 1875 of twenty Lee's breech loading rifles for testing through experimental use. "Company Commanders will be particular to place them in the hands of their best men," stated a directive. Another job often requiring special talent or interest was that of post gardener, and in February 1876 Private Henry Homer of Company C, First Infantry, took over that office. The gardens encompassed thirty acres in disparate plots generally maintained by the individual companies until 1879, when the plots were consolidated into one large garden. In 1876 and 1877, the gardens yielded, respectively, more than 3,000 bushels of potatoes and 7,000 heads of cabbage. On the centennial Fourth of July, a post special order directed that "a salute of thirteen guns will be fired at the dawn and also at the close of the day, and a National Salute [thirty-eight guns] will be fired at Meridian."[10] Although a post chaplain had resided at Fort Randall before 1873, in October of that year the fort was designated a legitimate "Chaplain Post." The chaplain also conducted classes in the post school. In June 1878, a notice was given that "all soldiers' children above five (5) years of age" were required to attend. As a precautionary measure in case of fire anyplace in the garrison, the four companies of the garrison were assigned "Hook and Ladder," "Bucket," "Hose," and "Tank" duties, respectively.[11]

The post trader's store continued offering a variety of goods to the Fort Randall garrison. The trader throughout most of the 1870s was James H. Pratt, a Massachusetts native who had garnered experience in the Quartermaster Department during the Civil War. He augmented his income while at Fort Randall by raising cattle and contracting for government provisions. Pratt gradually became more closely engaged in the cattle-raising operation and in July 1878 resigned his position with the army. He was succeeded at Fort Randall by John Cunningham. During the 1870s, the sale of alcohol to enlisted men became an issue meriting constant attention. Early in 1873, for instance, the men were limited to but two drinks per twenty-four-hour period, and the post trader was prohibited from dispensing more than that quantity. Occasionally, orders shut down liquor sales altogether. Such restrictions came and went, seemingly on the whim of the commanding officer. By 1878, the trader was dispensing beer freely and was in the process of opening an adjoining bar.[12] Next year, he received authorization to serve not only beer but malt liquor and wine, "subject to inspection by the Commanding Officer, Surgeon, or a Board of Officers . . . to determine [acceptable] quality."[13] Profits among the post traderships were enormous by the 1870s, when influence peddling was rampant on the frontier. In 1876, the post trader's establishment at Fort Randall came under at least marginal inquiry during congressional investigations of profiting from political influence and the "sale" of post traderships and Indian traderships that centered on Secretary of War William W. Belknap's involvement and resulted in his subsequent resignation and impeachment. Fort Randall was one of ten upper Missouri posts that had at least been suspected in bribery, paybacks, and other corrupt dealings.[14]

Other diversions for officers and enlisted men of the Fort Randall garrison during the 1870s included (as earlier suggested) membership in Echo Lodge No. 2, IOOF (at least one soldier passed muster in the fraternity by riding the Odd Fellows goat) and organization of a "Frontier Lodge" chapter of the Independent Order of Good Templars, devoted to promoting the abstinence of soldiers from drinking. (A previous garrison club, composed of men of Companies B, C, G, and H, Twenty-second Infantry, and known as the Twenty-second U.S. Infantry Temperance Association, had been founded in January 1871.) Private John E. Cox of the First Infantry recalled that he was elected chief templar. "The officers of the garrison gave hearty support, . . . particularly Col. Lugenbeel. . . . The lodge became a sort of corrective agency. When a soldier got drunk the Commander would suspend sentence on condition that the offender joined the Good Templars and took the abstinence pledge."[15] In October 1876, the annual meeting of the Grand Lodge of Dakota Territory convened at the post for a two-day session. On one occasion, the Dakota Odd Fellows met at a log inn at White Swan known as the Chamberlain before assembling at the post for regular meetings and a grand ball. The organizations also joined together to celebrate July 4, 1872, with a baseball game and wheelbarrow races. Baseball, in fact, became a staple at the post, with a team named "The O'Reillys." The existing stagecoach operation permitted occasional trips by the team to Yankton, where the players engaged "The Coyotes." Dances, masquerades, and cotillions were held frequently, while band performances occurred almost nightly. (An invitation ball commemorating George Washington's birthday took place in the Company G mess hall in February 1872.) The post library now boasted more than 1,500 volumes, along with assorted news tabloids and periodicals. Another newspaper flourished, albeit briefly, in 1873, and a theatrical ensemble was formed. Irish soldiers organized an "Irish National Association" as well as a Catholic church, which temporarily held services in a spare building. An Episcopal church, organized by settlers on the military reservation, also attracted soldiers from the post.[16]

Occasionally, the arrival of a famous personage energized the garrison. On June 27, 1872, dime novel protagonist and hunter and scout William F. Cody, well known as "Buffalo Bill," rode in on a cream-colored horse. He was trailing Indians with a unit of the Third Cavalry operating out of Fort McPherson, Nebraska, and stopped at the post for supplies and to obtain fresh horses. Although Cody's visit to Fort Randall was brief, it must have charged the men of the Twenty-second who were present. In September of the same year, Lieutenant General Philip H. Sheridan, Missouri Division commander and legendary Civil War figure, stopped at the fort en route downriver back to his Chicago headquarters. Eight months later, Lieutenant Colonel George A. Custer, the army's celebrated Indian fighter, passed through Fort Randall while transferring north to Fort Abraham Lincoln with companies of the Seventh Cavalry. Division commander Sheridan returned in May 1879, this time inspecting the post and reviewing the garrison with General Alfred H. Terry, the departmental commander, and their respective staffs. In one instance, a prominent person was already stationed at Fort Randall. Assistant surgeon and Captain Elliot Coues, posted there through the winter of 1872–73 and already known for his work as a naturalist, would later edit the journals of Lewis and Clark and other explorers as well as those of noted fur traders.[17] As surgeon, Coues accompanied the Northern Boundary Commission in 1873. Of the post and his time there, he recollected:

Randall was not a bad sort of a place, for a military post. I have pleasant memories of wintering there, 1872–73, though I was not well housed, did not fare sumptuously at table and sometimes had to go to bed to keep warm. The post was almost buried under the snow after a blizzard we had in April [1873], when some of the drifts were level with the roofs. I made large collections in natural history that season and wrote my Field Ornithology, which appeared in 1874. The best poker-player I ever faced . . . was Capt. John Hartley of the 22nd Infantry [at Fort Randall].[18]

Disease and the threat of disease occasionally caused alarm. Cases of pneumonia, syphilis, diphtheria, typhoid fever, rheumatism, catarrh, insanity, and "acute diarrhea" filled beds in the post hospital during the 1870s. A smallpox scare on the upper Missouri in the winter of 1872 forced the vaccination/revaccination of the entire command in February; another during the summer of 1873 focused on Peace Island, some fifteen miles above the post. As precaution against infection, boats approaching from upstream were prohibited from stopping at Fort Randall. Meantime, sexual contact between Indians and soldiers, also a diversion, proceeded as in previous years, and it continued to generate venereal diseases; by 1874, syphilis ranked fourth among contagious diseases at Fort Randall (as well as at Fort Buford and Fort Stevenson), despite edicts barring Indians from the military reservation and against enlisted men crossing the Missouri River to access the Yankton Reservation. Other medical cases involved frostbite, childbirth, and gunshot wounds, some of which resulted in surgery. Desertion remained a problem. In January, on the day following their being paid, three soldiers vanished, and a guard detachment was sent after them. It was later revealed that the men composing the guard spent a night with the fugitives in the cabin of an Indian who had been bribed to hide them. More desertions occurred following the discovery of gold in the Black Hills, with the subsequent departure of at least two musicians in 1875. Another soldier complained that an officer's continued exploitation of the men as cheap labor to enhance a private bathhouse project resulted in several desertions.[19]

Concurrent with the inner activities of the Fort Randall garrison were assorted external operations in which the soldiers took part. These comprised movements of parts of the post command to protect white settlers and Indians from each other and from other groups of

Indians. Troops constantly moved between the fort and the surrounding Indian agencies (Whetstone, Lower Brulé, Ponca, and, later in the decade, New Red Cloud and Spotted Tail agencies) as detachments were alternately assigned and relieved on a rotational basis. Others bolstered or switched places with companies at Fort Sully.[20] Meantime, because of expansionistic impulses and the resultant Indian situation on the northern plains during the fast-moving 1870s, troops from the upper Missouri posts were flying in all directions to participate in expeditions both for exploration and punitive reasons. In this vein, late in the summer of 1871 Companies C and H, Twenty-second Infantry, along with elements of Companies G and K, two companies of the Seventeenth Infantry and one of the Twentieth, plus a detachment of Indian scouts, composed the escort guarding surveyors of the Northern Pacific Railroad from Fort Rice to the Yellowstone River, an expedition headed by Lieutenant Colonel Joseph N. G. Whistler of the Twenty-second Infantry. The probe continued during the summer of 1872, when Companies D and G of the Twenty-second departed Fort Randall to accompany the expedition pushing farther up the Yellowstone; besides the infantrymen, the post component included five six-mule wagons and their teams, along with thirty head of cattle. The Fort Randall soldiers joined Company F from Fort Sully, along with two companies of the Seventeenth Infantry and a detachment of scouts. The expedition reached the mouth of the Powder River on the Yellowstone on August 18 and engaged Indians on the 21st and 22nd near O'Fallon's Creek. An officer of the Twenty-second, First Lieutenant Lewis D. Adair, was one of two men killed in a skirmish with warriors on October 5 as the column returned to Dakota. The Fort Randall men returned to their post in late October 1872.[21]

The Yellowstone Expedition of 1873—the third and largest thrust west in as many years—which traced the lands along the Yellowstone deep into the Montana hinterland of the nontreaty Lakotas, laid much of the groundwork for ensuing government demands on those tribesmen and helped provoke army operations against them in subsequent years. It also garnered the most public attention, encouraging imminent white settlement of the Yellowstone country. Headed by Colonel Stanley, the expedition organized at Fort Rice and, besides the engineering party, consisted of ten companies of the Seventh Cavalry commanded by Lieutenant Colonel Custer (some of which had passed through Fort Randall in April and May), four companies of the Sixth Infantry, six companies of the Ninth Infantry, four companies of the Seventeenth Infantry, headquarters and five companies of the Twenty-second—three (B, H, and K) from Fort Randall and two (E and I) from Fort Sully—a contingent of Indian scouts, and two M1861 Ordnance Rifles. The expedition outfitted at Fort Rice and departed June 20. It reached the Yellowstone on July 31 and traversed the north bank, the Seventh Cavalry engaging Sioux warriors on August 4 and 11. Following the latter clash, Twenty-second Infantry soldiers manned an artillery piece and shelled the Sioux along the banks of the river. Later that night, the battalion of the Twenty-second exchanged shots with Sioux attempting to stampede cattle, horses, and mules accompanying the expedition. Thereafter, the troops pushed up the Yellowstone to the Musselshell River with minimal opposition from the Indians before starting on their return. They reached Fort Abraham Lincoln on September 22, closing out a march of more than 1,200 miles. Companies B and H returned to Fort Randall on October 9, along with Company F, which had exchanged stations with Company K, posted to Fort Sully.[22]

Within a year of the Yellowstone Expedition of 1873, another military outing penetrated the Black Hills looking for potential sites on which to build a post as part of a design by General Sheridan to encircle the reservation and keep watch over the agency Sioux. Commanded by Custer, the Black Hills Expedition passed through and around the Hills in July and August 1874 and returned to Fort Abraham Lincoln bearing word from accompanying geologists that the low mountains of western Dakota contained substantial gold ore deposits. The Black Hills had long been rumored to harbor gold, and Custer's expedition seemingly offered credible proof. Over succeeding weeks, the news spread quickly, spawning parties of ragtag prospectors bent on illicitly entering the Black Hills—Lakota land according to the Fort Laramie Treaty of 1868—and seeking the Hills' newly confirmed wealth.

The government's reaction was to discourage intruders and to send troops to halt trespassers onto the Great Sioux Reservation. Sheridan directed department commander Terry to halt the interlopers and "use the force at your command to burn the wagon trains and destroy the outfit and arrest the leaders, confining them at the nearest military post."[23] To that end, the soldiers at Fort Randall, Fort Sully, the Lower Brulé and Cheyenne River agencies, Fort Laramie, and the new post of Camp Robinson on the White River prepared to execute that policy. The first citizen group of fortune hunters to invade the Black Hills, headed by John Gordon and others (under the aegis of promoter Charles Collins), departed Sioux City on October 6, 1874, entered the restricted country in December, and near French Creek raised a bastioned stockade for protection. A mounted command of thirty soldiers, accompanied by Indian scouts, departed Fort Sully and the Cheyenne River Agency in December. They found evidence of the intruders along the east side of the Black Hills but were forced by diminishing rations to return to their posts within sixteen days without making contact. Troops sent out from Fort Laramie, west of the Hills, also returned empty-handed. In December and January, a company of Third Cavalry operating with mounted infantry from Camp Robinson (built to guard the New Red Cloud Agency) also failed to locate the miners and were enveloped by freezing blizzard conditions en route back to their home station. In April 1875, a command under Captain John Mix from Fort Laramie located the Gordon party and escorted them from the Black Hills.

In the spring of 1875, a 150-man armed relief expedition led by Gordon (who had returned for supplies) set out from Sioux City to reach the miners in the Black Hills. At Fort Randall, Colonel Lugenbeel readied a force to overtake and stop it and others so inclined. He mounted Companies C, G, and I, First Infantry, under Captain Fergus Walker. "[Brevet] Major Walker's Black Hills Expedition," as one of the men dubbed the movement, was "a rather insignificant affair," destined to be an ordeal of bad weather for all.[24] Plagued by blizzards, sleet, and rain, Walker and Companies C, G, and I left Fort Randall on April 10. On May 6, they apprehended a group under Ben Andrews near a crossing of White River and sent them under escort to Fort Randall. Walker, with fewer than thirty men remaining, confronted the Gordon relief train on May 12 near Reunion Creek along the Niobrara River (near present Gordon, Nebraska). The miners at first agreed to go back but later refused to do so. Walker's undersized detachment regardless kept the filibusterers under observation. On May 21, joined by two companies of the Third Cavalry and a Gatling battery under Captain Anson Mills from Camp Sheridan, adjoining Spotted Tail Agency, the troops confronted Gordon's train near Reunion Creek. The command took the men into custody, destroyed most of their arms and wagons, and delivered them to Fort Randall.

Because the incident occurred before the group had entered the Sioux reservation, there arose controversy over the legality and justification for the arrests that reflected negatively on the Fort Randall garrison in the regional press. A district court case later upheld charges by some miners that Walker's actions, including looting, were illegal, while an army board of inquiry concluded that the accusations had been unfounded. The legal wrangling persisted, and ultimately verdicts favoring the miners encouraged further ventures.

The movements to eject trespassers continued through the spring and summer of 1875, augmented by the arrival at the post in May of three companies (A, E, and H) of the Seventh Cavalry under Captain Frederick W. Benteen, sent from the Department of the Gulf. Together with the cavalry adjunct, the soldiers from Forts Randall and Sully and Camp Robinson and the surrounding agencies stepped up their patrols and succeeded in covering an area stretching from the Missouri River to the Black Hills. In July and August, Benteen's troopers ranged into the Black Hills while Company D, First Infantry, covered the territory between the South Fork of the White River and Wounded Knee Creek. During this foray, the Seventh Cavalry captured several prospectors, returning with them to Fort Randall, where they were paroled after signing oaths not to return. As the year wore on, however, and as the numbers of trespassers into the Hills increased during the controversy over Walker's actions, government policy toward them softened. The military vigil relented as officials opened negotiations with the Sioux in the fall of 1875 seeking a cession of the mineral-rich country. Without immediate success in these councils, federal authorities decided to press the issue with the Sioux, forcing the nontreaty bands in Wyoming and Montana onto the reservation while using threats and coercion with the agency people in pursuing their objectives.[25]

Between March 1876 and September 1877, the army prosecuted the Lakotas and their Northern Cheyenne allies in several campaigns resulting in various engagements in Wyoming, Nebraska, Dakota, and Montana, including the defeat of Custer and the Seventh Cavalry at the Battle of the Little Big Horn in June 1876. Three companies of the Seventh had served earlier at Fort Randall; the members of one of them, Company E, had all been killed with Custer's battalion in the fighting. News of the Little Bighorn battle reached Fort Randall in early July, although the telegraph line had been disabled. Sergeant

Cox and several men were on holiday in Springfield, forty-five miles from the post when on July 5 a merchant beckoned him. As Cox recalled,

> I sprang through the open door and found myself in a telegraph office. The lone operator evidently was greatly agitated. "Can you write fast?" was his query. I sat down at a table and grasped a pencil and a sheet of paper. "I will read and you write," he whispered hoarsely. The dispatch was dated at Cheyenne, Wyo., and stated that a messenger had brought the news of the battle ten days before, and that Custer and his command were wiped out. I got that far, dropped my pencil and dashed from the telegraph office, ran to the hotel and hunted my comrades. After a moment's conference we were agreed that we must get back to Randall as quickly as possible. . . . We . . . made the best speed possible, reaching the fort up in the morning. We found a dispatch had gotten through and two or three companies were packing up to start for the fighting zone, my company being one of them."[26]

The Great Sioux War ultimately involved the participation of numerous cavalry, infantry, and artillery units from around the country. Six companies of the Fifth Infantry from Fort Leavenworth entrained for Yankton, where they boarded the steamer *E. H. Durfee* to head northwest into the war zone. On July 17, as they passed Fort Randall, members of its close-knit community gathered on the shoreline to wave encouragement. Six companies of the Twenty-second Infantry from Fort Randall, among them Cox's, also arrived in late July along the Yellowstone from their stations in the East to reinforce General Terry's command, ravaged following the Indians' defeat and destruction of the Seventh Cavalry. They took station at Glendive Cantonment and joined Colonel Nelson A. Miles in prosecuting the tribesmen through the winter of 1876–77 and the spring and part of the summer of 1877. During the summer of 1876, companies from Fort Sully continued to be sent to "prevent immigration to the Black Hills," while soldiers from Fort Randall moved to protect settlers along the Niobrara River. Although Acting Governor George H. Hand, following a resolution of Yankton citizens, offered the War Department a regiment of mounted troops to help prosecute the Indians, the gesture was declined as premature. In September 1876, companies of the First Infantry from Fort Randall traveled to Standing Rock Agency on the upper Missouri, taking part there in administering Sheridan's policy of disarming and dismounting the Sioux. During the early summer of 1877, four companies (B, G, H, and K) of the First Infantry from Fort Sully and Standing Rock also joined Miles's Yellowstone Command, helping pursue the Indians into the Dakota agencies and tracking down pockets of warriors in the wake of the major campaigns. Meanwhile, in September 1876 a commission had cajoled the reservation Sioux into signing away the Black Hills. Within seven months, the Military Division of the Missouri designated three routes to the gold country, one of which followed portions of the Niobrara and Keya Paha rivers and Porcupine Creek as "the shortest and most practicable route to Custer City" in the southern Hills. In May 1878, Companies C and I, First Infantry, were dispatched from Fort Randall via Fort Sully, along with Company K from that station, to Bear Butte, near the eastern edge of the Black Hills, to join soldiers of the Seventh Cavalry and Eleventh Infantry in building a post from which to protect the mining communities. The "camp near Bear Butte" would evolve into a major army installation, Fort Meade, near present Sturgis, South Dakota.[27]

Troops from Fort Randall also played a role in quelling the national labor riots that erupted in the East and Midwest during the summer of 1877. Fueled by wage cutbacks resulting in strikes that disabled the railroad industry, the unrest produced disturbances in several major cities, including Chicago, necessitating the placement of soldiers there. Among the nineteen companies of infantry and dismounted cavalry brought into the city to keep peace were Companies C and E, First Infantry, which departed Fort Randall on July 27, arrived on the 30th, and returned on August 19. Their primary duty while in Chicago was to protect government warehouses and utility firms.[28]

While Fort Randall proper played but a tangential role in the operations against the Sioux and Northern Cheyennes in 1876–77, relations with the neighboring Yankton and Ponca tribes continued to be much more direct. By the early 1870s, the Yanktons were considered a peaceful people "making rapid progress toward civilization," and under the Grant administration's Peace Policy the tribe continued its farming practice, beset by frequent drought, grasshopper infestation, and hail that repeatedly destroyed the yield. Episcopal and Presbyterian churches were located at Greenwood, across and downriver from Fort Randall, and by the early 1870s these institutions developed mission schools, promoting further acculturation. Attempts to introduce the people to cattle raising repeatedly failed, the Indians tending to eat the animals for survival, and in 1871 some of the tribesmen fled to Montana where they might hunt buffalo; most had apparently returned to the Yankton Reservation by late in the decade. Various reservation communities grew as the tribesmen abandoned their tipis and built houses, although an epidemic of measles in 1873 killed more than a hundred people.

Fort Randall's role vis-à-vis the Yanktons gradually diminished during the 1870s, although soldiers went to the reservation whenever trouble occurred, such as the killing of citizens' livestock by the Yanktons and incidents involving liquor among them, and whenever rumors arose that disaffected Yanktons might leave the agency to go north. In 1872, the Yanktons filed a complaint that an unidentified enlisted man had introduced "spirituous liquors" on the reservation, causing the post commander to decree that "any person connected with this garrison detected in the crime mentioned will be turned over to the civil authorities for trial and punishment."[29] Moreover, the frequent "misconduct" of enlisted men among the Yanktons living near the White Swan community in 1873 finally caused Colonel Otis to issue a proscription on soldiers crossing the Missouri "without permission from proper authority," an exclusion that continued, variously, through the balance of Fort Randall's occupation. In the summer of 1878, a group of Yanktons petitioned the commanding officer of Fort Randall for help in dealing with their agent over delayed annuity payments and inferior subsistence supplies, but when nothing happened a number of Yanktons departed the reserve and headed downriver toward the Omaha agency. Although a detachment started from Fort Randall to retrieve them, the Yanktons returned on their own.[30]

Because of the susceptibility of the Poncas to continued raiding by Lakotas during the 1870s, particularly by the Brulés, Fort Randall maintained its close relationship with the Poncas much as before. Like the Yanktons, the Poncas experienced repeated crop failures during the decade (although they enjoyed some successes), and the presence of the Lakotas forced them to curtail many of their former buffalo-hunting activities. By 1872, the Ponca reserve was in the charge of the Episcopalian mission. Most of the 750 or so tribal members occupied log homes and practiced agriculture, yet they maintained an incessant fear of the Sioux. Under the Fort Laramie Treaty of 1868, their reservation was mistakenly designated part of the Great Sioux Reservation, a factor that increasingly aggravated the age-old intertribal enmity. The raids by the Brulés were especially brutal as they sought to steal ponies, plunder homes, and kill and scalp the people. Occasionally, the Poncas, though poorly armed, mounted strong defenses, in December 1870, for instance, repelling an attack after killing three Sioux warriors. To help protect the Poncas, detachments of a dozen or fifteen men under an officer from Fort Randall began regular rotations to the agency. "It was forty miles from the fort," recalled one soldier, "and lonesome enough to suit a hermit."[31] In 1874, the Poncas centralized their homes at the agency headquarters. Even then, however, the attacks continued.

One of the fiercest Brulé assaults came on the morning of July 6, 1875, when a group of 100 to 150 warriors appeared before the agency. Eleven Fort Randall soldiers of Company G, First Infantry, under Sergeant Arthur C. Danvers, opened a lengthy engagement with the attackers. Improvising with material on hand, Danvers's men raised breastworks of cordwood and employed an old 12-pounder cannon repeatedly filled with stones and scrap iron to turn back three assaults by the Sioux. Infantryman John Cox described the discharge: "The sergeant set fire to his home-made fuse, and turned a somersault over an embankment just as the old gun 'spoke!' . . . It was like an earthquake! Such a cloud of smoke! The boys rushed forward and found that the brave old piece had . . . turned clear over, and was standing up on its muzzle."[32] The warriors satisfied themselves with long-range shooting and managed to wound slightly two soldiers before withdrawing without apparent casualties.[33] "This affair," stated General Orders No. 15, "shows that with proper precaution, coolness and discipline that professional Soldiers are equal to almost any number of Indians in combat."[34]

Mindful of the repeated sallies by the Sioux, who resented Ponca occupation of lands given them in 1868, as well as the Poncas' own desire to relocate, the government concluded in 1876 to remove the Poncas to the Indian Territory (present Oklahoma). The decision coincided with a plan to relocate the Brulé and Oglala Sioux (including recently surrendered tribesmen) from their White River locations back to the Missouri River for economy in provisioning them. The anticipated proximity of their enemies caused Colonel Lugenbeel at

Fort Randall to urge the Poncas' removal. "It will require a large force to protect the Poncas and they cannot carry on any kind of business while being so constantly annoyed by so numerous and so warlike a tribe of hostile Indians."[35] In April 1877, thirty soldiers of Company I, First Infantry, under Captain Walker, departed the post to escort the 736 Poncas south. The relocation occurred with catastrophic results for the Ponca people, some of whom chose to remain north with their Omaha kin. Those who resisted were briefly incarcerated in the Fort Randall guardhouse. Many of those who journeyed under guard to Kansas and the Indian Territory met untimely deaths from malaria, other sicknesses, and starvation. In 1878, Standing Bear, in defying the authority of the government, led sixty-five of his people back to Nebraska, where troops arrested him, precipitating, with the help of white activists working on the Poncas' behalf, a court case, *Standing Bear v. Crook*, which resulted in a momentous federal decision affording the Indians recognition and protection of their individual rights. The Poncas with Standing Bear won restoration of part of their Niobrara reservation, and an agreement with the Lakotas returned to them part of their former reservation, although sharing an agency with the previously removed Santee Sioux; eventually, the Poncas' land was allotted to them in severalty.[36] Meantime, the Spotted Tail Agency, instead of relocating at the mouth of Whetstone Creek on the Missouri River, went to the vacated Ponca Agency on the Niobrara, while Red Cloud's people removed from near Fort Robinson to the mouth of Yellow Medicine Creek, above Fort Randall on the Missouri. Neither group was happy, and late in 1878 soldiers accompanied both groups to new agencies in southwestern Dakota; Red Cloud's followers settled at White Clay Creek at a point thereafter called Pine Ridge Agency, while Spotted Tail's people settled on Rosebud Creek, thereafter called Rosebud Agency. In the spring of 1879, Company A, First Infantry, served as escort to an engineering crew surveying the new agencies.[37]

Beyond local Indian matters, the soldiers at Fort Randall allotted considerable time and effort to dealing with area settlers. Settlement in southeastern Dakota Territory and northwestern Nebraska flourished in the 1870s. "As the last and greatest of the public domains which offer free homes, liberal laws, and unparalleled prospective prosperity in the future to its people, Dakota stands preeminently alone," editorialized the *Sioux City Daily Times*.[38] Throughout the decade, as the Indian threat continued to subside, the arable land drained by the Missouri continued to beckon, offering not only rich parcels to emigrant farmers but also the possibility of new markets for their produce. Since the early days, the officers and men at Fort Randall interfaced regularly with area residents, and improved transportation allowed more frequent access to the growing downriver communities. Yankton and Sioux City, as well as intervening towns, became favorite retreats for officers and soldiers. Conversely, guests from those settlements participated in post functions, too.[39]

Military attention continued to be directed to legal and illegal settlers—protecting those legitimately occupying lands along the Niobrara south of the post or removing those who continued to take up residence on the military reservation. Through the decade of the 1870s, detachments of soldiers periodically rotated southeast from the post to safeguard foreign-born "Bohemian" (Czech) settlers near the former Ponca Agency (present Niobrara, Nebraska) from attack by Indians or white marauders, as well as from natural disasters. The Bohemians had gradually been moving into Nebraska since the late 1850s, but their numbers increased after the Civil War, some emigrating there from Wisconsin. Throughout 1871, with their supplies exhausted and crops failing, the destitute immigrants received from the army such food supplies as corn, flour, and barreled pork. Much as the Poncas had been, these people, too, were subjected to occasional attacks by Lakotas, and calls went out to Fort Randall for help in dealing with threatening tribesmen. First Infantry and Seventh Cavalry soldiers sent from the post in 1875 helped dissuade the Lakota warriors, but the 1878 occupation of the former Ponca lands by Spotted Tail's Brulés, albeit temporary, proved disquieting to the settlers, promoting the establishment of an interim military camp along the Keya Paha River in Holt County and continuation of the guard detail.[40]

Closer to home, the Fort Randall garrison contended with squatters on the military reservation, many of whom had settled in the vicinity of the post before the establishment of the reservation in 1860 and who claimed a previous right of occupancy, but some who were more recent trespassers. Of immediate concern to army authorities were those individuals trafficking in liquor, selling or bartering the product among the Indians, as well as selling to or otherwise enticing enlisted men at the post. Those squatters resided on a portion of the reserve on the east side of the Missouri and west of the Yankton Reservation that had been relinquished by the government in 1867 then re-claimed in 1870. When the post commander prohibited sales of alcohol by the post trader, "whiskey ranches" and bootlegging schemes proliferated around Fort Randall. In early December 1870, Colonel Otis warned some of the settlers either to quit the liquor business or "depart in peace," but by late that month, with no evidence of compliance, a detachment of soldiers threatened to remove "all persons engaged in illegal traffic & all those whose character is considered improper."[41] The issue of preemption remained, however, and a board of officers convened at Fort Randall in March 1871 to examine individual claims. Finally, in 1874 Congress endorsed the rights of the earlier settlers, instructing the War Department to turn over to the Interior Department for claims areas of the military reservation that had been settled upon before its establishment. Congress further directed the War Department to relinquish portions of the reservation north and east of the Missouri River that had been settled upon "in good faith" during 1867–70. The act thus permitted individuals who had formerly occupied any of these lands to secure legal title to them. A board of officers met at Fort Randall to determine what property improvements, or values thereof, had to be made by the government. The issue of squatters on the military reservation on the north side of the Missouri River continued, and as late as 1879 men of the First Infantry were forcibly evicting violators.[42]

By the time the decade of the 1870s closed, Fort Randall had either participated in or witnessed a large part of the passing of the American frontier. On the northern plains, the gold rush to the Black Hills had come and gone, bringing with it the death knell for the Lakotas and Northern Cheyennes. The major Indian conflicts passed into history, with the tribes finally impounded on reservations, and exploration, settlement, and commerce had proceeded in their course. Fort Randall, once the most advanced government outpost on the upper Missouri, once stalwartly poised at the vanguard of the pre– and post–Civil War westward thrusts by Euro-Americans, by the advent of the 1880s had been effectually circumscribed as a major force in the unfolding drama of the West, relegated to the periphery by inexorably changing times. In the years ahead, the post would enjoy but a few brief resurgences of notice before fading altogether from the scene.

Waning Years

Fort Randall's days appear to have been numbered even before the 1870s had ended. In 1879, the post emerged on a list of military installations under review for consideration for abandonment, a notice that drew protests from Dakota Territory residents and politicians who recognized a good thing and wanted to ensure its continuation. Fort Randall had by then become a mainstay in the area, recognized for its protective qualities as well as for its role in nurturing booming white settlement and the regional economy, and no eastern Dakotans (or Nebraskans, for that matter) wanted to see its status change. By the advent of the 1880s, however, it was clear to many people that the days of Indian warfare were largely over, and the proliferation of railroads permitting the rapid transit of troops from more urban stations to regional hot points commensurately required changes in the military infrastructure throughout the West. (In Dakota, an extension of the Chicago, Milwaukee, and St. Paul Railroad by 1885 had reached Springfield, just forty-five miles from Fort Randall; in 1886, the line extended to Armor, just twenty-five miles from the post, and mail and telegraph contact was maintained from there.) The Lakotas, Arapahos, and Cheyennes, who had been major threats to white occupation and settlement, were now on reservations and undergoing acculturation through government-sponsored farming programs while being watched over by civilian authorities and troops stationed at adjacent military posts. The Yanktons were peaceful people, and most of the Poncas had been removed to the Indian Territory.

The movement to close posts deemed no longer useful gained momentum in 1882, when Commanding General William T. Sherman unveiled a plan for a "radical change in our whole system of piecemeal work in quartering troops of the United States." Sherman outlined and discussed several strategic frontiers, including those on the Atlantic, Pacific, and Gulf coasts, as well as on the northern frontier, and explained how the coming of railroads had altered the necessity of maintaining so many army posts nationwide. Fort Randall was considered an interior post—one of many that had "grown up in the progress of the settlement of the Continent, were absolutely demanded by the necessities of the country at the time, . . . and having fulfilled their purpose should be allowed to die out." Sherman had briefly visited Fort Randall in July 1880 and had surveyed conditions there. In his 1882 report, the commanding general estimated Fort Randall to be necessary for retention for ten years, "the repairs to which should consequently be temporary and paid for out of the annual appropriation for barracks and quarters." Other posts were to be considered for immediate abandonment.[1]

Thus, as early as the first years of the 1880s, realization grew among the officer corps, at least, that Fort Randall was on the road to deactivation and likely abandonment. Despite that, the post continued operating much as before and would proceed to do so until circumstances warranted otherwise. In May 1880, the First Infantry, which had garrisoned the fort for six years, departed by steamer for Texas, changing stations with the Twenty-fifth Infantry, one of four regiments in the army composed of African American enlisted men and white officers and commanded by Colonel George L. Andrews. Regardless of the ongoing debate over whether black soldiers could withstand the winter cold on the northern plains, by mid-August 200 soldiers of Companies B, F, G, and I of the Twenty-fifth, along with the regimental band, occupied the barracks, while the field and staff took up residence in appropriate quarters. Other companies of the Twenty-fifth reaching Fort Randall transferred immediately to Fort Meade, in western Dakota near the Black Hills. The headquarters and three companies of the Twenty-fifth Infantry remained at Fort Randall for two and a half years, until November 1882, when part of the regiment departed Dakota Territory for Fort Snelling, Minnesota. Company G transferred to Fort Hale, up the Missouri River near the Crow Creek Reservation, where it remained until that post's abandonment in 1884; four companies of the Twenty-fifth remained at Fort Meade until 1888.

Companies C and D, Fifteenth Infantry, with field, staff, and band, Lieutenant Colonel Peter T. Swaine commanding, arrived in November 1882 from Colorado. They were followed by Companies A and H. Garrison strength at Fort Randall then stood at more than 200 men but generally fluctuated thereafter between 160 and 175. In November 1883, regimental headquarters transferred to Fort Buford, Montana, with Colonel Joseph N. G. Whistler (formerly of the Twenty-second Infantry), leaving Companies A, C, D, and H with Lieutenant Colonel Swaine at Fort Randall. After Swaine was promoted and reassigned six months later, Lieutenant Colonel Richard F. O'Bierne arrived to take command in September 1884. O'Bierne himself departed temporarily two years later and was replaced as commanding officer of Fort Randall by Major Hugh Theaker and subsequently by Captain Casper H. Conrad, who commanded the post until O'Bierne's return in May 1889.[2]

Because of its appointed temporary status, building activity at Fort Randall, especially after 1882 and for the balance of its existence, was limited mainly to repairs and necessary improvements to ensure maintenance of post functions. Some physical changes did occur, however, including construction of a new flagpole on the parade ground in 1880. Inspections of the post through the decade indicate that its overall condition had begun to suffer, not only as regarded construction programs but also available supplies and equipment. By 1882, the quartermaster storehouses were "old and dilapidated," while "there is hardly a [barracks] building which does not require repairs, many of them extensive." As on other posts, fire posed a constant threat, and in the winter of 1881–82 the kitchen and mess room of the Twenty-fifth Infantry band burned. In December 1884, fire destroyed a building housing the carpenter and blacksmith shops. "The protection against fire is a supply of ladders, conveniently placed, fire buckets, and the water wagon filled at all times." In addition, the hospital needed repairs, the post school had stopped operating for want of anyone capable of teaching, the fort's artillery complement of two 12-pounder Napoleon guns and two 10-pounder mountain howitzers were mounted upon decaying carriages, and the single Gatling gun was rusty. Ammunition for the 12-pounders, moreover, consisted of torn bags of powder left over from the Civil War. River water was still being distributed from a reservoir via a water wagon. The telegraph line, situated across the Missouri at White Swan, was nonfunctional because the line from Springfield to Chamberlain had been in disrepair for eight or nine months. Weeds grew high and thick around the garrison.

Inspectors had occasions to report on successes at Fort Randall, however, apparently many of them due to the labor of soldiers of the Fifteenth Infantry. One assessor described the post library, housed in the chapel, as being comfortable, well-lighted, and supplied with "760 books of Post library and 820 of Regimental library." By the summer of 1882, the post school was again operating, and by 1885 it occupied a building formerly used as band quarters, with sessions running from September 1 to July 1. (In 1889, methods of instruction were described as being "orally and by means of blackboard.") A brick building to contain commissary and quartermaster goods was under construction in 1882, and by September 1883 the two old frame commissary and quartermaster buildings had each been cut in two and their halves annexed to the rears of two barracks in L fashion to help relieve congestion in those quarters. In similar innovation, early the following year $350 was allotted the post quartermaster to arrange three old storehouses in a cross alignment and "line them with building paper and common siding" to form a double shooting gallery practice range "sufficient for four companies—two ranges running in each direction from the center point. The cross wings will afford accommodations for the men not firing, and heating stoves." A year later, the hospital was deemed "in excellent condition," the post in an "excellent state of police and in good sanitary condition." But as the years wore on, it was clear that proper expenditures were no longer forthcoming to keep up with needs. (Hospital repairs in 1881–82 amounted to $362; in 1884–85, they were $196 and in 1885–86, $258.) Repairs were still needed in the two-story barracks, officer quarters, guardhouse, and other structures. "In all instances," wrote an inspecting officer, "flooring, plastering, painting, [and replacing] stairways and steps are much needed, and in fact are absolutely necessary if it is the intention of the Department Commander to continue a garrison at this station for any length of time." (Repairs for barracks, officer quarters, and other buildings and quarters in 1884–85 totaled $1,199.80; for 1885–86 and 1886–87, repairs totaled only $500.00 and $600.00, respectively, for the entire garrison.) By 1887, the stables and corral were reported as being "liable to tumble down any day." Even the chapel, by 1889, needed repointing and roof repairs "to prevent permanent injury to the building."[3]

A typical annual post inspection of Fort Randall occurred on September 23 and 24, 1886, conducted by the army's inspector general, Lieutenant Colonel Edwin C. Mason, who critiqued the appearance and drill proficiency of the Fifteenth Infantry companies comprising the command:

> At 9 A.M. the 24th the troops were paraded in full dress for review and inspection. The review was faulty in the following particulars: Lines not well dressed; music did not wheel out of column before the reviewing officer; double time too slow. The "march past" in quick and double time very well done in regard to dress and military appearance, — the officers, however, saluted too soon — beginning the salute at about fifteen yards instead of six yards as prescribed by Tactics. Inspection: The troops were not brought to "order arms" after inspection of the "field & staff" until attention was called to it; a number of the cartridge boxes in each company had been whitened; — this should be prohibited as contrary to Regulations. The dress, arms and equipment, with the exceptions noted, were all in fine order. The general military appearance of the troops was good, although here and there a badly "set up" man marred the general effect. All the companies are fairly well instructed in the bayonet drill. . . . At 1.30 P.M. the troops paraded in field belts, haversacks and canteens. These articles were all in good order. None of the companies have any means of carrying their clothing — I recommend they be required to make requisition for the blanket bag. . . . [As for drill,] the marching [for the School of the Company, as contained in the infantry tactics manual] was good, but many of the movements were very poorly executed — notably the "turn." This movement was badly done in all cases. . . . Such commandants of companies as were called upon to exercise a squad in the "school of the soldier" manifested unfamiliarity with this essential part of the drill. . . . In the battalion drill the commands were correctly given and the movements were fairly well executed. There was in all the drills . . . an absence of the life and spirit that should characterize the performance of military duty.

Colonel Mason's major complaint had not to do with disorderly permutations of the soldiers, however. He believed that the procedure for crossing the Missouri River needed improving, and he elaborated on it in his report.

> The present mode is to wait until the weather is favorable. This frequently requires a delay of days, and sometimes weeks. Then, when

the auspicious moment arrives a flatboat is pushed out from the shore and, after much labor, is poled to the other side of the river. But if the wind changes while the passage is being made, the boat, with its load of mules, wagons or stores, may float down the river — to be regained only after much toil and long delay. A more unbusinesslike way of communicating with a military post I have never seen. . . . There are many times when if a call was made from the Indian agency, or other emergency required the presence of troops, it would be impossible for them to cross the river, except a few at a time in the small boat and then without stores or transportation.

To rectify this problem, which had existed for thirty years, Mason recommended the acquisition of a steam engine for mounting on the flatboat. "I think the matter is of such importance as to warrant a thorough examination by the Quartermaster Department."[4]

By the close of the 1880s, some construction needs and repairs had been addressed. A new stable and teamster quarters had been erected (cost: $1925.53 and $284.84, respectively), and the barracks and some other structures had been fixed up (cost in 1888–89, $969.05). An inspector remarked of the post that "when all the buildings are painted it will present a very neat and attractive appearance." Yet the barrack porches still needed flooring, the interiors needed plastering, and ceilings were required in the storehouses to prevent the entry of dust and snow. Lieutenant Colonel O'Bierne had plans to build a gymnasium for the command. At the beginning of 1886, an artesian well was created, with a delivery capacity of 600 gallons of water per minute (later increased to 1,400 gallons per minute), but within a few years its pipe corroded, rendering it practically useless. As of 1889, a "bathing or swimming tank" measuring thirty by sixty feet was available most of the time to the enlisted men and to officers and their families for one and a half hours each day. A bathhouse with a bathing tank for officers, moreover, had been built over a nearby hot sulphur spring wherein water temperature ranged between 80 and 84 degrees. It was envisioned that in the future, water from this spring or the artesian well might profitably be conveyed via pipes to service water closets and for bathing purposes in the barracks and officer quarters. Still other improvements during the decade concerned the military roads around Fort Randall, with principal notice directed to those leading to and from Springfield and Yankton that accessed the railroad. Examination of the route in 1880 disclosed sloughs and grade variables that needed addressing, and in 1882 Congress appropriated $5,000 to complete the necessary repairs.[5]

The issue of squatters on the Fort Randall Military Reservation reappeared in June 1883. A detachment of the Fifteenth Infantry forded the Missouri and marched to evict thirty-seven families residing in the northeast part of the reserve but instead issued warnings to the trespassers pending an alternative resolution. That came in July 1884, when Congress again modified the tract by turning over to the secretary of the interior for restoration to the public domain all of that portion remaining on the east side of the Missouri River (not impacting the Yankton Reservation) that had not previously been opened to white settlement by Congress in 1874. It appears that during the interim decade, attempts by the army to keep trespassers out had been half-hearted at best. Remembered one man who settled there illegally in 1883: "I took over the claim I squatted on from a fellow who had no more right there than did I. He had a cabin and some improvements and I took over from him. Twice while I lived there the soldiers came up from Ft. Randall to order us off and they did [that], but so far as I was concerned they never put me off and so I stayed. Later the Government, who [sic] had already surveyed this land, opened it to settlement, and I was allowed to use the time I had put in as a squatter against the time required for homesteading and so I finally got title to this land."[6]

The 1884 act, which applied to other military reservations as well, reflected changing conditions on the frontier. The lands would be surveyed, appraised, and auctioned for settlement. Moreover, as indicated, individuals who had resided on the lands before January 1, 1884, might seek ownership via homestead entry. Surveying of the adjoining Yankton Reservation boundary got under way in the summer of 1884, with men of the Fifteenth Infantry from the post assisting the engineers. The 1884 act affected disposition of more than 24,000 acres and represented a trend that would continue into the 1890s, paralleling the closure and abandonment of Fort Randall.[7]

Throughout the 1880s, the health of the garrison was generally good, and the post received high marks for its sanitary condition. An incidence of smallpox near Sioux City necessitated post surgeon J. D. Hall's vaccination of soldiers in the spring of 1881. In March 1884, "a slight endemic of Mumps" appeared among the troops, thought to have been introduced by arriving recruits. Late in the decade there was a minor outbreak of diphtheria, apparently introduced through post trader D. L. Batt and his family, who had been visiting in Michigan, where cases of the disease existed. Assistant surgeon William C. Gorgas recounted his efforts to diagnose and contain the sickness:

> I examined . . . [one of the post trader's four children] on November 12, [1887] and found its tonsils enlarged and congested, and am inclined to think that it had a mild attack of diphtheria. On the 6th of November two of the children were attacked with a disease which turned out to be diphtheria. On the 28th of November another child, who had been a constant companion of these children, was attacked. As soon as the disease was recognized, on the 11th these two families were isolated, and every attention given to the general condition of both families. The sick child was kept in one house and the others sent to another house.

Two of the children subsequently died from the disease, but Dr. Gorgas succeeded in his intent to keep diphtheria from infecting the soldiers.[8]

Ensuring good health of the command was but one element of maintaining the well-being of the Fort Randall garrison. The arrival of the black soldiers of the Twenty-fifth Infantry afforded certain relief for that regiment, which had been stationed at remote Texas outposts since 1870 and the disposition of whose officers and enlisted men toward their service needed rejuvenating. The men of the regiment, some of them former slaves, were proud of their unit, as their military readiness made clear.[9] A Yankton newsman visiting the post remarked on their appearance: "I have never seen such good-looking men as the 25th are composed of. They are, every inch of it [sic], good, strong, martial looking soldiers. Most of them will, after being discharged, make Dakota their home. They are all good Republicans and rejoice in the election of Gen. Garfield. They take just pride in their officers, and adore their regimental commander."[10] In May 1881, the year's first dress parade took place, the men marching across the "beautiful lawn" of the parade ground "impatient to show the fair ladies of the garrison what they could do. . . . Line was formed and the carry and order arms and parade rest was [sic] perfect. . . . The sight was a pretty one—the long steady line of the battalion, with the rays

of the setting sun reflected from their bayonets, looked the personi-
fication of 'grim visaged war.'"[11]

As was usually the case in any military organization, however, all
was not perfect within the Twenty-fifth Infantry. Garrison courts-
martial occurred routinely, their subjects charged with various petty
offenses. Occasionally, however, the infringements were more serious. In January 1881, two men convicted of stealing were sentenced
to eighteen months' imprisonment at the Fort Leavenworth military
prison and were conducted south by a detachment of their peers.
More sinister, perhaps, were anonymous complaints from Fort Randall to department headquarters "relative to the treatment the colored
soldiers have to endure at this post" during a hot spell in August 1881,
when the men allegedly performed guard mount daily in full dress attire. Moreover, a prisoner in irons was reportedly denied food for five
days. An unknown enlisted man complained directly to General Terry
that at Fort Randall, "very few old soldiers reenlist [in the Twenty-
fifth Infantry] like they did in Texas; the most of them go to the 10th
Cavalry, under General [Colonel Benjamin H.] Grierson." These particular grievances were returned to the post for Colonel Andrews's
information and attention.[12]

Officers occasionally faced the indignity of courts-martial at Fort
Randall. In the autumn of 1880, Captain Andrew Geddes went on trial
for drunkenness on duty, a common infraction among army personnel on the frontier. The testimony against Geddes was replete with
fellow officers' statements that indicted him for staggering about during parade; others supported the notion that he had simply become ill,
and the preponderance of the testimony favored his cause. Yet the testimony, in fact, reflected continuing factiousness within the Twenty-
fifth Infantry over Geddes following his 1879 court-martial conviction
for scandalously accusing a fellow officer of incest while the regiment
was stationed at Fort Stockton, Texas. Presidential disapproval of the
findings had permitted Geddes to continue his career, although the
army hierarchy clearly wanted him cashiered. At Fort Randall, that objective was realized, and Geddes, who the evidence, in fact, had largely
exonerated in the incest trial, left the service in disgrace on December 31, 1880, following his conviction for drunkenness.[13]

Desertion proved a continuing problem during the 1880s. In September 1884, it was reported that thirty-two men of the Fifteenth In-

fantry had taken "French leave" from Fort Randall during the past year, and in one month, September 1883, nine had deserted. An inspecting officer assured his superiors that the cause had nothing to do with excessive labor. It was, he stated, "from dissatisfaction due to being unacquainted with the duties of a soldier, want of amusements, and, in many instances [was] premeditated at time of enlistment; desiring free transportation to the West." Exactly how these conclusions were determined remains unclear. In any event, the problem persisted, although in declining numbers; only eleven men deserted in 1888–89.[14]

While at Fort Randall, the men of the Twenty-fifth Infantry, as well as those of the succeeding Fifteenth Infantry, drew the patterns of clothing and equipment then in vogue throughout the army. Basic daily fatigue attire consisted of lined or unlined blue wool blouses adorned with eagle buttons and light blue wool trousers adopted by the Quartermaster Department in the 1870s. They wore black campaign hats with blue tasseled cords and dark blue, billed forage caps with brass crossed rifles insignia, each with the regimental numeral above. Arms and equipment variously consisted of the following: Model 1873 Springfield rifle, caliber .45, with leather slings; cartridge belts; cartridge boxes; leather waist belts and belt plates; leather carrying braces; clothing bags and haversacks for carrying rations and meat cans (mess kits); knives, forks, spoons, and tin cups; entrenching tools and scabbards; bayonets and scabbards (Hoffman's patent); and canteens and straps. The dress uniform consisted of the aforementioned wool trousers together with a wool dress blouse of dark blue with light blue facings, besides the chasseur-style blue-trimmed infantry shako adopted by the army in 1872. Changes to army uniforms and equipment as introduced in the 1880s were reflected among the men of the Fifteenth Infantry then stationed there. (A major revision in dress headgear after 1881 saw pressed felt dress helmets substituted for the shakos.) But for slight modifications during the decade, small arms remained the same.[15]

Change also extended to Fort Randall's operations. With the close of the major Indian wars and removal of the Indians to reservations, operations at Fort Randall through most of the 1880s refocused on performance of routine duties within and in the vicinity of the garrison, although certain activities and responsibilities of the troops beyond the local orbit of the post continued much as before. As of the summer of 1880, the Twenty-fifth Infantry soldiers practiced a regimen of fatigue and drill that followed prescribed direction:

Reveille	4.55 A.M.
Breakfast call	5.30 A.M.
Sick call	6.00 A.M.
Fatigue call	6.30 A.M.
Guard mount	7.55 A.M.
Target practice (Mondays)	6.30 A.M.
Inspection (Sundays)	8.00 A.M.
Drill call and band practice	9.55 A.M.
Recall from drill	11.00 A.M.
First sergeants' call	11.45 A.M.
Officers' school on Tuesdays and Fridays	12.00 M.
Recall from fatigue	12.00 M.
Dinner call	12.20 P.M.
Fatigue call	1.00 P.M.
Recall from fatigue	5.30 P.M.
Retreat and parade	Shortly before sunset
Tattoo	8.50 P.M.
Taps	9.30 P.M.[16]

Target practice, utilizing .45 caliber Springfield breech loading rifles, took place each Monday unless bad weather intervened, when it occurred on the next favorable day of the week. In 1881, Colonel Andrews received orders to turn over to Rock Island Arsenal the Gatling and mountain howitzer and all ammunition and appurtenances, doubtless because it was anticipated that these armaments would likely no longer be used by troops stationed at Fort Randall. Nearly three years later, during refurbishment of the quartermaster storehouses, three of the old wooden buildings were relocated away from the garrison and fitted out for small arms target gallery practice. The target season that closed in September 1885 was pronounced successful, with sixty sharpshooters, 103 marksmen, and two first-classmen being identified among the Fifteenth Infantry companies stationed there.[17]

Besides target practice, drill, and road repair, there occurred occasional off-post training. In the fall of 1888, for example, the four companies of the Fifteenth Infantry stationed at Fort Randall—minus a guard detachment left to safeguard the post—debarked for a week of field instruction along the Niobrara River, accompanied by four wagons and an ambulance. Inspections occurred regularly, generally weekly and monthly, and usually were conducted by the post commander. Maintaining a smart and ready appearance was always a mainstay of U.S. soldiers, and at Fort Randall the importance of adhering to that standard was conveyed on more than one occasion. In October 1886, the commander saw need to publish a circular precisely directing the men on matters of garrison attire. Henceforth, "the waist and cartridge belts should be worn so that the plate covers the lower button of the dress or undress coat," and "the cartridge belt for ordinary garrison duty [should have its thimbles filled] with twenty rounds, ten on each side of the belt plate." In winter, review reflected the seasonal elements, as pronounced in a late January 1886 directive calling on the troops to "be paraded at 9 A.M. . . . in overcoats, fur caps and gloves . . . for the monthly inspection."[18]

As indicated, in accordance with existing circumstances, the troops at Fort Randall scaled back most external operations after the 1870s. In 1884, an inspector noted that "but little detached service has been required of this garrison during the year." By then, such activities were limited to escorting paymasters, overseeing the issue of Indian annuities at the Yankton Agency, the participation of officers in courts-martial at various department stations, inspecting telegraph lines, escorting survey teams, and pursuing deserters. Despite the curtailment of extended time afield, there occasionally arose need for the presence of troops under emergency or threatening circumstances. Repeated blizzards in the winter of 1880–81 produced such ice buildup on the Missouri that severe flooding in March and April 1881 inundated fields and property from Pierre to below Sioux City. The community of White Swan was destroyed by the rising water and its livestock lost, although its residents managed to gain high ground and survived. People in Yankton and Vermillion were especially hard hit, and some 8,000 settlers were reported destitute from loss of clothing, fuel, and shelter. Military authorities in the department and division, along with civil offices in St. Paul, Minnesota, raised nearly $6,000 for the relief effort. In April and May, Company F, Twenty-fifth Infantry, under Captain H. Baxter Quimby, repeatedly journeyed to settlements along the Keya Paha River to assist homeless settlers. The men of the Twenty-fifth donated personal funds to help the people survive; in one instance, they drove a farmer's cattle onto the military reservation to prevent high water from sweeping the animals away. Again, in June and July 1882 settlers along the Keya Paha and Montana rivers, generally fearful of Indian depredations following the murder of Spotted Tail the previous summer, became particularly alarmed by Indians passing by en route to a Sioux sun dance at Rosebud Agency. Two companies from Fort Randall marched onto the reservation and scouted the roads until after the events concluded a month later. No incidents happened, and the soldiers returned to the post.[19]

With congressional passage of the Dawes Act of 1887, allotment in severalty was introduced on the Yankton Reservation the following year. Troops from Fort Randall were dispatched to oversee and assist the work of the surveyors on the reservation. In one instance, a number of tribesmen who opposed individual allotment tried to disrupt the process, and four companies of the Fifteenth arrived from Fort Randall to quell the trouble. Two companies remained temporarily at the agency to guard against further disturbances. In 1889, looking to imminent statehood, a federal agreement forged with the Lakotas on the Great Sioux Reservation shortly created six smaller reserves and apportioned most of the remaining nine million acres for sale to white farmers and cattlemen, an action that helped aggravate future confrontation between the government and the Sioux.[20]

Beyond formal operations, the Fort Randall garrison maintained its lively social life much as before. As soldiers from the post had done earlier, the men of the Twenty-fifth and Fifteenth infantry regiments affected after-hour trysts with women on the Yankton Reservation. Some soldiers wed Yankton women, and a number of infants born on the reservation bore features reflecting the post's proximity. While the ready access of the Yanktons afforded social relationships, another local source appeared in a place called Bradley's ranch, located perhaps one and a half miles from the post. Besides the pursuit of female companionship and alcohol, some soldiers liked simply to loaf, while others consumed their free time gambling, especially right after payday, when poker, monte, high five, and euchre games abounded. Modes of more athletic recreation included baseball, billiards, walking, hiking, and hunting. Horse racing remained a popular fixture, especially on holidays.[21] In a race on the Fourth of July 1882, one of the participants, a well-liked man named Frank St. Clair, suffered fatal injuries when his horse stumbled over a picket rope and somersaulted. "St. Clair fell, striking his head, and the horse fell with its entire weight on him, the pummel [*sic*] of the saddle striking him on the breast. He was carried to the post hospital, but never moved again or became conscious." St. Clair's funeral service was held in the IOOF Echo Lodge hall of the chapel.[22]

The more sedate side of social life at Fort Randall during the 1880s usually resided with officers and their families. While the officers enjoyed certain freedoms and reflected more worldly interests than did most enlisted men, they were nonetheless aware of certain restraints presented by the garrison community. "Life was a constant routine of going to the same dinners, listening to the same stories, laughing at the same jokes," reminisced Dr. Gorgas. "Whist and euchre parties . . . now and then afforded relaxation; the inevitable quarrels of such a small society added a little spice, and a whiff of scandal came as an occasional godsend." Intragarrison disputes among officers, as elsewhere, were common. Occasionally, they impacted performance of duties. In January 1889, there arose issues of insubordination and disrespect among the commissioned cadre, eliciting sharp admonition from post commander Major Hugh A. Theaker: "The Commanding Officer has noticed officers passing another to whom they were unfriendly to look in another direction, so they would not be compelled to pay the courtesy properly due. . . . This must cease at this Post in the future. . . . Officers will on all occasions . . . be courteous to their superiors and one another." The tedium of garrison life, especially in winter, was difficult to overcome. Early in 1885, when the mercury plummeted to well below zero and remained there for weeks, the officers grew beards, likely for the sake of conversation as well as for warmth. "The diversity of color, style and general ugliness causes one to wish for spring," piped one wag. "Progressive euchre" was the rage in quarters that winter. At one gathering, "there were players enough for five tables, and the games were so hotly contested that even without well-known fondness for good things we hated to stop playing long enough to do justice to the escalloped oysters, the chicken salad, the cream, jellies, cakes, and above all the 'Punch,' that comprised the menu."[23]

Social enterprises included band concerts, school activities, celebration of national holidays, and dances, some of which involved participation by officers and enlisted men. The bands of the Twenty-fifth and Fifteenth infantry regiments contained accomplished musicians;

both played not only in garrison but also in neighboring communities. School exhibitions showcased the educational accomplishments of children of the garrison. In 1880, schoolmaster Eugene P. Messier proudly oversaw recitations, songs, and comic medleys by his charges, with music performed by the First Infantry band. The post commander and officers, together with their wives, enlisted parents, and citizens from nearby communities, partook of the festivities, which "evidenced the intelligence of the pupils and reflected credit upon the teachers." One officer's daughter, Edith Heiner, along with an enlisted man's daughter, Maggie Coleman, received "medals of honor" for their superior achievements. Public holidays still afforded a break in the regimen, as on February 22, 1887, when Washington's birthday permitted the suspension of duties, except guard and police. Dances infused energy and gaiety into garrison life, at least the commissioned side of it. Such events as hops and "theme" dance parties as occurred in the summer of 1889 helped officers and their spouses endure the monotony of Fort Randall.[24] At the latter events, masquerade-type performances took place; one in August entitled "The Minuet de la Cour" featured four women, each fitted out "in cavalier cloak," as gentlemen wooing ladies dressed in "Empire costumes." "The pompadour pinks and blues of the dresses [and] . . . the soft puffs of gray hair piled high on the pretty heads made the always lovely young faces twice as entrancing."[25]

Garrison community life notwithstanding, the most significant event of the decade—indeed, one of the most noteworthy in Fort Randall's history—was the army's incarceration there of the Hunkpapa Lakota medicine man and political leader Sitting Bull and his immediate followers from 1881 to 1883. In the spring of 1877, toward the end of the Great Sioux War and after confrontations with army commands in the Yellowstone and Missouri valleys, the frustrated chief had led his people across the border into Canada, where he remained until the summer of 1881. Beset by diminishing food resources, Sitting Bull finally passed back into American territory, tracing the steps of other Sioux leaders who had recently yielded. At noon on July 19, he and 187 Lakotas turned themselves in to army authorities at Fort Buford, Dakota Territory, on the Missouri River, near its junction with the Yellowstone. Ten days later, the chief and his band embarked under guard via steamboat for Fort Yates, named for one of Custer's fallen officers, 280 miles down the Missouri, where they arrived on August 1. Three weeks later, as concerns mounted over Sitting Bull's potential disruptive demeanor vis-à-vis the Indians at the adjacent Standing Rock Agency, as well as over the sudden need to feed so many Indians arriving from Canada during the spring and summer of 1881, Secretary of War Robert T. Lincoln instructed Commanding General Sherman to direct the removal of the chief and his immediate followers south to Fort Randall, there to be held prisoners of war until their final disposition might be determined. The order for removal countered the general belief of the Indians that they were to receive amnesty and live with their friends on the reservation. Despite resistance by the Hunkpapa leader, on September 10 soldiers of the Seventeenth Infantry surrounded the band with bayonets at the ready, and he and his followers reluctantly boarded the steamer *General Sherman* for the trip downstream. Colonel Charles C. Gilbert, commanding at Fort Yates, wired Colonel Andrews at Fort Randall: "The Sitting Bull party left early this afternoon for Fort Randall, one hundred and seventy-two in all. Tepees plenty."[26]

On September 18, 1881, 172 heavily guarded Lakotas debarked at the Fort Randall wharf in the charge of Captain Henry S. Howe of the Seventeenth Infantry, accompanied by the scout Edward H. Allison, who would remain for a time with them at Randall. A few of the Indians were sick, noted post surgeon William H. Faulkner, but the majority were "healthy specimens of humanity." Almost immediately, two children required medical treatment, one for a partially severed finger needing amputation, the other for being scalded with hot coffee in the Indian camp.[27] Sufficient food resources for the people, including several thousand pounds of shelled corn stored at Yankton, were not immediately forthcoming. Authorities urged its shipment to the post via steamer or wagons, and within a week the Indians at Yankton Agency collected a wagon load of corn for delivery to the prisoners. Besides food, to help prepare for the onset of cold weather, Sitting Bull's people needed supplies of cloth, deerskins, blankets, assorted knives and kettles, shawls, mittens, socks, bed sacks, scissors, axes, buffalo robes (for moccasins), rope, sinew, and "canvas for 4 lodges, or equivalent to 12 A tents."[28]

Presumably, the disparity between the number of tribesmen who surrendered at Fort Buford with Sitting Bull (187) and the number who embarked from Fort Yates to Fort Randall (172) can be explained by the likelihood that some who came in with Sitting Bull belonged to other bands at Standing Rock and were permitted to remain there with their families. It is clear that at the time of their embarking from Fort Yates on September 10 and their debarking at Fort Randall, the prisoners evidently numbered 172 souls, as an itemized list accounts for that many and provides names for most. They comprised fifteen members of Sitting Bull's immediate family, plus the members of families belonging to White Dog, Four Horns, One Bull, Fire Cloud, Elk Horn, Bone Tomahawk, Spotted Eagle, Brave Thunder, Black Bird, Hairy Coat, Scarlet Thunder Jr., Took Their Guns, Blue Cloud, Yellow Dog, Fought the Bear, Brave Bear, Hunted Alone, Deaf Woman, Big Leg, Bear that Looks Back, Scarlet Thunder Sr., Mosquito, and High in the Clouds. Included, too, was Steps, a Shoshone Bannock whose feet had frozen and whose legs were subsequently partially amputated. Steps had joined Sitting Bull in Canada following the Nez Perce War in 1877 and was now listed as a member of the family of White Dog.[29]

On their arrival, the Lakotas raised their camp on a hill back from the Missouri and south of the fort. In late October, as the weather cooled and rainstorms increased, they were moved to the shelter of the timbered bottom near the post. On November 4, their camp moved yet again "from its damp location to a pleasant little knoll not more than seventy-five yards from the old camp, but better protected and sheltered from the storms of winter, with good drainage, and near to wood and water." Dr. Faulkner allowed that "they seem well pleased with the present site." An inspecting officer added: "They are guarded by two non-com'd officers and twelve men; are counted daily by the Officer of the Day. [They] are well supplied with tepees and rations, but have not sufficient clothing; are apparently well contented, but desire to have children educated and lands given them for farming. In reference to the clothing: the Post Quartermaster has made the necessary requisition. There are at post 100 buffalo overshoes. These are now not used by the troops; the Indians state they can make moccasins of them."[30]

During their first weeks of incarceration, the Lakotas became objects of extreme interest to diverse parties. Almost immediately, the Yanktons wanted to visit with them and repeatedly beseeched Colonel Andrews for permission to send their chiefs—among them, Strike the Ree—to talk with Sitting Bull and give him "good advice as the friends of whites." Within weeks, too, Rev. Martin Marty, Catholic missionary in Dakota, asked Andrews for permission to place a priest among them to impart religious instruction. "They are kept in one place, at leisure in body & mind & in every way ready to learn & improve."[31] Marty's request was not granted, however. Instead, a proposal by Episcopal bishop William E. Hare to provide education for Lakota children at the Yankton Agency school met approval, and eventually five children, including a son of Sitting Bull, entered St. Mary's School there.[32]

While generally compliant with the government's wishes for him, Sitting Bull remained concerned over the ultimate disposition of his people. To that end, he urged Colonel Andrews to request that he and other headmen be allowed to visit Washington to determine the intention of government authorities for his people. Andrews obligingly filed a request, stating that "failing at this, he [Sitting Bull] desires a visit from someone especially commissioned by the President, and failing in this he desires to be informed 'over the President's own signature' just what it is proposed to do with him and his people and when."[33] Sitting Bull was not allowed to travel to the East, nor did he receive the desired information. But he was grateful to Andrews, thanking him for his kindness. "I am very sad and distrustful," he related, "for I am like a man who enters a land for the first time. It is not easy for me to sit down as a prisoner and dream out the future. It is all dark to me." Had he gained an audience, he likely would have told officials, as he had told the colonel, of his interest in providing for his followers in the manner of other Sioux leaders. Nonetheless, in an interview with an Indian named Walking Elk, witnessed by one Running Bull and translated and delivered to Andrews, the Hunkpapa leader explained the reasons for his surrender and expressed hopes for his people's future:

Many of my brethren sold their lands to the Grand Father and said they would settle down and be civilized. And they sent word to me to come down to them. I said, Friends, wait a little. There are a great many buffalo up here yet. . . . By and by, when you get fixed up and able to make a good living at civilized ways I will come down to you. . . . Then the soldiers came and hunted my tracks and as soon as they got in sight of me shot at me. . . . [Finally,] I said—Since the Grand Father has been waiting for me to come for a good many years, let us go and see what he wants us for. . . . And so I sent word to my friends who were being civilized at Standing Rock, and

Cheyenne River, and Pine Ridge, and Rosebud, and Lower Brulé, and Crow Creek, and Yankton Agency and tell [?] them to help me to civilized life. So I came down. . . . I want my children taught. I want schools and teachers the same [as] you have. That is what I understand the Grand Father wanted me to come in for. So I want my children to have those advantages.[34]

Sitting Bull's presence at Fort Randall drew wide attention, and visitors often came to the post to meet him. Many of the sentiments that the Hunkpapa leader had expressed to Andrews were repeated to others during the fall and winter of 1881, including the anthropologist Alice Fletcher, who was becoming known for her work among the Omahas. In his willingness to inform, Sitting Bull detailed an extensive account of his movements in the weeks and months after Little Bighorn until he crossed into Canada, which the Reverend John Williamson, Lakota-speaking Presbyterian missionary at the Yankton Agency, transcribed and mapped in a significant contribution to knowledge of the Indians' side of the Great Sioux War. In furtherance of the historical vein, while at Fort Randall in December 1881, Sitting Bull identified copies of pictures drawn by him and contained in a "Hieroglyphic Autobiography" acquired by an army surgeon at Fort Buford in 1870 and forwarded from the Surgeon General's Office in Washington, D.C., for verification. He was naturally cautious about those depictions showing his encounters with soldiers and other white men. Some of the pictures had earlier appeared in the *New York Herald* and *Harper's Weekly* in the months following Custer's fall. Later, Sitting Bull made additional sets of the drawings, two for army officers who had been kind to him and a third for the post trader at Fort Randall. Another caller on Sitting Bull was most unusual. Adventurer Paul Boyton had invented a rubber suit that enabled him to float on water. In September, in an apparent test run, Boyton had plunged into the Yellowstone River at Glendive, Montana, intending to float his way to St. Louis. In October, he stopped en route at Fort Randall, where he met the famed Hunkpapa chief.[35]

Perhaps Sitting Bull's most enjoyable visitor during the first weeks of his imprisonment was the German artist Rudolf Cronau, who arrived at Fort Randall on October 22. Cronau had spent considerable time painting Indian portraits at Standing Rock, and he anticipated meeting and painting one of the famed Hunkpapa. He and Sitting

Bull immediately bonded. "I found him thoroughly informed about my person, as he had always remained in secret contact with his tribesmen in Fort Yates. So I found it easy to invite him to pose for his portrait," Cronau remarked. When Cronau finished his watercolor of Sitting Bull, the Lakota signed his own name at the bottom. Cronau remained at the post for several weeks, and during that time his friendship with the Hunkpapa leader flourished. Sitting Bull implored him, if he should visit the president, to "tell him that we wish to be treated like human-beings, entitled to the same rights as all the white people." Before he left Fort Randall, the artist opened an exhibition of his paintings. After the officers and the women at the fort had viewed the gallery, the Indians were ushered in to enjoy portraits of their friends and family members at far-off Standing Rock.[36]

Despite the evident amity existing between the Indians and the officers, there occurred some serious incidents that marred the relationship between the tribesmen and the enlisted men of the Twenty-fifth Infantry. On December 27, 1881, three soldiers attacked a Lakota woman out retrieving wood, and two of them raped her. The episode outraged Colonel Andrews, who assembled the garrison so that the perpetrators might be identified and arrested. Without hesitation, the victimized woman pointed out two of the men. The third culprit deserted the post. Preferring to avoid all publicity of the affair, which would not have happened had he transferred the accused for civil justice, Andrews peremptorily discharged the soldiers. Possibly as precaution against further fraternization between the Indian women and the enlisted men that might escalate into similar incidents, Captain Charles Bentzoni, who took over as post commander after Colonel Andrews's departure, ordered a proscription on all dealings "between soldiers and Indians held as prisoners of war," even forbidding the troops from visiting the post trader's store during periods designated for the Lakotas.[37]

At Fort Randall, the Indians fell into a routine that, while monotonous, ensured generally good relations with the garrison. Occasionally, squabbles erupted among them. An elderly man named Spotted Eagle had his arm broken in one such scuffle, while another named White Swan was admitted into the post hospital with a severe forehead wound inflicted by an ax. Meantime, the women endured the daily drudgery of hauling firewood for cooking and heating the lodges. Annuity goods were issued periodically. An unofficial inventory had each

Sioux family receiving a bake oven, camp kettle, frying pan, coffee mill, coffee pot, various tin cups, and an ax. Each man received one buffalo robe, one blanket, one blouse, one pair of trousers, three yards of cloth to make leggings, one hat, two undershirts, two pairs of socks, two overshirts, one tin cup, two combs, and one butcher knife. Each woman received one shawl, one blanket, two undershirts, two pairs of socks, one scarf, one handkerchief, one comb, and a variety of flannel, calico, and muslin, besides assorted scissors, thimbles, needles, and thread. Attempts by the army to procure sinew for sewing moccasins proved unsuccessful, and the women had to use thread for the task.[38]

Maintenance of sanitary conditions likely necessitated movement of the camp from place to place around the fort. In August 1882, an inspecting officer noted that "the Indian prisoners of war are now encamped on bluff near post, tepes [sic] in a circle. Two sentinels post[ed] over camp. . . . Police of camp good, and tepes are also good. Supplied with sufficient rations, and fairly supplied with clothing."[39] With Sitting Bull lived his two wives and three of his children. He dressed in plain attire, rarely wore a feather in his hair, and managed to keep his camp in good order. It became clear that, since his surrender, Sitting Bull had mellowed. He embraced concepts of education for his people yet resisted sending his children to off-reservation boarding schools. When the Indian school at Carlisle Barracks in Pennsylvania received authorization to recruit ten students from among Sitting Bull's followers, the chief opposed sending them, and none went while the people remained at Fort Randall.[40] In the summer of 1882, Sitting Bull expressed his views regarding aspects of his internment there:

> We are living here well and comfortable but would like, though, to be sent to the Ree [Red?] River country where our grandfathers are buried, and which is a good country for raising cattle. Some of my young men are dissatisfied; two went off yesterday,—five altogether since I have been here. Some of the women are getting crazy, as they think they will have to be here all their lives. Each family gets their rations all right. [We] have enough clothing, although some of it is getting ragged. I do the best I can to control my people, but when they do anything wrong it is always blamed on me. My friends here, though, all treat me well. The soldiers guard my camp, which I like, as no one comes here to bother me.[41]

While at Fort Randall, Sitting Bull made the acquaintance of a young officer fresh from West Point, Second Lieutenant George P. Ahern. When Ahern was assigned the duty of handling the chief's mail, the two had frequent business. The young officer described Sitting Bull as having "a vivid personality." He was "a man who knew his ground. . . . I learned to admire him for his many fine qualities." Ahern observed the Hunkpapa leader closely for several months during his assignment and left a reasoned account of his association with him that repeatedly addressed his human side: "One night as I sat in Sitting Bull's tipi, a squaw sat between us holding a one-year-old baby girl. The baby was very ill and had several convulsions while I was present. After one severe convulsion, when it looked as if the end was near, Sitting Bull took hold of its little wrist to feel the pulse, and imagine my amazement to see the tears rolling down his cheeks, and he actually sobbing like a woman. The baby died the following morning at daybreak."[42]

As the imprisonment proceeded, the Indians at Fort Randall occasionally welcomed relatives from Rosebud, Pine Ridge, Standing Rock, and the other Sioux agencies. The visitors carried credentials authorizing their presence among Sitting Bull's people, and application for such exchanges had to be arranged, coordinated, and approved by both the concerned agencies and the army well in advance. The visits promoted nostalgia among the prisoners for friends and relatives at Standing Rock and perhaps helped to erode the army's iron grip over the tribesmen.[43] In early 1882, the Bailey, Dix, and Mead photography firm of Fort Randall captured a series of twenty-four scenes of Sitting Bull and the Sioux camp, many of which show the circle of tipis interspersed among a heavy growth of box elder trees not far from the Missouri. Some of the pictures depict the men wearing outmoded army clothing, including the previously much-distained pattern 1872 fatigue blouse. Taken together, the photographs provide significant documentation for this special period at Fort Randall with Sitting Bull and his people.[44]

As the months of enforced tedium passed, Sitting Bull continued lobbying for his people's return to Standing Rock. Probably with the assistance of an army officer—possibly Ahern—he appealed directly to the commissioner of Indian affairs for transfer of his people to civilian control. Moreover, the Yankton chief Strike the Ree joined in the effort, through Rev. Williamson penning a plea on Sitting Bull's behalf directly to the secretary of war. "What has Sitting Bull been convicted of doing that you hold him a prisoner for so many long moons? . . . He is kept in prison just across the river from me, and his moaning cry comes to my ear."[45] During much of 1882, reported Indian Agent James McLaughlin at Standing Rock, the Hunkpapa leader had made repeated entreaties for his own intercession, and in February 1883 McLaughlin wrote the commissioner of Indian affairs that he had learned that the army would not object to such a transfer and that relatives and friends of the prisoners at the agency were willing to help them and share provisions with them as they resettled in the Grand River country. McLaughlin suggested that if his request were approved, the Indians should travel up the Missouri "by one of the first boats in the spring, which would be about the middle of April next, and which would enable them to plant some crops . . . [this] coming season, thus placing them as not entirely dependent upon subsistence issues of the Government."[46] If their transfer be delayed beyond the start of May, he warned, the Indians would lose an entire year before they would be able to help themselves. Accordingly, Secretary of War Lincoln directed the removal of Sitting Bull's people. The army would provide transportation and rations to subsist the Indians for four weeks following their arrival.[47]

By Special Orders No. 54, Headquarters, Department of Dakota, March 29, 1883, Sitting Bull and his people were to be conducted to Standing Rock Agency "by the first available contract boat going up the river." Scarcely a month later, on April 28, 160 Lakotas boarded the steamboat *W. J. Behan* for the journey north from Fort Randall, their twenty-month-long internment at an end. First Lieutenant Thomas F. Davis headed a detachment of twenty-four men from the Fifteenth Infantry, along with acting assistant surgeon William H. Faulkner as medical officer, accompanying the Indians. They reached Fort Yates on May 10 and passed on to Standing Rock. For most of the remaining seven years of his life, Sitting Bull would occupy a home along the Grand River.[48]

The period of Sitting Bull's tenure at Fort Randall clearly marked a highlight in the post's annals, for the presence of the celebrity Hunkpapa brought a rush of attention, coupled with visitations, which it had hardly known in years past. Consequently, the balance of the 1880s saw no comparable events of such magnitude there. In the aftermath of the Lakota eminence, Fort Randall settled back into a period of mounting quietude much as before, consisting, as indicated, of the daily routine of garrison life, a pattern rarely broken by extraordinary proceedings. Late in the decade, state constitutional proponents overcame sectional differences to encourage congressional passage of an act dividing Dakota Territory. On January 22, 1889, President Grover Cleveland signed the Omnibus Bill, creating North Dakota, South Dakota, Montana, and Washington. The South Dakota constitution ceded jurisdiction of Fort Randall, along with that of Forts Sully and Meade, to the federal government, and territorial government formally ended on November 2, 1889.[49] For the immediate future, the post would continue to be administered by the Department of Dakota in St. Paul, Minnesota.

GALLERY OF STEREOPTICON VIEWS *produced in 1882 by Bailey, Dix, and Mead (possibly from photographs taken by Stanley J. Morrow) to record the imprisonment of Sitting Bull's Hunkpapa Lakotas at Fort Randall, 1881–83. The titles and captions, which appeared on the reverse of the views, are repeated here, complete with original errors. Source: Sitting Bull Collection, Photograph Vault, State Archives, South Dakota State Historical Society, Pierre.*

TATON KAIYOTONKA. *Sitting Bull*

The above is a true Photo and Auto-
graph of "Sitting Bull," the Sioux Chief
at the Custer Massacre.

Copyrighted, 1882, by Bailey, Dix & Mead.

SITTING BULL,

AND TRUE AUTOGRAPH.

This noted Chief, With his band of Uncapapa Souix Indians, now prisoners of war at Fort Randall. D. T., is 43 years of age ; Weight 200 pounds ; Height, 5 ft. 9 in. Has had over 100 engagements with their natural enemies, the Crows, of which he proudly boasts, but is too shrewd to acknowledge to having killed any whites. He has had 9 wives. The two now living with him appear with descriptions in Nos. 5, 11 and 20. Has had one child by each of his first 6 wives.

1. Sitting Bull.
2. Winter Quarters.
3. Steps.
4. Medicine Teepe.
5. Sitting Bull and Favorite Wife.
6. Winter Quarters.
7. One Bull.
8. Winter Quarters.
9. Issuing Rations.
10. Woman's Rights.
11. Sitting Bull, Squaw and Twins.
12. True to Nature.
13. Morning Visit.
14. Stealing the Trade.
15. Batallion Drill.
16. One Bull and Black Prairie Chicken.
17. Issuing Supplies.
18. Morning Roll Call.
19. Squaws Carrying Wood.
20. Sitting Bull, Two Wives and Three Pappooses.
21. Winter Quarters.
22. Eat Dog and Family.
23. Summer View.
24. Summer View.

Address, *BAILEY, DIX & MEAD*, Fort Randall, D. T.

No. 2. Winter Quarters.
These views numbers 2, 6, 8
and 21, are sectional of the
Winter Quarters. They show
but little if any snow, as it has
been such an open winter, but
we have endeavored to give to
them a much richer and more
attractive appearance than is
shown in the bleak and dreary
character of such views in
general. This camp circular in
form is situated in a beautiful
grove of box elders, just under
the hill at Fort Randall, and
near the banks of the Missouri
River. The scenery in each view
is so different that it hardly
seems possible that they are of
the same camp.

No. 3. Steps.
A Nes Perce Indian, who
escaped from his band, while
surrounded in the bad lands of
Nebraska, by Gen'l Miles, in
1878. He then joined Sitting
Bull's band of Uncapapa
Souix Indians in the British
possessions and has followed
their fortunes ever since. He
lost his feet above the ankles,
also his right hand by being
frozen, having been caught in
one of the severe snow storms,
21 years ago.

Copyrighted, 1882, by Bailey, Dix & Mead.

No. 4. Medicine Teepe.
This is the largest Teepe
belonging to the camp. Here
the Indians congregate
evenings, to sing and dance,
until the medicine man, who
sits by the side of a drum,
"made of a tin boiler,"
beating it with a stick, calls
out that he has made his
medicine, "in thoughts,"
when they all retire to their
Teepes' to await the morning
dawn, when they again
congregate in front of the
medicine teepe to learn the
medicine man's dream or
vision. Also the old squaw,
90 years old, watching the
work of some preparation on
a wolf skin she is tanning.

No. 5. Sitting Bull
and his Favorite Wife.
This is a most excellent
likeness of Sitting Bull and
his favorite wife, with their
Teepe in the back ground.
He with his pipe and tobacco
pouch in his lap, she with her
blanket wrapped around her,
and her earrings of musell
shells, showing as plain as in
life. She is his eighth wife, has
six children and is thirty years
of age.

No. 6. Winter Quarters.
[see No. 2 for caption]

Copyrighted, 1882, by Bailey, Dix & Mead.

No. 7. One Bull.
Twenty-seven years of age,
is a nephew of Sitting Bull,
and a skillful warrior. He it
was who had to be knocked
down and carried aboard the
boat to be brought as a
prisoner to the fort. He has
had 10 wives. 9 of whom are
now living. Only two of them
are living with him now. His
second wife is his favorite.
She has had two children—
one but four hours old as
we squat by the side of the
Teepe to obtain his history
by the assistance of the Post
Interpreter. He weighs 145
pounds, height 5 feet 6 inches.

No. 8. Winter Quarters.
[see No. 2 for caption]

No. 9. Issuing Rations.
April 18th, 1883. Giving four distinct views.
An Indian with a pipe in his hand in the
foreground watching the artist, some officers
and their families with Indians standing and
squatting around them. Behind them the
camp, and in the distance the hills covered
with snow.

A Ration is the amount of food furnished each
individual every twenty four hours, and is
proportioned as follows, for every one hundred
rations.
300 lbs of Fresh Beef gross or, 3 lbs Beans,
150 lbs   "   "   net, 4 lbs Coffee,
10 lbs Pork or Bacon, 8#lbs Sugar,
50 lbs Flour, or 1 lb Soap,
50 lbs Shelled Corn, or 1 lb Salt,
in lieu of either 1/2 lb Tobacco.
55 lbs Hard Bread,

No. 10. Women's Rights.
An Indian's idea of the same.
Showing two squaws sitting
beside their Teepe, resting
after carrying the wood seen
beside them, on their backs,
as seen in view No. 19, for
over half a mile, while their
leige lords and masters, (the
noble red men,) are smoking.

No. 11. Sitting Bull,
Squaw and Twins.
This is his last squaw. No. 9,
age 29, who has 6 children,
three of whom are shown in
this view. The youngest one,
on her back, is one year old,
and the two twins, five years
of age, are sitting one upon
each side of "Little Bell."

No. 12. True to Nature. Showing the Indian Camps at their summer quarters. The guard tent in the foreground. The sentinel walking his beat, etc.

No. 13. Morning Visit. The Officers and Ladies' morning call, after morning roll call by the new officers of the day, showing Steps, Teepe, Squaw and Pappoose.

No. 14. Stealing the Trade. Our Artist's first arrival at the Indian Camp. Sitting Bull trying to steal the trade. The result.

No. 15. Battalion Drill. Headquarters, band and four Companies 25th, Infantry Colored, garrisoning the Fort and guard over the Uncapapa Souix Indians, prisoners of war at Fort Randall, D.T. Beginning at the right, you see the Post Hospital, Quarters of Company G, the Magazine and Guard House.

No. 16. One Bull and Black Prairie Chicken.
This view shows the commanding Officer inspecting the Indian Camp, also the
Medicine Teepe and flag of red flannel, with One Bull and Black Prairie Chicken
watching a hide that had just been stretched by his squaws, previous to their
departure for wood.

No. 17. Issuing Supplies.

The issuing of annuity goods to the prisoners of war at Fort Randall, April 17, 1882, by the Post Quartermaster, with a list of what each Indian, Squaw and family received.

Each Buck: 1 Blanket, 1 Buffalo Robe, 1 pair Pants, 1 Blouse, 1 Hat, 2 Undershirts, 2 Outershirts, 3 yards of Cloth for Leggings, 2 pair Stockings, 1 Butcher Knife, 1 Tin Cup, 1 coarse Comb.

Each Squaw: 1 Shawl, 1 Blanket, 6 yards Calico, 5 yards heavy Flannel, 3 yards Flannel, red for Leggings, 3 yards Bleached Muslin, 2 Undershirts, 2 pair Stockings, 1 pair Scissors, 1 doz. spools Thread, 1 paper Needles assorted, 1 Thimble, 1 fine comb, 1 coarse Comb, 1 scarf, 1 Handkerchief.

Each Family: 1 Bake Oven, 1 Camp Kettle, 1 Coffee Pot, 1 Frying Pan, 1 Coffee Mill, 1 Ax, Tin Cups from 1 to 10, according to size of family.

No. 18. Morning Roll Call.

Every morning the Indians are required to sit or stand in front of their Teepes, to be counted by two commissioned Officers, consisting of the old and new officers of the day. When a child is born, (a frequent occurrence,) they are brought out in the line to be registered, that they may draw their regular rations the same as an adult. Number of Indians, May 19th, 1882, are as follows:

Males.	16 years of age and over,	38
	under 16 years of age,	30
Females,	16 years of age and over,	52
	under 16 years of age,	41
	Total,	161

No. 19. *Squaws Carrying Wood.*
This view represents the Indian Women in one of their most arduous duties which is done every day, having to pack their wood over half a mile.

No. 20. Sitting Bull, Two Wives and Three Pappooses. This shows the renowned chief with his interesting family, two wives, the twins and little pappoose.

No. 21. Winter Quarters. [see No. 2 for caption]

No. 22. Eat Dog and Family.
Eat Dog received his name from stealing dogs, of which he is very fond.
He will give all his food to the dog until he gets fat, when he is killed for
food for his master. Eat Dog is a skillful horse thief.

No. 23. Summer View.
Showing their camp on the
open prairie, which is as true a
picture as art can produce.

No. 24. Summer View.
This view gives a section of
their summer quarters,
showing a full brother
of the noted Indian, Brave
Bear, (under sentence of
death for murder) and
Brave Bear's squaw.

Last Days and After

The creation of the new state of South Dakota resulted from cumulative and inexorable changes that were transforming the political landscape of the northern plains. Throughout the 1880s, as railroad spur extensions spread across eastern Dakota, siding towns proliferated, and long-haul steamboat traffic largely ended. More settlers arrived from Minnesota and adjoining states, all seeking land. The population of Sioux Falls grew to more than 10,000 by 1890, and it replaced Yankton as the state's major city. The railroad companies, cattle syndicates, and town-site boomers had much to do with the liquidation of the Great Sioux Reservation and the land boom that resulted. In the early 1890s, thousands of homesteaders filed onto the former Indian lands and set up claims. Although troops were sometimes called out to restrain sooners, the need for an army presence had by 1890 waned significantly, and Fort Randall, which had been there at the threshold of settlement since the mid-1850s, now stood as something of an anachronism amid the forces of civilization that were circling rapidly from all directions. Consolidation of remote garrisons at rail points and population centers became the order of the day; by the late 1880s, Fort Niobrara, approximately one hundred miles west near Valentine, Nebraska, fulfilled most duties previously prescribed for Fort Randall. Furthermore, the land boom quickly changed the region, and Fort Randall's ever-shrinking military reservation contributed to the growing South Dakota economy. In October 1890, the remaining lands in that portion of the reservation lying east of the Missouri River and north of the former Yankton Reservation were thrown open for white settlement.[1]

The Fort Randall garrison, now consisting of but three companies of the Fifteenth Infantry, was reduced again on April 30, 1890, with the transfer to the Department of the East of Companies A and D, Fifteenth Infantry, leaving Company C (fifty-six men) under Lieutenant Colonel O'Bierne at the post. On February 6, 1891, the fort and what remained of the military reservation were transferred from the Department of Dakota to the Department of the Platte, headquartered in Omaha and commanded by Brigadier General John R. Brooke. On May 21, 1891, Company G, Twenty-first Infantry, consisting of three officers and forty-seven enlisted men, lately at the newly created Rosebud Reservation, arrived from Fort Sidney, Nebraska, to replace Company C of the Fifteenth, which departed permanently the next day for Illinois. In August, Companies F and H, Twenty-first Infantry, joined Company C. In September, a new Company I began enlisting Indians (see below), and in November Lieutenant Colonel William J. Lyster assumed command. On April 21, 1892, Company G departed for Fort Sidney and was followed on the 29th by Company H, leaving Companies F and I, Twenty-first Infantry, totaling ninety-four enlisted men and two lieutenants, to garrison Fort Randall under the command of Captain Willis Wittich. When Company F finally transferred, Company I remained the last army unit stationed there. By then, the post was accessed six days a week by buckboard carriage from the Chicago, Milwaukee, and St. Paul Railroad station at Armour, South Dakota, twenty-four miles distant, and three times weekly by stagecoach from the Fremont, Elkhorn, and Missouri Valley Railroad station at O'Neill, Nebraska, forty-seven miles away.[2]

Necessarily, with the prospect of abandonment hovering, Fort Randall enjoyed few structural changes requiring substantial monetary investment. In fiscal year 1890, the only new construction was for a frame addition to the guardhouse at a cost of $239, while repairs authorized to the hospital, barracks, quarters, and icehouse totaled $940. In 1891, neither construction nor repairs were authorized, and in the following year the cost for repairs to the hospital and other buildings stood at $129.[3] In 1889, the post surgeon had presented detailed plans, specifications, and estimates for a new ward addition on the hospital, dead house (morgue), ambulance shed, storeroom, and stable, besides repairs for the old building, in all totaling more than $2,000 for labor and material. The grandiosity of it all defied reality, however, and only a scaled-down dead house was authorized and built. In July 1890, the newly completed dead house was struck by lightning, requiring repair.[4]

Buildings that needed attention included civilian employee quarters, which were deemed "unsightly" by post commander Captain Casper H. Conrad in March 1891. "The quarters known as 'Laundry row' cannot be improved," he lamented, "as the authorities will not allow an appropriation for repairs. The location of this row of buildings does not materially affect the good appearance of the post." Other problems related to the sanitary condition of Fort Randall. These included ensuring proper ventilation and air circulation in at least one of the barracks and the continued antiquated means of retrieving water from the Missouri River. As the post surgeon noted, "the muddy river water has been drunk for years with apparent impunity, but this should [now] be no argument against its further purification when this . . . can be effected with small cost and labor."[5]

As early as 1890, plans were being studied as to the future non-military use of Fort Randall. The commander of the Department of Dakota, following up on an inquiry from the Department of the Interior, solicited the commanding officer's view "as to the practicality of yielding a portion of the post [including certain buildings] for use for Indian school purposes," based on the anticipated presence of a downsized garrison of one or two companies.[6] A more specific proposal from the Bureau of Indian Affairs in the spring of 1892 called for converting the post into an industrial school for Lakotas from the Rosebud Reservation, but availability of insufficient funds nullified the application.[7]

As far as the garrison was concerned, life proceeded much as before, with the troops continuing to participate in drill (albeit irregularly), target practice, and normal fatigue duty. Inspections continued to be held in conformance with army regulations, periodic muster took place as required, and the overall tedium of the late 1880s carried over into the new decade. In February 1891, the troops were variously ordered out in "regulation overcoats, fur caps, and gloves" for the occasion of inspection and muster; the Post Council of Administration convened its normal meeting; courts-martial and boards of survey proceeded; and military life went on. On February 20, a special parade honored former commanding general William T. Sherman, who had died in New York City. A post circular directed that "seventeen guns will be fired at half-hour intervals commencing at 8 o'clock A.M. . . . During the firing of the salute the National flag will be at half staff."[8] Late in the year, another death drew more immediate attention. In early December, Colonel Joseph S. Conrad, commander of the Twenty-first Infantry, while visiting Fort Randall on an inspection tour died unexpectedly at the post. As before, bugle calls still governed the operation of the garrison, from reveille at 6:25 A.M. through some twenty more calls until tattoo pierced the evening air at 9:20 P.M. School continued to be held for children, although teachers appear to have been in short supply. A request went out for a recruit to be selected from among those at the Columbus Barracks, Ohio, depot who might be competent to teach.[9]

In the spring of 1891, a flap evolved over use of the "natatorium," or indoor bathhouse with swimming pool (a tank sixty feet by eighteen feet by five feet) ever filled by the artesian well, when an unknown enlisted man defecated in the water "causing complaint and disgust from all good soldiers." Captain Conrad prescribed specific times during which the enlisted men henceforth might use the facility. Previously, the men had enjoyed unlimited access between reveille and retreat, except for a daily period, 3:30-5:00 P.M., appointed for officers and their families. Post surgeon Junius L. Powell protested the change as being detrimental to the maintenance of the good health of the garrison, but Conrad justified his decision based on the overall decline in the number of troops present requiring access to the pool. The matter was dropped.[10]

Fire prevention and control, always important, seem to have increased in attention in the 1890s, possibly because of the moribund building program. Notices about fire drills appeared frequently and called for repeated evening and nighttime inspections of quarters and kitchens. "In case fire call is sounded, Company G, 21st Infantry will assemble on its parade ground and on being divided into two platoons, the first platoon under charge of the first sergeant will proceed on a run to the artesian well, man the water wagon and take it to the fire. The second platoon in charge of the senior sergeant present will proceed on a run to the guardhouse and man the hook and ladder wagon and take it to the fire. All officers present at the post will proceed at once to the scene of the fire, the senior officer present taking charge and directing the operation of extinguishing the fire." A later directive ordered that half the men first assembled proceed with buckets directly to the fire while the water wagon was being readied.[11]

By 1892, regardless of ongoing military requisites, new changes were occurring regularly. Recruits still arrived at Fort Randall, but they were assigned there rather than to posts farther upstream. The clothing of the soldiers remained much the same as before, although certain modifications, such as white duck-covered cork solar helmets, were now authorized for wear at the post during the summer. While rations stayed the same, certain exigencies arose needing special attention. In October 1892, the commanding officer requested that he be allowed to issue baking powder to the troops "as it has been found necessary to issue the flour ration, there being no one . . . competent to bake bread for the command."[12] The emergency action proved unnecessary, for the chief commissary officer in the Department of the Platte detailed an experienced baker to Fort Randall from Fort Sidney.[13]

One new change effected throughout the army during the 1880s introduced the concept of the post canteen, initially an experimental replacement for the old post sutler-trader system that had existed for decades. Inspired by similar facilities instituted in the British army, canteens consisted of social clubs with rooms for reading and refreshments like beer (no hard liquor) and food that offered soldiers alternative forms of leisure and amusement to off-base watering holes. A post council oversaw the canteen, with the whole administered by the post commander. Funds generated by sales went into acquiring recreational facilities, such as bowling alleys. By 1889, the War Department endorsed canteens, and they rapidly multiplied at posts throughout the country. Post trader appointments formally ended in 1895, leaving the canteen system and its succeeding post exchange system firmly in place.[14]

The post canteen at Fort Randall started operation in 1891 in a building set aside for that purpose and designated "the canteen building." With the arrival of the Twenty-first Infantry troops (the regiment had earlier "pioneered" the canteen concept at Vancouver Barracks, Washington), the facility expanded by two rooms. By that time the post trader store was failing, and J. B. Brown, the appointee since 1888, had moved to St. Paul, Minnesota, making only occasional visits to the fort before quitting altogether. A former post trader, businessman D. L. Pratt Jr. of Sioux City, took over as trustee for the creditors and was permitted time to dispose of the abandoned holdings.[15] Meantime, the sale of beer became suspended at the post in April 1891 by virtue of an army appropriation act that prohibited the sale of alcoholic beverages in states or territories where such sale was illegal, and South Dakota had included such a provision in its constitution. The circumstance not only denied the sale of beer to the soldiers, it kept the new canteen from thriving from such sales, thereby nullifying much of its purpose. The men resorted to other avenues to acquire beer and liquor, largely from communities near Fort Randall that more or less ignored the state proscription.[16] The commanding officer complained to departmental headquarters, citing "the absurdity . . . of the sale of liquors in almost every part of South Dakota, except Fort Randall." The situation continued as described, with the canteen profiting only from the sale of hard cider. As the commanding officer noted, "the principal reason why this canteen is able to support itself . . . results from the isolated position of the post, no other place of amusement being accessible to the men."[17]

Beyond the confines of the garrison, post operations became increasingly minimal in the early 1890s. As mentioned, troops variously monitored the former Great Sioux Reservation lands to prevent civilian intrusion prior to opening them for white settlement, as when Company A, Fifteenth Infantry, took station at Lower Brulé Agency near Chamberlain in February 1890. During the same approximate period, troops under Second Lieutenants William N. Blow and Robert C. Williams also scouted through the area southeast of Fort Randall, monitoring conditions along the Keya Paha River and Spotted Tail Road, while a detachment under First Lieutenant Alexis R. Paxton trailed a deserter named Eggleston up the Missouri then south to the Niobrara. Although the post maintained relations with the Yanktons, its role in Indian matters was not the same as in previous years because circumstances had altogether changed. By 1892, nearly three-quarters of the Yanktons occupied allotted lands; in 1894, all unallotted lands of the former reservation were opened for white settlement.[18]

During the so-called Ghost Dance confrontation between the Lakotas and the army that followed the sale, division, and allotment of the former Great Sioux Reservation lands in 1890, the soldiers at Fort Randall played but a tangential role. The fort was one of nine such installations that ringed the former Sioux lands, and its troops could have been called upon if necessary. As the crisis mounted on the Standing Rock, Cheyenne River, Pine Ridge, and Rosebud reservations, Major General Nelson A. Miles, commanding the Military Division of the Missouri, expected far-flung infantry commands "to be used in guarding trains, protecting supplies, and, if necessary, . . .

to give as much protection as possible to scattered settlements requiring their protection."[19] Yet an incident involving a Brulé Lakota peace chief created certain alarm at Fort Randall and in the surrounding area during the days leading up to the Wounded Knee Massacre of December 29, 1890. On December 5, Swift Bear and thirteen followers, bent on avoiding imminent trouble on the Rosebud Reservation, appeared at the post to consult with Captain Conrad, asking that their people be permitted to receive their rations at Fort Randall or on the Yankton reserve. The presence of the Indians caused excitement among area settlers, and some visited the post to give the alarm and to purchase arms and ammunition in preparation for an anticipated raid. But fears soon subsided, and the Indians camped at nearby Ponca Creek until informed that it was safe for them to return to their reservation.[20]

The Swift Bear incident was not the last matter involving Indians at the post. The final and perhaps exceedingly significant development regarding Indians there during the months preceding its closing centered not on further military efforts to control the Indians, but on the army's enlistment of them to serve there in a formal military capacity. The trial plan to recruit Indians during the administration of Secretary of War Redfield Proctor was an attempt to acculturate and assimilate them into the dominant culture while capitalizing on their perceived qualities and abilities. By General Orders No. 28, March 9, 1891, the War Department directed that Company L of certain cavalry regiments and Company I of certain infantry ones would each be filled by as many as fifty-five Indians. Enacting orders to Fort Randall from the Department of the Platte came down in September 1891. Accordingly, the hospital staff was increased for the purpose of examining the enlistees, and post commander Captain William H. Boyle dispatched Second Lieutenant Samuel Seay Jr., the new company's commander, to the Yankton Agency to consult with the agent and begin the recruitment process. As word got around, tribesmen from other agencies arrived to sign up, and before long the Fort Randall Company I contingent numbered thirty-seven men with anglicized names. Although most of the new soldiers were from the Yankton Agency, Boyle expressed concern that more could not be recruited there "to fill the company to the standard." Others were consequently enlisted from among Brulés at the Lower Brulé and Rosebud reservations. As late as October 9, 1892, likely because no officers were then available, Private Hugh M. Jones received directions "to proceed to Yellow Breast's camp, S.D., for the purpose of obtaining four more recruits at that place." Primarily because of cultural differences, including language problems, the army considered the Indian experiment a failure, and it was terminated in 1897.[21]

The extended recruitment of Company I, Twenty-first Infantry, coincided with events that concluded the active tenure of Fort Randall. With removal of the need for a sustained military presence, political and economic concerns combined to dictate its end. By the 1890s, the expansion of railroads afforded alternative means of distributing troops under emergency conditions, and as the Indian frontier receded, so did the frontier of white settlement and thus the need for retaining the venerable post. The end came on October 31, 1892, when Fort Randall was turned over to the Quartermaster Department. Nine days later, it officially became an abandoned military post, and the enlisted staff, consisting of commissary and hospital personnel together with the post baker, were reassigned to other venues. On October 1, Company F, Twenty-first Infantry, the sole remaining unit composed of white soldiers, had departed the post for Fort Sidney, Nebraska. On November 14, a post edict allowed that "all drills are suspended at this Post until further orders." Little more than three weeks later, on December 7, 1892, Company I of the regiment, consisting of forty-three enlisted Indian men and two white officers, vacated the premises for Fort Sidney.[22] In a historic quirk of irony, as well as perhaps a fitting reflection of changing times, the post established thirty-six years earlier to help prosecute Indians on the upper Missouri now witnessed the departure of its final army command composed entirely of them.

Likewise, with the abandonment of the post, the Fort Randall Military Reservation ceased to exist. What remained of the property was turned over to the Department of the Interior on October 20, 1893, in accordance with the July 5, 1884, act that legislated the relinquishment of military reservations. At the time of the transfer, the land embraced 96,160 acres and some fifty structures. Under an existing act of March 3, 1893, Congress tendered the reservation property in South Dakota to that state for school uses, and in 1897 an authorization permitted the state to select appropriate lands. The state initially refused the offer because the lands were pronounced of little worth. Ultimately, the state took certain lands, and those remaining were appraised and disposed of to homesteaders under an amend-

ing act of August 1894, which required payment based upon appraisal of the property. As a result of an earlier state boundary re-
alignment, a piece of the reservation amounting to 35,838 acres lay in
Holt County, Nebraska, and odd-numbered sections of the land likewise were conveyed for school purposes to that state, while that remaining was opened for homesteading.[23] The closure of Fort Randall
followed closely the passing of the frontier as officially pronounced
by the national census of 1890. It marked a significant change on the
upper Missouri, and with the subsequent abandonment of Fort Sully
in 1894 and Fort Buford in 1895, the days of the Missouri River posts
were gone.

In the autumn of 1893, less than a year after the Twenty-first Infantry vacated the premises, a group of Brulés attempted to settle at the
fort. The intrusion resulted from an interreservation dispute regarding Indians at the Lower Brulé Reservation who desired to transfer to
Rosebud. When approval for the move was not forthcoming, one hundred of the Brulés peremptorily left Lower Brulé and moved to Fort
Randall, where they took over the vacated barracks. Indian police from
the Lower Brulé and Crow Creek reservations pursued them and, following a brief melee, managed to disarm the dissenters. Several of the
Brulés fled Fort Randall to the Yankton Reservation, where they were
apprehended. All returned to Lower Brulé, where the leaders of the
revolt were jailed.[24] One observer described the takeover of the post:

> I saw a lot of horses out west of the church and when I got inside
> the parade ground I saw a lot of Indian wagons standing at each of
> the buildings and on inquiry they said they had come down from
> Lower Brulé to take over the fort as it belonged to them now that
> the soldiers were gone. There was an old man among them who
> said he had been there when they signed the treaty and that the
> Government would have it so long as they used it as a fort, to pro-
> tect the Indians, but when they left that the Indians were to have it
> back. [A few days later I] . . . saw a file of men on horse back coming
> into the fort. It proved to be the mounted Indian police from the
> Lower Brulé [Reservation].[25]

Immediately following the abandonment of Fort Randall, John H.
McLaughlin, a custodian hired to oversee the buildings and reservation, took up residence there. A veteran soldier and former forage
master at the post who had homesteaded nearby, McLaughlin con-

tinued as postmaster at the fort following its closure until 1895, when the buildings were sold and McLaughlin ceased his $40-per-month duty. That summer, the fort became the site for festivities by neighborhood settlers, who cleaned out a mess hall for the occasion. "The old post resounded again with the gay music of the dance and the laughter of the merrymakers."[26] Thereafter, most of the structures were dismantled or moved by area farmers to new locations. In 1894, the government exhumed the soldiers' remains in the post cemetery for reinterment in the Fort Leavenworth National Military Cemetery in Kansas. At the same time, the headstones were removed, crated, and shipped away. In the following year, the post grounds became targeted for firewood by drought-stricken local settlers who entered the lands and extensively cut trees in the area, including those around the parade ground; the infringement was duly reported to the federal authorities, but apparently no indictments resulted.[27] Soon afterward, the fort was described as the "scene of solitude and desolation. . . . High winds have carried clouds of dust and sand, which have sifted into the buildings for a depth of an inch or more. The skeleton of a rattlesnake over four feet long, which was caught in coming through a crevice in the roof of a shed, still hangs where the reptile died and sways with every passing breeze."[28]

Following the sale of public buildings, McLaughlin purchased much of the fort land and continued residing there. Beyond the commanding officer's home and cognate structures where McLaughlin and his family lived, his stepson, Denny Moran, resided in a nearby officer quarters, which he later demolished for the lumber. In about 1900, all that remained were the two officers' homes and the stone church erected in 1875. "The old parade grounds are just as they were left by the troops, except that they are overgrown with wild grass. At the four sides of the grounds are handsome cottonwood trees which were set out fifteen years ago."[29] The gravel walks remained, as well as "the stub of a gigantic flag pole that floated the stars and stripes while the fort was occupied." Along the south side of the post, "an ancient sun dial" still marked the passing of days, while to the southeast lay the foundations of the vaunted bathhouse, its pipe still spewing its thermal bounty. In the abandoned chapel, pigeons now nested, although the adjacent Echo Lodge No. 2 saw occasional use by the sixteen Odd Fellows' members still living in the area. After McLaughlin died in 1907, Moran moved into the commanding officer's home. "It contained twelve rooms," he recalled, "and was built of red cedar logs and was certainly a well built place." Moran stayed on the property until 1916 and sold it several years later.[30]

In September 1922, an aged Civil War veteran named Henry Dunkelman was brought to the site of Fort Randall by his daughter. Dunkelman had served at the post from 1863 to 1865. The changes by then were profound. "Right over there between that row of trees was the flag-staff; over here . . . were the barracks," he recalled, "and at this the extreme north end was my bunk. My goodness! Here is where I slept 58 years ago."[31] With the passage of years, the remaining resources of Fort Randall continued to decline. Interest in preserving the site as a park for future generations came from Gustave Reider, an elderly former soldier who had been discharged at the post in 1878, who had settled at nearby Gregory, and who in the 1920s was serving as mayor of that community. By then, only the chapel and the commanding officer's home remained, although the artesian well still flowed. The commanding officer's home burned sometime after that.[32]

Because the imposing chalk rock chapel continued to dominate the scene, it became the immediate and long-lasting focus of preservation efforts. Despite extensive tornado damage to its roof in the 1890s, it had survived relatively intact and was considered in excellent condition, although "the doors stand open . . . and the floor, pews, and altar are half buried in dust."[33] Following the sale of the public buildings in 1895, McLaughlin purchased the chapel for $70. In 1896, Mrs. T. J. Thompson of Fairfax, South Dakota, purchased from McLaughlin for her home many of the black walnut inner fixtures, including altars, one of which was donated to a local church and another sold. A pulpit and a pew were later donated to the South Dakota State Historical Society. The 550-pound steel chapel bell ended up in nearby Springfield, where it served as a fire bell. In the 1940s (and still present into the late 1950s), a building reputed to be the quarters of the post commissary sergeant was located on land adjoining the old tract, having been removed there earlier by local residents. Renewed interest in saving what remained of Fort Randall arose in the 1940s and 1950s in conjunction with establishment of the massive Corps of Engineers–Bureau of Reclamation Missouri River flood control–reservoir project, which included construction of the Fort Randall Dam within sight of the old fort grounds. At that time, the property comprising the former fort land was transferred once again to the United States. In the latter decade, it became the goal of Will G. Robinson, secretary of the South Dakota State Historical Society, to work with federal agencies to rehabilitate the ruined chapel and the parade ground and to mark the sites of former structures for interpretation, so that the history of the post might be accessible to visitors. This, to a large degree, was accomplished during succeeding years.[34]

So passed Fort Randall. Archaeology and preservation efforts acknowledge the significant contributions of the upper Missouri River post during an active tenure of thirty-six years, five months, and eleven days between 1856 and 1892.[35] They were decades of change that witnessed the full flower of American expansionism in the pre- and post-Civil War eras. For a brief moment, as the only permanent federal station on the upper river, Fort Randall stood as an enticing beacon astride the ever-advancing frontier, a stabilizing influence for a generation of white Americans bent on carving livelihoods from the trans-Mississippi wilderness. As sole government authority in a region broadly embracing parts of modern Iowa, Minnesota, Nebraska, and North and South Dakota, it proved a bulwark of the democratic system, promoting Euro-American emigration, settlement, capitalism, and community, with all of their ramifications, and for a time played a role in the subjugation of native peoples who defied those objectives.

For the Yanktons, Dakotas, Poncas, Lakotas, and other area tribes, Fort Randall brought change that was not necessarily good. In its duty as promoter of white settlement and protector of white populations, Fort Randall commensurately subordinated the interests of native peoples in accordance with perceived national interests. Hence, troops from the post took part in campaigns against the Indians, participated in the establishment of agencies and reservations, promoted the military domination of tribes and their placement on designated tracts, and thereafter controlled their activities, generally to the advantage of whites and to the detriment of the Indians. In the preeminent event of the incarceration of Sitting Bull and his people, Fort Randall served, in effect, as a federal detainment center—a prison—intended to punish as well as to ensure against the promulgation of discord by the Hunkpapa leader among his own people. Thus, for the Indians that its presence affected, Fort Randall caused cultural trauma and upheaval that in one form or another likely continues to pervade their families and societies.

In its task as purveyor of the national agenda, Fort Randall assisted in the exploration of the Black Hills and environs and of the upper Missouri and its tributaries, which led to further government expansion into those regions, while continuing as a depot for troops and supplies for emerging upriver installations as well as for ongoing and projected military campaigns against more distant Indian adversaries. In time, as the frontier passed, the post assumed a less rigorous posture. During its final years, as with other regional military stations whose usefulness had expired, it stood amid prosperous communities whose origins it had fostered and whose citizens its garrison had served. Changing times and circumstances made its survival tenuous. In the years following Fort Randall's abandonment, most of its tangible remains were removed or slowly melted away, the account of its existence consigned to history.

Appendix A Commanding Officers, Fort Randall, 1856-92

First Lieutenant David S. Stanley, First Cavalry
    June 26, 1856–June 30, 1856
First Lieutenant George H. Paige, Second Infantry
    July 1, 1856–Aug. 4, 1856
Captain Nelson H. Davis, Second Infantry
    Aug. 5, 1856–Aug. 9, 1856
Colonel Francis Lee, Second Infantry
    Aug. 10, 1856–Sept. 22, 1857
Major Hannibal Day, Second Infantry
    Sept. 23, 1857–July 2, 1858
Captain Henry W. Wessells, Second Infantry
    July 3, 1858–May 2, 1859
Captain Christopher S. Lovell, Second Infantry
    May 3, 1859–July 15, 1859
Lieutenant Colonel John Munroe, Fourth Artillery
    July 16, 1859–May 10, 1860
Captain John P. McCown, Fourth Artillery
    May 11, 1860–July 13, 1860
Lieutenant Colonel John Munroe, Fourth Artillery
    July 13, 1860–Jan. 11, 1861
Captain John P. McCown, Fourth Artillery
    Jan. 12, 1861–Apr. 9, 1861
Captain George W. Getty, Fourth Artillery
    Apr. 10, 1861–Apr. 24, 1861
Captain John A. Brown, Fourth Artillery
    Apr. 25, 1861–Aug. 6, 1861
Second Lieutenant Thomas R. Tannatt, Fourth Artillery
    Aug. 7, 1861–Nov. 30, 1861
Captain John Pattee, Fourteenth Iowa Infantry
    Dec. 1861–Jan. 1862*
Major William P. Lyman, Dakota Volunteers
    Feb. 1862–Mar. 1862*
Captain Bradley Mahana, Fourteenth Iowa Infantry
    Apr. 1862–Apr. 1862*

Source: Adapted from War Department listing, Adjutant General's Office,
January 11, 1934
*Precise dates of state occupying forces are incomplete.

Captain John Pattee, Fourteenth Iowa Infantry
  May 1862–Apr. 1863*
Captain George H. Wolfe, Forty-first Iowa Infantry
  May 1863–Aug. 1863*
Major J.H. Pearman, Second Nebraska Cavalry
  Sept. 1863–Sept. 1863*
Major Thomas H. Shepherd, Sixth Iowa Cavalry
  Oct. 1863–Oct. 1863*
Lieutenant Colonel Samuel M. Pollock, Sixth Iowa Cavalry
  Nov. 1863–Nov. 1863*
Major Thomas H. Shepherd, Sixth Iowa Cavalry
  Dec. 1863–Jan. 1864*
Lieutenant Colonel Samuel M. Pollock, Sixth Iowa Cavalry
  Feb. 1864–Mar. 1864*
Major Thomas H. Shepherd, Sixth Iowa Cavalry
  Apr. 1864–Apr. 1864*
Lieutenant Colonel Samuel M. Pollock, Sixth Iowa Cavalry
  May 1864–May 1864*
Major Thomas H. Shepherd, Sixth Iowa Cavalry
  June 1864–Sept. 1864*
Lieutenant Colonel Samuel M. Pollock, Sixth Iowa Cavalry
  Oct. 1864–Mar. 1865*
Captain L. L. Ainsworth, Sixth Iowa Cavalry
  Apr. 1865–Apr. 1865*
Lieutenant Colonel Samuel M. Pollock, Sixth Iowa Cavalry
  May 1865–May 1865*
Captain L. L. Ainsworth, Sixth Iowa Cavalry
  June 1865–Aug. 1865*
Captain Francis H. Cooper, Seventh Iowa Cavalry
  Sept. 1865–Oct. 1865*
Lieutenant Colonel Charles C. G. Thornton, Fourth U.S. Volunteers
  Nov. 1865–Jan. 1866*
Captain Mortimer Neely, Mounted Battalion Cavalry
  Feb. 1866–Feb. 1866*
Lieutenant Colonel Charles C. G. Thornton, Fourth U.S. Volunteers
  Mar. 1866–May 1866*
Major Hiram Dryer, Twenty-second Infantry
  June 1, 1866–Feb. 27, 1867
Captain Joseph Bush, Twenty-second Infantry
  Feb. 28, 1867–Mar. 25, 1867
Lieutenant Colonel Elwell S. Otis, Twenty-second Infantry
  Mar. 26, 1867–May 26,1867

Captain Joseph Bush, Twenty-second Infantry
    May 27, 1867–Aug. 9, 1867
Major Alexander Chambers, Twenty-second Infantry
    Aug. 10, 1867–Apr. 5, 1869
Captain Joseph Bush, Twenty-second Infantry
    Apr. 6, 1869–June 29, 1869
Captain Charles A. Webb, Twenty-second Infantry
    June 30, 1869–July 19, 1869
Major Joseph N.G. Whistler, Twenty-second Infantry
    July 20, 1869–July 2, 1870
Lieutenant Colonel Elwell S. Otis, Twenty-second Infantry
    July 3, 1870–Sept. 12, 1870
Captain Joseph Bush, Twenty-second Infantry
    Sept. 13, 1870–Oct. 22, 1870
Lieutenant Colonel Elwell S. Otis, Twenty-second Infantry
    Oct. 23, 1870–June 6, 1873
Captain Charles A. Webb, Twenty-second Infantry
    June 7, 1873–Nov. 23, 1873
Lieutenant Colonel Elwell S. Otis, Twenty-second Infantry
    Nov. 24, 1873–Mar. 13, 1874
Captain Charles A. Webb, Twenty-second Infantry
    Mar. 14, 1874–June 26, 1874
Lieutenant Colonel Pinkney Lugenbeel, First Infantry
    June 27, 1874–Dec. 24, 1874
Captain Kinzie Bates, First Infantry
    Dec. 15, 1874–Jan. 9, 1875
Lieutenant Colonel Pinkney Lugenbeel, First Infantry
    Jan. 10, 1875–June 20, 1875
Captain Kinzie Bates, First Infantry
    June 21, 1875–July 26, 1875
Lieutenant Colonel Pinkney Lugenbeel, First Infantry
    July 27, 1875–Jan. 25, 1876
Captain Kinzie Bates, First Infantry
    Jan. 26, 1875–Feb. 9, 1876
Lieutenant Colonel Pinkney Lugenbeel, First Infantry
    Feb. 10, 1876–Aug. 4, 1876
Captain Robert H. Offley, First Infantry
    Aug. 5, 1876–Sept. 5, 1876
Lieutenant Colonel Pinkney Lugenbeel, First Infantry
    Sept. 6, 1876–Dec. 28, 1876
Captain Robert H. Offley, First Infantry
    Dec. 29, 1876–Mar. 24, 1877

Lieutenant Colonel Pinkney Lugenbeel, First Infantry
    Mar. 25, 1877–Jan. 13, 1878
Captain Robert H. Offley, First Infantry
    Jan. 14, 1878–May 14, 1878
Lieutenant Colonel Pinkney Lugenbeel, First Infantry
    May 15, 1878–Oct. 30, 1879
Captain Fergus Walker, First Infantry
    Oct. 31, 1879–Dec. 20, 1879
Colonel William R. Shafter, First Infantry
    Dec. 21, 1879–May 31, 1880
Captain John Hamilton, First Infantry
    June 1, 1880–June 29, 1880
Colonel George L. Andrews, Twenty-fifth Infantry
    June 30, 1880–Sept. 25, 1880
Captain Charles Bentzoni, Twenty-fifth Infantry
    Sept. 26, 1880–Oct. 27, 1880
Major Joseph Bush, Twenty-fifth Infantry
    Oct. 28, 1880–Nov. 27, 1880
Colonel George L. Andrews, Twenty-fifth Infantry
    Nov. 28, 1880–Oct. 27, 1881
Captain Charles Bentzoni, Twenty-fifth Infantry
    Oct. 28, 1881–Nov. 9, 1881
Colonel George L. Andrews, Twenty-fifth Infantry
    Nov. 10, 1881–Mar. 30, 1882
Captain Charles Bentzoni, Twenty-fifth Infantry
    Mar. 31, 1882–May 3, 1882
Colonel George L. Andrews, Twenty-fifth Infantry
    May 4, 1882–Sept. 25, 1882
Captain Gaines Lawson, Twenty-fifth Infantry
    Sept. 26, 1882–Nov. 18, 1882
Lieutenant Colonel Peter T. Swaine, Fifteenth Infantry
    Nov. 19, 1882–May 20, 1884
Captain Casper H. Conrad, Fifteenth Infantry
    May 21, 1884–Sept. 10, 1884
Colonel Richard F. O'Bierne, Fifteenth Infantry
    Sept. 11, 1894–Sept. 6, 1886
Captain Henry R. Brinkerhoff, Fifteenth Infantry
    Sept. 7, 1886–Sept. 21, 1886
Captain Casper H. Conrad, Fifteenth Infantry
    Sept. 22, 1886–Oct. 9, 1886
Major Hugh A. Theaker, Fifteenth Infantry
    Oct. 10, 1886–Apr. 22, 1887

Captain Casper H. Conrad, Fifteenth Infantry
    Apr. 23, 1887–Apr. 26, 1887
Captain Henry R. Brinkerhoff, Fifteenth Infantry
    Apr. 27, 1887–Apr. 28, 1887
Captain Casper H. Conrad, Fifteenth Infantry
    Apr. 29, 1887–May 24, 1887
Captain Henry R. Brinkerhoff, Fifteenth Infantry
    May 25, 1887–June 11, 1887
Major Hugh A. Theaker, Fifteenth Infantry
    June 12, 1887–Apr. 25, 1888
Captain Casper H. Conrad, Fifteenth Infantry
    Apr. 26, 1888–May 3, 1889
Colonel Richard F. O'Bierne, Fifteenth Infantry
    May 4, 1889–Sept. 9, 1890
Captain Casper H. Conrad, Fifteenth Infantry
    Sept. 10, 1890–May 21, 1891
Captain William H. Boyle, Twenty-first Infantry
    May 28, 1891–Nov. 6, 1891
Lieutenant Colonel William J. Lyster, Twenty-first Infantry
    Nov. 7, 1891–Dec. 19, 1891
Captain William H. Boyle, Twenty-first Infantry
    Dec. 20, 1891–Mar. 27, 1892
Lieutenant Colonel William J. Lyster, Twenty-first Infantry
    Mar. 28, 1892–Aug. 25, 1892
Captain Willis Wittich, Twenty-first Infantry
    Aug. 26, 1892–Sept. 20, 1892
First Lieutenant Francis E. Eltonhead, Twenty-first Infantry
    Sept. 21, 1892–Oct. 10, 1892
Second Lieutenant Samuel Seay, Twenty-first Infantry
    Oct. 11, 1892–Dec. 7, 1892

Appendix B Regiments stationed at Fort Randall, 1856-92

1856–59	Second U.S. Infantry
1856–57	Second U.S. Dragoons
1859–61	Fourth U.S. Artillery
1861–65	Fourteenth Iowa Volunteer Infantry
	(Forty-first Iowa Volunteer Infantry)
1862–65	First Dakota Cavalry
1863–65	Sixth Iowa Cavalry
1863–63	Thirtieth Wisconsin Volunteer Infantry
1863–65	Seventh Iowa Volunteer Cavalry
1863–64	Second Nebraska Volunteer Cavalry
1865–66	Fourth U.S. Volunteer Infantry
1865–66	Brackett's Minnesota Cavalry Battalion
1866–66	Thirteenth U.S. Infantry
	(reorganized 1867 as Twenty-second U.S. Infantry)
1867–74	Twenty-second U.S. Infantry
1874–80	First U.S. Infantry
1880–82	Twenty-fifth U.S. Infantry
1882–91	Fifteenth U.S. Infantry
1891–92	Twenty-first U.S. Infantry

Appendix C "List of Indian Prisoners of War, Sitting Bull's Band," 1881

No.	Name	Sex	Age	Remarks
	Sitting Bull's Family			
I	Sitting Bull	Male	Adult	
2	Hunt in the Cold	Male	Adult	Cousin
3	Saw Nation	Female	Adult	Wife
4	Stand Sacred	Female	4 yrs.	Daughter
5	Crow Foot	Male	7 yrs.	Son
6	Stood By Him	Male	15 yrs.	Son
7	Four Blankets	Female	Adult	Wife No. 2
8	Infant	Female	1 day	Daughter
9	Her Lodge in Sight	Female	5 yrs.	Daughter
10	Blue Turtle	Male	14 yrs.	Nephew (or son)
11	On the Hill and Not Afraid on Train	Male	3 yrs.	Son ⎫ Twin
12	Fled and Left Him on Train	Male	3 yrs.	Son ⎭
13	Seen While Walking	Female	15 yrs.	Daughter
14	Many Horses	Female	18 yrs.	Daughter
15	Lost Woman	Female	Adult	Mother-in-law
	White Dog's Family			
I	White Dog	Male	Adult	
2	Black Prairie Chicken	Male	Adult	Nephew
3	Good Bird	Male	15 yrs.	Son
4	Eagle Wing Woman	Female	17 yrs.	
5	The Good Natured Woman	Female	Adult	Mrs. White Dog
6	Ran Be-Hind	Male	6 yrs.	Son

Source: "List of Indian Prisoners of War, Sitting Bull's Band, turned over by Captain H. S. Howe, 17th Infantry, to Colonel G. L. Andrews, 25th Infantry, on the 18th day of September 1881," NA, RG 393, Entry 6, Letters and Telegrams Received, Fort Randall, S.D., Box 6; and "List of Indians (Sitting Bull's Party) Turned over at Fort Randall (D.T.) Sept 18, 1881," Stamped received, June 13, 1883, NA, RG 393, Entry 7, Letters Received, Fort Yates, N.D. (reproduced in: James McLaughlin Papers, Assumption Abbey Archives, microfilm roll 31). I am grateful to Ephriam Dickson, Utah Museum of Natural History, for his assistance in the transcription.

No.	Name	Sex	Age	Remarks
7	Winter	Male	10 yrs.	Son
8	The Lodge Beyond	Female	23 yrs.	Daughter
9	Killed	Male	2 yrs.	Grandson
10	Steps	Male	Adult	Son Nez Perce–Shoshone Bannock

Four Horns Family

No.	Name	Sex	Age	Remarks
1	Four Horns	Male	Adult	
2	Four Horns Jr.	Male	22 yrs.	
3	Mrs. Four Horns	Female	Adult	Wife
4	Red White Cow	Female	18 yrs.	Daughter

One Bulls Family

No.	Name	Sex	Age	Remarks
1	One Bull	Male	Adult	
2	Killed In the Lodge	Male	19 yrs.	Brother ⎱ Half
3	Killed Standing	Male	19 yrs.	Brother ⎰ brothers
4	Sacred Girl	Female	Adult	Mrs. One Bull
5	Infant Daughter	Female		
6	Growl Boy	Male	14 yrs.	Brother
7	The Pretty Plume	Female	Adult	Mother to One Bull & sister to Sitting Bull
8	Stormy Cloud	Female	Adult	Grandmother. Sitting Bull's mother

No.	Name	Sex	Age	Remarks
1	*High Bull*	Male	Adult	Family absent

No.	Name	Sex	Age	Remarks
1	*One Iron Horse*	Male	Adult	

Fire Cloud's Family

No.	Name	Sex	Age	Remarks
1	Fire Cloud	Male	Adult	
2	The Four Frozen	Female	Adult	Wife
3	The Four Generations of Buffalo	Male	10 yrs.	Son
4	The Tongue	Male	12 yrs.	Son

Elk Horn's Family

No.	Name	Sex	Age	Remarks
1	Elk Horn	Male	Adult	
2	Iron Heart	Male	Adult	Son

No.	Name	Sex	Age	Remarks
3	The Mercy	Female	18 yrs.	Daughter
4	Asked of	Male	9 yrs.	Grandson
5	Old Woman	Female	Adult	Wife

Bone Tomahawk's Family

No.	Name	Sex	Age	Remarks
1	Bone Tomahawk	Male	Adult	
2	Mrs. Bone Tomahawk	Female	Adult	Wife
3	Charges	Female	8 yrs.	Daughter
4	Their Benefactor	Female	11 yrs.	Daughter
5	Mrs. Bone Tomahawk	Female	Adult	Wife No. 2
6	Killed the Crow	Male	2 yrs.	Son
7	Red Horned Woman	Female	Adult	Sister-in-law
8	Red Headed Woman	Female	Adult	Mother-in-law

Broken Arrow's Family

No.	Name	Sex	Age	Remarks
1	Broken Arrow	Male	Adult	
2	Mrs. Broken Arrow	Female	Adult	Wife

Spotted Eagle's Family

No.	Name	Sex	Age	Remarks
1	Spotted Eagle	Male	Adult	
2	Mrs. Spotted Eagle	Female	Adult	Wife
3	Run With Them	Male	8 yrs.	Son
4	White Chief Woman	Female	24 yrs.	Daughter
5	White Cow Girl	Female	4 yrs.	Granddaughter
6	Went Ahead	Female	2 yrs.	Daughter
7	Deformed	Female	20 yrs.	Daughter

Brave Thunder's Family

No.	Name	Sex	Age	Remarks
1	Brave Thunder	Male	Adult	One wife and two daughters absent
2	Mrs. Brave Thunder	Female	Adult	Wife
3	Infant	Female	2 yrs.	Daughter

Black Bird's Family

No.	Name	Sex	Age	Remarks
1	Black Bird	Male	Adult	
2	Wife	Female	Adult	
3	Girl	Female		
4	Girl	Female		

No.	Name	Sex	Age	Remarks
	Hairy Coat's Family			
1	Hairy Coat	Male	Adult	
2	Mrs. Hairy Coat	Female	Adult	Wife
3	Infant	Female	2 months	Daughter
4	The Bull	Male	3 yrs.	Son
5	Day Woman	Female	17 yrs.	Daughter
6	Scabby Face	Male	13 yrs.	Son
	Shoot the Bear's Family			
1	Shoot the Bear	Male	Adult	
2	Mrs. Shoot the Bear	Female	Adult	
3	Killed Living	Male	13 yrs.	Son
4	Red Maisn	Female	14 yrs.	Daughter

Returned to Standing Rock Agency on steamer *Sherman.*

No.	Name	Sex	Age	Remarks
	Scarlet Thunder's Family			
1	Scarlet Thunder Jr.	Male	Adult	
2	Mrs. Scarlet Thunder	Female	Adult	Wife
3	Drove Them	Male	1 yr.	Son
4	Plundered Them	Female	4 yrs.	Daughter
5	Her Horse	Female	17 yrs.	Daughter
	Zume's Family			
1	Zume	Male	Adult	
2	Mrs. Zume	Female	Adult	Wife
3	Hunted in the Centre	Male	6 yrs.	Son
4	Scarlet Girl	Female	4 yrs.	Daughter
5	Bears Nest	Male	1 yr.	Son
	Took Their Gun's Family			
1	Took Their Guns	Male	Adult	
2	Mrs. Took Their Guns	Female	Adult	Wife
3	Owl Old Man	Male	8 yrs.	Son
4	Climbed the Lodge	Male	13 yrs.	Son
5	Medicine	Female	4 yrs.	Daughter
6	Beaver	Female	7 yrs.	Daughter
7	Yellow Horned Woman	Female	10 yrs.	Daughter
	Blue Cloud's Family			
1	Blue Cloud	Male	Adult	
2	Mrs. Blue Cloud	Female	Adult	Wife

No.	Name	Sex	Age	Remarks
3	Mrs. Blue Cloud	Female	Adult	Wife No. 2
4	Killed Alive	Male	16 yrs.	Son
5	Lifted Up	Male	6 yrs.	Son
6	Strange Hair	Male	1 yr.	Son
7	Kidney	Female	14 yrs.	Daughter
8	Jumped In	Male	1 yr.	Son

Yellow Dog's Family

No.	Name	Sex	Age	Remarks
1	Yellow Dog	Male	Adult	
2	White Haired Cow	Male	Adult	Brother
3	Smeller	Female	20 yrs.	Niece
4	Smeller	Male	1 yr.	Son
5	Yellow Dog's Mother	Female		Mother

Fought the Bear's Family

No.	Name	Sex	Age	Remarks
1	Fought the Bears	Male	Adult	
2	Old Woman	Female		Grandmother
3	White Cow Woman	Female	18 yrs.	Cousin
4	Her Many Horses	Female	15 yrs.	Sister
5	Iron Hitter	Female	19 yrs.	Cousin
6	Infant	Female	1 month	Daughter

| 2 | *Brave Bear's Wife & child* | | | |

Hunted Alone & Family

No.	Name	Sex	Age	Remarks
1	Hunted Alone	Male	Adult	
2	Sacred Pipe	Male	Adult	Son
3	Eagle Blanket	Male	12 yrs.	Son
4	They Cried For	Female	6 yrs.	Daughter
5	Mrs. Hunted Alone	Female	Adult	Wife
6	Infant	Female		Daughter
7	Loved	Female	5 yrs.	Daughter
8	Shell Girl	Female	8 yrs.	Daughter

The Deaf Woman's Family

No.	Name	Sex	Age	Remarks
1	Deaf Woman	Female	Adult	
2	Stood in Sight	Male	10 yrs.	Son
3	They Called Her	Female	3 yrs.	Daughter

No.	Name	Sex	Age	Remarks
	Big Leg's Family			
1	Big Leg	Male	Adult	
2	Mrs. Big Leg	Female	Adult	Wife
3	Saw Her	Female	12 yrs.	Daughter
4	White Coat	Male	8 yrs.	Son
5	Good Voice	Female	4 yrs.	Daughter
6	The Bread	Female	14 yrs.	Daughter
7	The Yellow	Male	2 yrs.	Son
1	*His Many Old Man*	Female	Adult	Wife
	The Bear That Looks Back Family			
1	The Bear That Looks Back	Male	Adult	
2	Hard to Beat	Male	7 yrs.	Son
3	Scarlet Girl	Female	9 yrs.	Daughter
4	Came Out Red	Female	6 yrs.	Daughter
5	Mrs. Bear That Looks Back	Female	Adult	Wife
6	Infant	Female		Daughter
7	The Many Shells	Female	8 yrs.	Daughter
8	Mrs. Bear That Looks Back	Female		Wife No. 2
9	Infant	Female		Daughter
10	White Robe	Female	9 yrs.	Daughter
11	His Mother-In-Law	Female		
	Scarlet Thunder's Family			
1	Scarlet Thunder Sr.	Male	Adult	
2	Mrs. Scarlet Thunder	Female	Adult	Wife
3	No Pillow	Female	20 yrs.	Daughter
4	Infant Daughter	Female		Granddaughter
5	Running Horse	Female	15 yrs.	Granddaughter
6	Girl	Female	8 yrs.	Daughter
7	Girl	Female	11 yrs.	Daughter
1	*Bad Head*	Male	Adult	
1	*Feeble White Cow*	Male	Adult	Two children and wife absent
	The Rider Family			
1	The Rider	Male	Adult	
2	Mrs. The Rider	Female	Adult	Wife

No.	Name	Sex	Age	Remarks
	Mosquito's Family			
1	Mosquito	Male	Adult	
2	Mrs. Mosquito	Female	Adult	Wife
3	Infant	Female		Daughter
4	The Great Spirit Girl	Female	14 yrs.	Daughter
	High in the Cloud's Family			
1	High in the Clouds	Male	Adult	
2	Mrs. High in the Clouds	Female		Wife
3	Rode Over	Male	6 yrs.	Son
4	Old Man Crow	Male	10 yrs.	Son
5	The Eagle Wing	Female	25 yrs.	Daughter
6	Infant	Male		Son
1	*Mrs. Crazy Horse*	Female		Man absent joined at Fort Randall afterward

Total: 172

Males, under 12 yrs.	Males, over 12 yrs.	Females, under 12 yrs.	Females, over 12 yrs.
27	49	35	61

Appendix D "List of Chiefs, Headmen, etc., of 'Sitting Bull's' tribe, en-route from Fort Randall to Standing Rock Agency, D.T. [April 13, 1883]"

Sitting Bull	Chief
Red Thunder	old chief, (1st)
Tall as the Cloud	Head man
The man that takes the gun away	"
Looking back Bear	Chief (2nd)
Young red Thunder	"
Mad Dog	"
Bone Club	" Head soldier # 1
White Slow Buffalo	" " " whom S.B. wants as chief
Brave Thunder	Chief
Four Horns	" (oldest chief)
Fire Cloud	"
One Hand	" Head soldier
One Bull (nephew)	Head of police
Black Prairie Chicken	Head soldier. Police man
Standing Kill	" " " "
Yellow Dog	Soldier
Standing Cloud	Head Soldier (chief)
Roan faced Bear	Chief Soldier
Big Legs	Headman
His Speared Pipe	Soldier
Iron Heart	"
Four Horns Jr.	"

Source: NA, RG 393, Entry 19, Letters and Telegrams Received, 1892, Fort Randall Orders Received, 1867–74, Miscellaneous Records 1817–92. See also, for variances, Stanley Vestal, *New Sources of Indian History, 1850–1891* (Norman: University of Oklahoma Press, 1934), pp. 293–94.

Notes

I. NEW POST ON THE UPPER MISSOURI

1. Herbert S. Schell, *History of South Dakota*, 4 ed., rev. John E. Miller (Pierre: South Dakota State Historical Society Press, 2004), pp. 32–36, 40–41, 43; J. Leonard Jennewein and Jane Boorman, eds., *Dakota Panorama* (Pierre, S.D.: Dakota Territory Centennial Commission, 1961), pp. 43, 45, 53; Moses K. Armstrong, "History of Dakota, Montana and Idaho," *South Dakota Historical Collections* 14 (1928): 25. Other expeditions that passed by the future site of Fort Randall included that of Manuel Lisa in 1811, Wilson Price Hunt and the Astorians in the same year, and Joseph Nicholas Nicollet, who topographically surveyed the Upper Missouri valley in 1839. Schell, *History of South Dakota*, pp. 46–47, 62–63.

2. Schell, *History of South Dakota*, pp. 41, 48.

3. Ibid., pp. 49–51.

4. Ibid., pp. 54–55.

5. Ibid., pp. 57–59. For the Leavenworth Expedition, see William R. Nester, *The Arikara War: The First Plains Indian War* (Missoula, Mont.: Mountain Press, 2001). See also, Roger Nichols, "Backdrop for Disaster: Causes of the Arikara War of 1823," *South Dakota History* 14 (Summer 1984): 93–113.

6. Schell, *History of South Dakota*, pp. 59–61, 64.

7. See Richard White, "The Winning of the West: The Expansion of the Western Sioux in the Eighteenth and Nineteenth Centuries," *Journal of American History* 65 (September 1978): 321, 324–25, 330–32.

8. Schell, *History of South Dakota*, pp. 65–66.

9. Ibid., p. 66. These synopses of the Grattan affair and Harney's attack on the Lakotas near Ash Hollow, along with precursor events, are drawn from Richmond L. Clow, "General William S. Harney on the Northern Plains," *South Dakota History* 16 (Fall 1986): 229–48; and Jerome A. Greene, *Reconnaissance Survey of Indian–U.S. Army Battlefields of the Northern Plains* (Denver: National Park Service, 1998), pp. 14–15. For a comprehensive treatment, see R. Eli Paul, *Blue Water Creek and the First Sioux War* (Norman: University of Oklahoma Press, 2004). Harney's biography appears in George Rollie Adams, *General William S. Harney: Prince of Dragoons* (Lincoln: University of Nebraska Press, 2001).

10. Augustus Meyers, "Dakota in the Fifties," *South Dakota Historical Col-*

lections 10 (1920): 132–34, 139; William Maxwell Blackburn, "A History of Dakota," ed. DeLorme W. Robinson, *South Dakota Historical Collections* 1 (1902): 105–6. Previous fur posts near the mouth of the Bad River were Fort Teton, 1817–22, and Fort Tecumseh, 1822–32. Doane Robinson, comp., *Doane Robinson's Encyclopedia of South Dakota* (Pierre, S.D.: Published by the author, 1925), p. 260; George W. Kingsbury, *History of Dakota Territory*, with George Martin Smith, *South Dakota: Its History and Its People*, 5 vols. (Chicago: S. J. Clarke, 1950), 1:63–64 (hereafter cited as Kingsbury and Smith, *South Dakota*). Harney had visited the area thirty years earlier as a member of the Atkinson-O'Fallon Expedition of 1825. Adams, *General William S. Harney*, pp. 28–29. The buildings are discussed in Parmenas Taylor Turnley, *Reminiscences of Parmenas Taylor Turnley, from the Cradle to Three-Score and Ten* (Chicago: Donohue and Henneberry, 1893), pp. 127–29, but see also Timothy R. Nowak, "From Fort Pierre to Fort Randall: The Army's First Use of Portable Cottages," *South Dakota History* 32 (Summer 2002): 95–116.

11. Meyers, "Dakota in the Fifties," p. 169.

12. "Official Correspondence Relating to Fort Pierre," *South Dakota Historical Collections* 1 (1902): 431; Adams, *General William S. Harney*, p. 136; Meyers, "Dakota in the Fifties," p. 169 (see also pp. 154–65 for an explicit remembrance of the winter of 1855–56 at Fort Pierre. A particularly graphic secondary account is in Robert G. Athearn, *Forts of the Upper Missouri* [Englewood Cliffs, N.J.: Prentice-Hall, 1967], p. 46); Ray H. Mattison, "Report on the Historic Sites in the Big Bend Reservoir Area, Missouri River, South Dakota," *South Dakota Historical Collections* 31 (1962): 280; and Robinson, *Encyclopedia of South Dakota*, p. 260.

13. Harney's remark, seemingly indicting Captain Wessells, is quoted from his December 1855 report in Frederick T. Wilson, "Fort Pierre and Its Neighbors," *South Dakota Historical Collections* 1 (1902): 286–87.

14. Wilson, "Fort Pierre," pp. 288–89; "Official Correspondence Relating to Fort Pierre," p. 431; Robinson, *Encyclopedia of South Dakota*, pp. 259–60; "Lyman County," *South Dakota Historical Collections* 12 (1924): 256; Brenda K. Jackson, "Holding Down the Fort: A History of Dakota Territory's Fort Randall," *South Dakota History* 32 (Spring 2002): 3. Details of the erection and brief existence of Fort Lookout can be found in Meyers, "Dakota in the Fifties," pp. 175–85. Troops from Fort Ridgely occupied Fort Pierre from 1856 to 1858. Kingsbury and Smith, *South Dakota*, 1:66. For the archaeology of the Fort Lookout fur-trading post, see Carl F. Miller, *The Excavation and Investigation of Fort Lookout Trading Post*

(39LM57) in the Fort Randall Reservoir, South Dakota, River Basin Surveys Papers, No. 17, Bureau of American Ethnology Bulletin 176 (Washington, D.C.: Government Printing Office, 1960).

15. Harney to Adjutant General, June 30, 1856, National Archives (NA), Record Group (RG) 393, Part 1, Entry 5504A, "Letters Sent by the Sioux Expedition, 1855–56"; "Official Correspondence Relating to Fort Pierre," p. 428. Daniel Randall, born in Maryland and appointed to the army from the District of Columbia, became assistant paymaster in 1814. Discharged after the War of 1812, he was appointed regimental paymaster (major) of the First Infantry in July 1818 and became deputy paymaster general of the army (lieutenant colonel) in March 1847. Randall died on December 17, 1851. Francis B. Heitman, comp., *Historical Register and Dictionary of the United States Army, from Its Organization, September 29, 1789, to March 2, 1903*, 2 vols. (Washington, D.C.: Government Printing Office, 1903), 1:814.

16. Harney to Adjutant General, June 30, 1856.

17. Wilson, "Fort Pierre," pp. 289–92; Kingsbury and Smith, *South Dakota*, 1:65–66; Carlton W. Kenyon, "History of Fort Randall" (master's thesis, University of South Dakota, 1947), p. 17.

18. Post Returns, Fort Randall, June, July, August 1856, NA, RG 94, Records of the Adjutant General's Office, NA Microfilm Publication M617, Roll 988, Post Returns, Fort Randall, 1867–79 (hereafter cited as Post Returns); Willard B. Robinson, *American Forts: Architectural Form and Function* (Urbana: University of Illinois Press, 1977), pp. 141, 183.

19. Post Returns, August, September 1856; *Report of the Secretary of War, 1856* (Washington, D.C.: A. O. P. Nicholson, 1857), p. 240; Fort Randall Medical History of Post, p. 4, NA, RG 94, Records of the Adjutant General's Office, Entry 547, Post Histories, Box 3, Microfilm copy, Nebraska State Historical Society, Lincoln (hereafter cited as Medical History); Turnley, *Reminiscences*, pp. 179–81. Harney's July 1856 directive, evidently subsequently modified, called for the placement at Fort Randall of Companies D, E, H, and K, Second Dragoons, along with regimental headquarters and four companies of the Second Infantry, all in the charge of the junior major of the Second Infantry. "Official Correspondence Relating to Fort Pierre," pp. 434–35. Despite the initial advantages of the location of Fort Randall, Colonel Lee concluded that the site lacked sufficient timber, building stone, and forage, and that the Missouri was undependable for transportation because it was either too low or frozen during parts of the year. He promoted yet another location near the bur-

geoning town of Sioux City and believed that the Indians could be effectively controlled from that point. Athearn, *Forts of the Upper Missouri*, pp. 54–55.

20. Meyers, "Dakota in the Fifties," p. 185.

21. Ibid., p. 186; Kingsbury and Smith, *South Dakota*, 1:292; Merrill J. Mattes, "Report on Historic Sites in the Fort Randall Reservoir Area, Missouri River, South Dakota," *South Dakota Historical Collections* 24 (1949): 482. The "beautifully situated" quotation is in a transcribed note from St. Louis's *Missouri Republican*, July 4, 1856, reproduced in *Nebraska State Historical Society Publications* 20 (1922): 285, copy in the O. B. Talley Collection, SC122, "Explorers, Roads, South Dakota," Sioux City Public Museum, Sioux City, Iowa. In later plats of Fort Randall, ca. 1870s, a number of "Old Indian Mounds"—possibly burial mounds—appear just west of the north end of the quadrangle. It appears that the presence and proximity of these knolls, if in fact identified as such in 1856, deterred neither the selection of the site or the construction of the post. See Plat, "Fort Randall, Dakota Territory," in John S. Billings, *Report on Hygiene of the United States Army with Descriptions of Military Posts*, Circular No. 8, War Department, Surgeon General's Office, May 1, 1875 (reprint, New York: Sol Lewis, 1974), following p. 418.

22. Meyers, "Dakota in the Fifties," p. 186.

23. *Report of the Secretary of War, 1857* (Washington, D.C.: William A. Harris, 1857), p. 255; Meyers, "Dakota in the Fifties," pp. 186–88; Kenyon, "History of Fort Randall," p. 16.

24. Fort Randall, Nebraska Territory, 1856, NA, RG 49, Records of the General Land Office. This map appears on the reverse of a town-site plat entitled "Townsite File, Bellevue, Nebraska."

25. *Missouri Republican*, September 18, 1858, reproduced in *Nebraska State Historical Society Publications* 20 (1922): 315.

26. John S. Billings, *Report on Barracks and Hospitals with Descriptions of Military Posts*, Circular No. 4, War Department, Surgeon General's Office, December 5, 1870 (reprint, New York: Sol Lewis, 1974), p. 387.

27. *Sioux City Eagle*, October 23, 1858.

28. Meyers, "Dakota in the Fifties," p. 187; Taylor, *Reminiscences*, p. 192; Kenyon, "History of Fort Randall," p. 21. Todd was cousin to Mary Todd Lincoln, a relationship he exploited with Washington, D.C., contacts. He and his trader partner, Daniel M. Frost, owned the largest wholesale storehouse in Sioux City. Todd's involvement in business and in area politics increased thereafter, and he later served as delegate to Congress from Da-

kota Territory. David M. Delo, *Peddlers and Post Traders: The Army Sutler on the Frontier* (Helena, Mont.: Kingfisher Books, 1998), p. 99; Ray H. Mattison, ed., "The Harney Expedition against the Sioux: The Journal of Capt. John B. S. Todd," *Nebraska History* 43 (June 1962): 130.

29. "Journal of Dr. Elias J. Marsh: Account of a Steamboat Trip on the Missouri River, May–August 1859," *South Dakota Historical Review* 1 (January 1936): 90.

30. *Sioux City Register*, March 31, 1859.

31. Adjutant General to Commanding Officer, Fort Randall, March 27, 1858, Captain Henry W. Wessells, Second Infantry, to Colonel Samuel Cooper, July 4, 1858, and Lieutenant Colonel George W. Lay to Wessells, September 4, 1858, all three in NA, RG 393, Entry 6, Letters and Telegrams Received, Fort Randall, S.D., Box 1; *Sioux City Register*, May 26, 1859. Boosters promoted the post as a future major depot affording markets for goods for use in regional garrisons throughout Minnesota and Nebraska (including Dakota), as well as for those projected farther up the Missouri. The depot issue became major, with supporters later blaming territorial congressional delegate John B. S. Todd (the former Fort Randall post sutler) for failing to create the depot. *Weekly Dakotian*, June 27, September 14, 1861, August 19, 1862.

32. Meyers, "Dakota in the Fifties," p. 186; Turnley, *Reminiscences*, pp. 180–84, 188–96; Athearn, *Forts of the Upper Missouri*, p. 55; Kenyon, "History of Fort Randall," p. 22.

33. *Sioux City Register*, May 19, 1859.

34. *Sioux City Eagle*, January 30, 1858.

35. *Sioux City Eagle*, November 7, 1857, April 17, 1858, May 21, 1859; *Sioux City Times*, January 30, 1858; *Sioux City Register*, April 21, 1859. One of the earliest beef contractors for Fort Randall was Alpheus G. Fuller of the Yankton Indian Agency. "The Census of 1860," *South Dakota Historical Collections* 10 (1920): 415.

36. Proceedings of Post Council of Administration, Fort Randall, August 13, 1856, December 31, 1858, February 1859, NA, RG 393, Part 5, Entry 14, Vol. 1, Fort Randall, S.D. Captain Nathaniel Lyon, while endorsing the school concept, did not support the notion of a chaplain's post, fearing that the religious component would produce an "indoctrinating school." See his discourse ibid. Similarly, post commander Wessells believed that the "employment of Chaplains for religious instruction of a Sectarian character is inexpedient and can be of no practical utility to the post." Ibid. Kenyon stated that a school for dependent children run by Dr.

Franklin Caulkins operated at the fort during the winter of 1856–57. Kenyon, "History of Fort Randall," p. 23.

37. "Inventory of the Effects of Private Daniel Harting of Comp'y 'H' 4th Arty, Deceased," Proceedings of Post Council of Administration, Fort Randall, August 12, 1859, NA, RG 393, Part 5, Entry 14, Vol. 1, Fort Randall, S.D.; Randy Steffen, *The Horse Soldier, 1776–1943*, 4 vols. (Norman: University of Oklahoma Press, 1978), 2:34ff; John Langellier and Bill Younghusband, *U.S. Dragoons, 1833–55* (London: Osprey Military, 1995), p. 45 and passim; Gregory J. W. Urwin, *The United States Infantry: An Illustrated History, 1775–1918* (London: Blandford Press, 1988), pp. 82–83. Augustus Meyers remembered that the formal change in uniform pattern instituted in 1855 occurred at Fort Randall during his tenure there. Among other things, the new uniform hat "was made of stiff black felt with a broad brim and a high crown [the M1855 Hardee hat]. The brim was looped up on the right side and fastened with a brass eagle, otherwise it would have interfered when the soldier had his gun at 'shoulder-arms.' On the front was a brass bugle with the regimental number in the centre of it and a brass letter of the company above it. Around the hat was a worsted cord with tassels of light blue for the infantry. A single black feather or plume was fastened on the left side of the hat, which few of the soldiers knew how or cared to keep curled neatly. In damp weather it looked like a drenched rooster's tail-feathers." Meyers, "Dakota in the Fifties," p. 188.

38. Meyers, "Dakota in the Fifties," pp. 187, 192; Athearn, *Forts of the Upper Missouri*, pp. 55–56. For an especially graphic description of flogging at Fort Randall, see Meyers, "Dakota in the Fifties," pp. 189–90.

39. Meyers, "Dakota in the Fifties," p. 188.

40. Patricia Y. Stallard, *Glittering Misery: Dependents of the Indian Fighting Army* (Fort Collins, Colo.: Old Army Press, 1978), pp. 53–55, 57, 59, 61. Laundresses are addressed in *Regulations for the Army of the United States, 1857* (New York: Harper and Brothers, 1857), paragraphs 124–26, 764, 1,026, 1,133 and page 212; and *Revised Regulations for the Army of the United States, 1861* (Philadelphia: J. B. Lippincott, 1861), pp. 24, 35, 112, 132, 284, 343. For insights into the lives of civilian dependents on the frontier, see Stallard, *Glittering Misery*, and Anne Bruner Eales, *Army Wives on the American Frontier: Living by the Bugles* (Boulder, Colo.: Johnson Books, 1996).

41. *Report of the Secretary of War, 1857*, pp. 72–73; Medical History; Post Re-

turns, July, September 1859; *Sioux City Eagle*, July 4, 1857, June 12, October 23, 1858, June 25, July 16, 1859.

42. *Sioux City Eagle*, July 4, 1857; Post Returns, January 1858; Medical History; Kenyon, "History of Fort Randall," pp. 24 (citing *Report of the Secretary of the Interior, 1857*, pp. 381–82), 27. For Fort Union, see Barton H. Barbour, *Fort Union and the Upper Missouri Fur Trade* (Norman: University of Oklahoma Press, 2001).

43. Quoted in "General Warren in South Dakota," *South Dakota Historical Collections* 11 (1922): 163.

44. "General Warren in South Dakota," pp. 59, 145, 163, 202–3; Vincent J. Flanagan, "Gouverneur Kemble Warren, Explorer of the Nebraska Territory," *Nebraska History* 51 (Summer 1970): 171, 190–93. See also James D. McLaird and Lesta V. Turchen, "Exploring the Black Hills, 1855–1875: Reports of the Government Expeditions," *South Dakota History* 3 (Fall 1973): 359–89.

2. INDIAN NEIGHBORS

1. *Missouri Republican*, September 18, 1858, reproduced in *Nebraska State Historical Society Publications* 20 (1922): 315.

2. For the Lakotas, see Royal B. Hassrick, *The Sioux: Life and Customs of a Warrior Society* (Norman: University of Oklahoma Press, 1964); for the Northern Cheyennes, see John H. Moore, *The Cheyenne Nation: A Social and Demographic History* (Lincoln: University of Nebraska Press, 1987); for the Santees, see Roy W. Meyer, *History of the Santee Sioux: United States Indian Policy on Trial* (Lincoln: University of Nebraska Press, 1967). See also the following articles in William C. Sturtevant, gen. ed., *Handbook of North American Indians*, vol. 13, *Plains*, ed. Raymond J. DeMallie, 2 parts (Washington, D.C. Smithsonian Institution, 2001), Part 2: Raymond J. DeMallie, "Teton," pp. 794–820; John H. Moore, Margot P. Liberty, and A. Terry Strauss, "Cheyenne," pp. 863–85; and Patricia C. Alberts, "Santee," pp. 761–76. In addition, for government treatment of the Yanktons, Poncas, and other area tribes, see the appropriate parts of David J. Wishart, *An Unspeakable Sadness: The Dispossession of the Nebraska Indians* (Lincoln: University of Nebraska Press, 1994).

3. Raymond J. DeMallie, "Yankton and Yanktonai," in DeMallie, *Plains*, 2:777–78. See also Frederick W. Hodge, ed., *Handbook of American Indians North of Mexico*, 2 parts (Washington, D.C.: Government Printing Office, 1910), 2:989–90.

4. See "Treaty with the Sioux, etc., 1825," "Treaty with the Teton, etc., Sioux, 1825," "Treaty with the Sauk and Foxes, etc., 1830," "Treaty with the Oto, etc., 1836," and "Treaty with the Yankton Sioux, 1837," all in Charles J. Kappler, comp., ed., *Indian Treaties, 1778–1883* (reprint of vol. 2 of *Indian Affairs: Laws and Treaties* [Washington, D.C.: Government Printing Office, 1904], New York: Interland, 1972).

5. Harney had President Franklin Pierce's assent to treat with the tribes over provisions relative to events extending mostly from the Grattan affair, in the aftermath of Harney's assault on the tribesmen at Blue Water Creek. See "Minutes of a council held at Fort Pierre, Nebraska Territory, on the 1st day of March 1856, by Brevet Brigadier General William S. Harney, United States army, commanding the Sioux expedition, with the delegations from nine of the bands of the Sioux," in *Senate Executive Documents*, 34th Cong., 1st sess., 1855–56, No. 94, Serial 859. An enlisted man's account of the proceedings appears in Meyers, "Dakota in the Fifties," pp. 167–69.

6. DeMallie, "Yankton," p. 779; *Dakota Union*, July 5, 1864.

7. Kappler, *Indian Treaties*, p. 779.

8. *Dakota Union*, July 5, 1864; Kappler, *Indian Treaties*, pp. 776–81; Will G. Robinson, comp., "Digest of Reports of the Commissioners of Indian Affairs—1853–1869," *South Dakota Historical Collections* 27 (1954): 249; Harold Edward Briggs, "Early History of Clay County," *South Dakota Historical Collections* 13 (1926): 76–77.

9. DeMallie, "Yankton," pp. 779–80.

10. Kappler, *Indian Treaties*, p. 772.

11. Donald N. Brown and Lee Irwin, "Ponca," in DeMallie, *Plains*, 1:416–22, 424–26; Hodge, *Handbook of Indians North of Mexico*, 2:278–79; Kappler, *Indian Treaties*, pp. 140, 225–27, 772–75; Anthony McGinnis, *Counting Coup and Cutting Horses: Intertribal Warfare on the Northern Plains, 1738–1889* (Evergreen, Colo.: Cordillera Press, 1990), pp. 96–97. Details of the conditions existing among the Poncas preceding and following their acceptance of the Treaty of 1858 are in Charles Mulhair, *Ponca Agency* (Niobrara, Neb.: privately published, 1992), pp. 1–9. Other treaties that historically affected what became the Fort Randall lands were: Treaty with the Delawares, July 17, 1854, Treaty with the Kickapoos, July 17, 1854, Treaty with the Omahas, June 21, 1854, Treaty with the Iowas, July 17, 1854, Treaty with the Sac and Fox Indians, July 17, 1854, and Treaty with the Oto and Missouri Indians, April 10, 1855, all in NA,

RG 393, Fort Randall, S.D., Letters and Telegrams Received, 1892, Fort Randall Orders Received, 1867–74, Miscellaneous Records, 1817–92.

12. Doane Robinson, "Before the Settlers Came," *South Dakota Historical Collections* 12 (1924): 196; Schell, *History of South Dakota*, p. 71; Athearn, *Forts of the Upper Missouri*, pp. 56–57; Armstrong, "History of Dakota," pp. 36–37; Blackburn, "History of Dakota," p. 115.

13. Robinson, "Digest of Reports," pp. 249–52; Athearn, *Forts of the Upper Missouri*, pp. 70–71.

14. Kenyon, "History of Fort Randall," p. 24; *Missouri Republican*, September 18, 1858, reproduced in *Nebraska State Historical Society Publications* 20 (1922): 315; "Journal of Dr. Elias J. Marsh," p. 120.

15. Meyers, "Dakota in the Fifties," p. 191.

16. "Journal of Dr. Elias J. Marsh," p. 90.

17. First Lieutenant Joseph C. Clark, Fourth Artillery, to First Lieutenant Louis H. Pelouze, March 10, 1860, transmitting "Survey of the 'Military Reservation' at this post," including map, copy in Vertical Files, State Archives Collection, South Dakota State Historical Society, Pierre; "Survey of the 'Military Reservation' at this post," in Billings, *Report on Hygiene of the United States Army*, pp. 417–18 (which states the boundary erroneously); Medical History, pp. 1–4 (including map); Charles L. Green, "The Administration of the Public Domain in South Dakota," *South Dakota Historical Collections* 20 (1940): 147–48. The haying agreement is contained in "Articles of agreement between Q.M. (& A.Q.M. of Fort Randall) & agent of Yankton Indians," NA, RG 393, Entry 6, Letters and Telegrams Received, Fort Randall, S.D., Box 1.

18. Charles E. Hanson, "The Fort Pierre–Fort Laramie Trail," *Museum of the Fur Trade Quarterly* 1 (Summer 1965): 3–7; James A. Hanson, "A Forgotten Fur Trade Trail," *Nebraska History* 68 (Spring 1987): 2–9.

19. Hyman Palais, "South Dakota Stage and Wagon Roads," *South Dakota Historical Collections* 25 (1950): 218, 249; F. M. Ziebach to O. B. Talley, December 7, 1922, O. B. Talley Collection, SC 122, "Explorers, Roads, South Dakota," Sioux City Public Museum; "Old South Dakota Trails," *South Dakota Historical Collections* 14 (1924): 152; *Weekly Dakotian*, July 6, 1861; *Dakotian*, October 6, 1863; *Union and Dakotian*, August 26, 1865; "Old Fort Randall Military Road Revisited," *Fort Randall Independent* 5 (October 1996): 4–5; Briggs, "Early History of Clay County," pp. 92–93. In the late 1850s, mail delivery between Sioux City and Fort Randall was via horseback. "Census of 1860," p. 417. In 1861, W. W. Marsh and Company

of Sioux City operated a "United States Mail and Express Line" that departed the city at 5 A.M. every Sunday and Wednesday, and departed Fort Randall at 8 A.M. each Sunday and Wednesday. *Weekly Dakotian*, July 13, 1861.

20. "General Warren in South Dakota," p. 202.

21. William H. Goetzmann, *Army Exploration in the American West, 1803–1863* (New Haven, Conn.: Yale University Press, 1959), p. 415; R. Jay Roberts, "History of Agate Springs," *Nebraska History* 47 (September 1966): 268–71; "Report of A. A. Humphreys," November 20, 1858, in *Report of the Secretary of War, 1858* (Washington, D.C.: William A. Harris, 1859), pp. 585–86 (much of this is reprinted in "General Warren in South Dakota," pp. 136–37, 145, 202–3).

22. "Report of Lieut. G. K. Warren," in *Report of the Secretary of War, 1858*, p. 669.

23. *Union and Dakotian*, May 6, 1865.

24. *Weekly Dakotian*, June 10, 1862; *Dakotian*, April 19, 1864; *Dakota Union*, July 26, 1864; LeRoy R. Hafen and Ann W. Hafen, comps., *Powder River Campaigns and Sawyers Expedition of 1865* (Glendale, Calif.: Arthur H. Clark, 1961), pp. 220–353, including James A. Sawyers's official report, pp. 224–85; *Union and Dakotian*, December 16, 1865, December 8, 1866. A concise description of the efforts to establish wagon roads across Dakota to the gold country is in Schell, *History of South Dakota*, pp. 80–82.

25. Palais, "South Dakota Stage and Wagon Roads," pp. 220 (map), 250–51, 254, 256; "Memorial and Joint Resolution Relative to a mail route, Dakota City to Fort Randall," transcribed copy in O. B. Talley Collection, SC 122, Vol. 5, File 2, "Road from Omadi to Omaha Indian Reservation," Sioux City Public Museum; Jennewein and Boorman, *Dakota Panorama*, p. 300.

26. *Weekly Dakotian*, June 27, 1861.

27. The impact of frontier forts as harbingers of settlement and as instigators of regional community and economic growth is discussed in Michael L. Tate, *The Frontier Army in the Settlement of the West* (Norman: University of Oklahoma Press, 1999), especially pp. 111–35.

3. WARTIME

1. The politics of the creation and existence of Dakota Territory, together with their interplay with and backdrop for the military institutions there, including Fort Randall, are thoroughly addressed in Howard Roberts Lamar, *Dakota Territory, 1861–1889: A Study of Frontier Politics* (New Haven, Conn.: Yale University Press, 1956).

2. *Report of the Secretary of War, 1860* (Washington, D.C.: Government Printing Office, 1860), pp. 216–17; Raphael P. Thian, comp., *Notes Illustrating the Military Geography of the United States, 1813–1880* (Washington,
   D.C.: Adjutant General's Office, 1881; reprint, Austin: University of Texas
   Press, 1979), pp. 67, 82, 106–7; Athearn, *Forts of the Upper Missouri*, pp.
   71–72; *Sioux City Times*, May 4, June 1, 1860;; Kingsbury and Smith,
   South Dakota, 1:67–68; Jennewein and Boorman, *Dakota Panorama*, pp.
   285, 287; *Report of the Secretary of War, 1861* (Washington, D.C.: Government Printing Office, 1861), p. 54; Jackson, "Holding Down the Fort,"
   p. 9. The *Sioux City Register*, June 6, March 9, and April 13, 1861, reported
   on several officers at Fort Randall who resigned and joined the Confed-
   erates. Cited in Jennewein and Boorman, *Dakota Panorama*, pp. 278–79.

3. John Pattee, "Dakota Campaigns," *South Dakota Historical Collections* 5
   (1910): 277; Sergeant Amos R. Cherry, Company A, Fourteenth Iowa Infantry, quoted in Athearn, *Forts of the Upper Missouri*, pp. 73–74.

4. William Waldron to uncle, March 2, 1862, Manuscripts Archive, H75.88,
   Folder 1, South Dakota State Historical Society, Pierre.

5. Pattee, "Dakota Campaigns," pp. 278–82; *Weekly Dakotian*, June 3, 1862;
   A. M. English, "Dakota's First Soldiers: History of the First Dakota Cavalry, 1862–1865," *South Dakota Historical Collections* 9 (1918): 241–42;
   Athearn, *Forts of the Upper Missouri*, p. 75; Jennewein and Boorman, *Dakota Panorama*, pp. 284–85, 290–91. Company A, First Dakota Volunteer Cavalry, was mustered in at Yankton on April 30, 1862, to serve
   three years or the duration of the Civil War. English, "Dakota's First Soldiers," p. 243. On May 29, 1862, Governor Jayne wrote Secretary of War
   Edwin M. Stanton asking permission to raise two companies of volunteers "to garrison Fort Randall . . . and thus relieve the three companies of
   the Fourteenth Regiment of Iowa Volunteers now garrisoning Fort Randall." *The War of the Rebellion: A Compilation of the Official Records of the
   Union and Confederate Armies*, 70 vols. (Washington, D.C.: Government
   Printing Office, 1880–1902), Series 3, 2:96.

6. Quoted in Athearn, *Forts of the Upper Missouri*, p. 77.

7. Ibid.

8. Ibid., pp. 78–79. Todd was a West Point graduate, class of 1837. Heitman,
   Historical Register and Dictionary, 1:964; Jennewein and Boorman, *Dakota Panorama*, p. 292.

9. Robinson, "Digest of Reports," pp. 308–9; *Weekly Dakotian*, July 1, November 11, 1862.

10. The Santee Sioux outbreak in Minnesota is covered in all its aspects in

Alvin M. Josephy, Jr., *The Civil War in the American West* (New York: Alfred A. Knopf, 1991), pp. 95–154. See also Robert M. Utley, *Frontiersmen in Blue: The United States Army and the Indian, 1848–1865* (New York: Macmillan, 1967), pp. 70–71ff.

11. *Weekly Dakotian*, November 11, 1862.

12. Hoffman to Gov. William Jayne, September 17–19, 1862, reproduced in Mulhair, *Ponca Agency*, pp. 15–19. The general atmosphere among friendly, or "treaty," tribes is recounted in Michael A. Sievers, "Westward by Indian Treaty: The Upper Missouri Example," *Nebraska History* 56 (Spring 1975): 77–78.

13. *Weekly Dakotian*, September 30, 1862.

14. Ibid.

15. Ibid., November 11, 1862.

16. Ibid., September 30, 1862.

17. Jennewein and Boorman, *Dakota Panorama*, pp. 292–96. Governor Jayne's proclamation of August 30, 1862, appears in the *Weekly Dakotian*, September 15, 1862.

18. For more details relating to the white captives and subsequent campaigning, see Pattee, "Dakota Campaigns," pp. 284–86; English, "Dakota's First Soldiers," pp. 260–64; *Weekly Dakotian*, November 19, 1862, January 29, February 3, 1863; "Lyman County," p. 255; Jennewein and Boorman, *Dakota Panorama*, pp. 299–300; Robinson, "Digest of Reports," pp. 342–43. See also the account of the trek by Private Horace Austin of Company A, First Dakota Cavalry, in his letters to mother and sister, December 3, 1862, and mother, December 1, 1862 (apparently should be January 1, 1863), Horace Austin Collection. I. D. Weeks Library, University of South Dakota, Vermillion.

19. English, "Dakota's First Soldiers," pp. 265 (and n. 79), 267–68; Pattee, "Dakota Campaigns," pp. 291–302; Jennewein and Boorman, *Dakota Panorama*, pp. 299–300; Robinson, "Digest of Reports," pp. 342–43; *Weekly Dakotian*, November 19, 25, 1862, May 26, June 23, July 7, September 22, 1863; "Lyman County," pp. 300–301; Richard N. Ellis, *General Pope and U.S. Indian Policy* (Albuquerque: University of New Mexico Press, 1970), p. 16. Many of the operations of the Dakota troops during this period are presented in English, "Dakota's First Soldiers," pp. 244–60. An account of the pursuit of the killers of Sergeant Trask appears in the *Weekly Dakotian*, September 29, 1863.

20. *Weekly Dakotian*, November 25, 1862. This military district was later reconfigured to the District of Iowa.

21. *Weekly Dakotian*, July 7, 1863, NA, RG 393, Entry 6, Letters and Telegrams Received, Fort Randall, S.D., Box 1.

22. *Weekly Dakotian*, June 9, 1863.

23. Ellis, *General Pope*, p. 17. The Sibley-Sully campaigns are treated at length in Josephy, *Civil War in the American West*, pp. 122–54, and Athearn, *Forts of the Upper Missouri*, pp. 108–15.

24. *Weekly Dakotian*, June 30, 1863.

25. Ibid., July 7, 1863.

26. Ibid.

27. Sully to Captain Wolfe, July 6, 1863, NA, RG 393, Entry 6, Letters and Telegrams Received, Fort Randall, S.D., Box 1.

28. *Report of the Secretary of War, 1863* (Washington, D.C.: Government Printing Office, 1863), p. 30; Pope to Major General Henry W. Halleck, February 9, 1864, "Official Correspondence Pertaining to the War of the Outbreak, 1862–1865," *South Dakota Historical Collections* 8 (1916): 174; *Weekly Dakotian*, July 7, September 29, 1863; Wilson, "Fort Pierre," pp. 301–11; Utley, *Frontiersmen in Blue*, pp. 270–75; Jennewein and Boorman, *Dakota Panorama*, pp. 300–304; Robert W. Frazer, *Forts of the West* (Norman: University of Oklahoma Press, 1965), pp. 137–38. General Pope's strategy, as explained to Secretary of War Stanton, was to "leave one entire regiment of cavalry (the Sixth Iowa) this winter on the Upper Missouri, at Fort Randall and Fort Pierre, as an additional precaution against any attempt of the Sioux to recross to the North (East) side of the Missouri River, and again in the spring to visit the entire Indian Nation East of the Rocky Mountains." Pope to Stanton, August 29, 1863, "Official Correspondence" (1916), p. 116.

29. Letter, Lieutenant Colonel John Munroe, April 8, 1860, and J. Shaw Gregory to Captain McGowan, Fort Randall, June 22, 1860, both in NA, RG 393, Entry 6, Letters and Telegrams Received, Fort Randall, S.D., Box 1; *Weekly Dakotian*, July 8, 1862; Mulhair, *Ponca Agency*, pp. 19–22.

30. *Weekly Dakotian*, September 22, October 21, November 19, 1862, January 6, August 4, September 15, December 1, 22, 1863, September 3, 1864; *Weekly Dakota Union*, July 26, 1864.

31. *Weekly Dakotian*, June 3, 16, August 18, 1863; Acting Assistant Adjutant General (Major) James F. Meline to Commanding Officer, Fort Randall, July 28, 1863, NA, RG 393, Entry 6, Letters and Telegrams Received, Fort Randall, S.D., Box 1; Frank Myers, *Soldiering in Dakota, Among the Indians, in 1863–4–5* (Huron, D.T.: Huronite Printing House, 1888; reprint, Pierre: South Dakota State Historical Society, 1936), p. 5. The dependents

took steamboats to Sioux City and dispersed to their homes, mostly in Iowa, for the duration of Sully's Indian campaigns. Because the troops were scattered among the upriver stations, the women and children likely did not return before the regiments were mustered out of service in the fall of 1865.

32. Special Order No. 32, Fort Randall, October 3, 1863, No. 33, October 4, 1863, No. 36, October 6, 1863, No. 38, October 8, 1863, No. 95, November 16, 1863, and No. 93, November 15, 1863, all in Ledger, "Orders 1863 & 1864," NA, RG 393, Part 5, Entry 9, Vol. 1, Fort Randall, S.D.

33. Special Order No. 109, Fort Randall, November 24, 1863, No. 110, November 24, 1863, No. 111, November 24, 1863, and No. 112, November 24, 1863, all ibid.

34. Special Order No. 100, Headquarters, Fort Randall, March 4, 1864, in Ledger, "Orders 1864 & 1865," NA, RG 393, Part 5, Entry 9, Vol. 2, Fort Randall, S.D.; Kenyon, "History of Fort Randall," pp. 41-42.

35. The Yanktonais attack on the mackinaw is detailed in *Weekly Dakotian*, October 28, 1862.

36. Special Orders No. 32, Headquarters, Northwestern Indian Expedition, June 11, 1864, NA, RG 393, Entry 6, Letters and Telegrams Received, Fort Randall, S.D., Box 1; Ellis, *General Pope*, pp. 52-53; Jennewein and Boorman, *Dakota Panorama*, p. 305.

37. Utley, *Frontiersmen in Blue*, pp. 275-79; Athearn, *Forts of the Upper Missouri*, pp. 131-48; Josephy, *Civil War in the American West*, pp. 147-52; Jennewein and Boorman, *Dakota Panorama*, pp. 304-8. For soldiers' accounts of the campaign, see Myers, *Soldiering in Dakota*, pp. 9-32, and English, "Dakota's First Soldiers," pp. 273-99.

38. Agent John W. Douglas to Commissioner of Indian Affairs, August 26, 1878, in *Report of the Commissioner of Indian Affairs, 1878* (Washington, D.C.: Government Printing Office, 1878), p. 544; Pope to Halleck, November 3, 1864, in *War of the Rebellion*, Series 1, Vol. 41, Part 1, pp. 136-37; Kenyon, "History of Fort Randall," pp. 42-43.

39. Sully to Major General Samuel R. Curtis, February 25, 1865, *War of the Rebellion*, Series 1, Vol. 48, Part 2, pp. 979-81; "Organization of troops in the Military Division of the Missouri, Maj. Gen. John Pope, U.S. Army, commanding, February 28, 1865, ibid., p. 1030; *Union and Dakotian*, November 19, 1864; Jennewein and Boorman, *Dakota Panorama*, pp. 302, 314, 316; Utley, *Frontiersmen in Blue*, pp. 322-23, 332-36; Sievers, "Westward by Indian Treaty," p. 80. Sully had earlier asked permission "to alter

the shape of Fort Randall. The buildings, store-houses, stables, etc., are so scattered it takes a guard of about forty-five men to post the necessary sentinels. It is more like a village than a military post." Sully to Assistant Adjutant-General (AAG), Department of the Northwest, February 7, 1865, "Official Correspondence" (1916), p. 534. For the former Confederate prisoners garrisoned along the Missouri River, see Michele Tucker Butts, *Galvanized Yankees on the Upper Missouri: The Face of Loyalty* (Boulder: University Press of Colorado, 2003).

40. Sievers, "Westward by Indian Treaty," pp. 79–82.

41. Pope to Major General Grenville M. Dodge, August 1, 1865, "Official Correspondence Pertaining to the War of the Outbreak, 1862–1865," *South Dakota Historical Collections* 31 (1962): 544–45; Jennewein and Boorman, *Dakota Panorama*, pp. 317, 318.

4. LIFE AT FORT RANDALL

1. Pattee, "Dakota Campaigns," p. 276.

2. Ibid., p. 277; Sergeant Amos R. Cherry, Company A, Fourteenth Iowa Infantry, quoted in Athearn, *Forts of the Upper Missouri*, pp. 73–74.

3. Pattee, "Dakota Campaigns," p. 277; Sergeant Cherry, quoted in Athearn, *Forts of the Upper Missouri*, pp. 74–75.

4. Richard D. Rowen, ed., "The Second Nebraska's Campaign against the Sioux," *Nebraska* History 44 (March 1963): 29 (quoting George P. Belden). See also Special Order No. 182, Fort Randall, December 20, 1863, Ledger, "Orders 1863 & 1864."

5. Athearn, *Forts of the Upper Missouri*, p. 183.

6. *Weekly Dakotian*, August 4, 1863. See also July 7, 1863, and March 1, 1864; Delo, *Peddlers and Post Traders*, p. 198. Late in 1864, the Fort Randall Theater presented several other performances, among them *The Splendid Melo-Drama of the Brigand and his Son*, *The Mischievous Nigger*, *Backwoods Echo*, *Bones*, *Banjo Lesson*, *Brass Band*, and *Front Seats for the Ladies*. *Weekly Dakotian*, December 17, 1864.

7. Martin to brother, December 14, 1861, "Typescript of Lambert Martin Letters," WA MSS S-1036, Yale Collection of Western Americana, Beinecke Rare Book and Manuscript Library, Yale University Library, New Haven, Conn. (hereafter cited as Martin Letters).

8. Martin to parents, December 29, 1861, January 18, March 15, 1862, Martin to brother, January 4, April 15, 1862, Martin to brother and others, January 26, 1862; and Martin to brothers, October 11, 1862, all in Martin

Letters. Similarly, Private William Waldron, also of Company B, echoed Martin's sentiment: "We have plenty to eat such as it is. Bread and coffee, beaf [sic] part of the time, pork part of the time which is marked B.C. and has now come to its resurrection." Waldron to uncle, March 2, 1862.

9. Martin to brother, January 26, 1862, and Martin to parents, March 15, 27, May 18, 1862, all in Martin Letters. Regarding the proximity of Indians, Private Waldron noted: "We . . . are not troubled by the Indians, although there is a band of the Sioux Tribe within 40 miles of the Fort. . . . The boys sometimes get frightened after going to bed. Night before last, after going to bed we heard . . . the report of a gun. One of our mess, Wm. L. Boyd jumped up, hunting for his pants, but could not find them, then declared that he was not going to be caught in bed in case of an actack [sic]. A second thought was his gun and caterages [cartridges] but declared he had no caps but plenty of caterages. In the morning we found that there was 9 shots fired down on the [Yankton] reserve, but it was said to be on the occasion of the death of a squaw." Waldron to uncle, March 2, 1862.

10. Martin to parents, March 27, 1862, and Martin to brother, June 18, 1862, both in Martin Letters.

11. Martin to brother, June 28, 1862, Martin Letters.

12. Martin to brother, July 16, 1862, August 3, 1862, Martin Letters.

13. Martin to parents, May 18, 1862.

14. Martin to parents, March 15, 1862.

15. Martin to parents, April 4, 22, 1862, and Martin to brother, April 23, July 9, 1862, all in Martin Letters.

16. Martin to friends, August 24, 1862, and Martin to parents, September 27, 1862, both in Martin Letters.

17. Martin to friends, August 24, 1862.

18. Martin to parents, February 8, 1862, Martin Letters. One of these ventures is detailed in Lambert A. Martin, "My Experience in Scouting in Dakota Territory," typescript in WA MSS S-1036, Yale Collection of Western Americana, Beinecke Rare Book and Manuscript Library.

19. Martin to parents, September 27, 1862, and Martin to friends, October 5, 1862, both in Martin Letters.

20. Martin to parents, November 11, 1862, Martin Letters.

21. Martin to brother, November 22, 1862, Martin Letters.

22. Martin to parents, December 1, 1862, Martin Letters. Martin went on to say that Major Pattee and the women spoke to the command, thanking the men for their generosity in collecting a purse for them: "We were

then ordered to go forward, leaving the women to go on their way to Randall and we on our way to punish the depridators [*sic*] who are within two days march of Fort Pierre." Martin elaborated on the former captives in a letter to friends dated December 9, 1862: "The children are from five to ten years of age, one a boy, the other girls. One woman [is] about 40 years and the other 25 (a good looking and very intelligent lady), who both are married. The older lady's name was Mrs. Duly, the younger Mrs. Wright."

23. On June 21, Martin wrote home a hearsay account of Lieutenant Colonel Samuel M. Pollock's arrival at Fort Randall: "He arrived on the bank of the river opposite the Fort with his battalion and found the boys of our battalion ferrying Indians across. He asked them what they were at that work for. Corporal of the whole squad [said] that it was the orders of Major Pattee. Says Colonel Pollock, 'I countermand the order, and if Iowa boys are here only to cross Indians they had better go home.'" When Pollock assumed command of the fort, the Indians tried to give him a feast. "He told them that he came there to feast them cold lead if they desired it and was ready to make his first issue at once. They took offense at this whereupon he ordered all the Indians to clear out giving them five minutes to begin to strike teepees and one day to get six miles from the fort." Martin to friends, June 21, 1863, Martin Letters.

24. Martin to parents, July 4, 1863, Martin Letters.

25. Martin to parents, August 2, 1863, and Martin to friends, August 17, 1863, both in Martin Letters.

26. Sergeant Amos Cherry to Alex, January 7, 1864, Martin Letters. Martin's illness was consistent with water-borne dysentery, a plague to large numbers of troops in humid country adjoining water bodies such as the Missouri River, but particularly those stationed in the South during the Civil War.

27. Austin to mother and sister, March 25, 1863, Austin Collection.

28. Ibid.

29. Austin to mother and sister, April 24, May 30, September 9, 1863, and Austin to mother, May 5, 1863, all in Austin Collection.

30. Austin to mother and sister, September 9, 1863, Austin Collection.

31. Austin to mother and sister, October 21, 1863, Austin Collection.

32. Austin to mother, November 17, 1863, Austin Collection.

33. Austin to mother and sister, January 15, 1864, Austin Collection.

34. Austin to mother and sister, February 3, 1864, Austin Collection.

35. Austin to mother, May 25, 1864, Austin Collection.

5. POSTWAR CHANGE

1. General Order No. 21, Headquarters, District of Iowa, Office of the Assistant Adjutant General, April 25, 1865, NA, RG 393, Entry 6, Letters and Telegrams Received, Fort Randall, S.D., Box 1.

2. Robert M. Utley, *Frontier Regulars: The United States Army and the Indian, 1866–1891* (New York: Macmillan 1973), p. 121.

3. Joseph Warren Arnold, "Joseph Warren Arnold's Journal of His Trip to and from Montana, 1864–1866," ed. Charles W. Martin, *Nebraska History* 55 (Winter 1974): 538.

4. Medical History, p. 14.

5. Robert G. Athearn, *William Tecumseh Sherman and the Settlement of the West* (Norman: University of Oklahoma Press, 1956), p. 50; Athearn, *Forts of the Upper Missouri*, p. 215; "Fort Randall, D.T." (Cusick's drawing), NA, RG 77, Records of the Office of the Chief of Engineers. Miscellaneous Forts File, Item 2, "Undated Sketch of Fort Randall." Philippe Regis Denis de Keredern de Trobriand arrived up the river and wrote: "Through the tall trees growing on the bank we saw the buildings, only part of which are surrounded by a palisade [fence]. It is more a post than it is a fort, for the fortifications do not amount to anything." De Trobriand, *Military Life in Dakota: The Journal of Philippe Regis de Trobriand*, trans., ed., Lucile M. Kane (St. Paul, Minn.: Alvord Memorial Association, 1951), p. 28.

6. Circular, Headquarters, Fort Randall, D.T., February 8, 1866, NA, RG 393, Part 5, Entry 8, Vol. 1, Fort Randall, S.D.

7. *Sioux City Times*, August 7, 1869.

8. *Sioux City Daily Times*, December 7, 1869.

9. Orders No. 23, Headquarters, Fort Randall, D.T., February 25, 1866, NA, RG 393, Part 5, Entry 8, Vol. 1, Fort Randall, S.D.; *Report of the Secretary of War, 1867* (Washington, D.C.: Government Printing Office, 1867), p. 42; Medical History, p. 20; Athearn, *Forts of the Upper Missouri*, pp. 215–18; Athearn, *Sherman*, pp. 51–52; Oskaloosa M. Smith, "The Twenty-second Regiment of Infantry," in *The Army of the United States: Historical Sketches of Staff and Line, with Portraits of Generals-in-Chief*, ed. Theophilus F. Rodenbough and William L. Haskin, (New York: Maynard, Merrill, 1896), p. 683; *Union and Dakotian*, July 31, 1869.

10. At the same time, the Third Battalion, Thirteenth Infantry, became the Thirty-first Infantry. See James B. Goe, "The Thirteenth Regiment of Infantry," in *Army of the United States*, ed. Rodenbough and Haskin, p. 580; Smith, "Twenty-second Regiment," pp. 680–81. The term "Galvanized

Rebels" was also used for the Fourth U.S. Volunteers stationed at Fort Randall. Medical History, p. 8.

11. Post Returns, November 1865–July 1869, and as cited in Kenyon, "History of Fort Randall," pp. 52–53, 57–58; Leonard W. Gilchrist, "The Missouri River Journal of Leonard W. Gilchrist, 1866," ed. James E. Potter, *Nebraska History* 58 (Fall 1977): 276 (includes reference to the presence of two companies of the Fourth U.S. Volunteers and one of the Seventh Iowa at the post as of May 22, 1866); General Orders No. 9, Headquarters, Middle District, Fort Sully, D.T., June 11 (?), 1869, NA, RG 393, Entry 19, Letters and Telegrams Received, 1892, Fort Randall Orders Received, 1867–74, Miscellaneous Records, 1817–92; *Report of the Secretary of War, 1867*, pp. 48, 50; *Report of the Secretary of War, 1868* (Washington, D.C.: Government Printing Office, 1868), pp. 33, 738–39; *Report of the Secretary of War, 1869* (Washington, D.C.: Government Printing Office, 1869), pp. 41, 43, 157; *Union and Dakotian*, March 24, November 3, 1866, August 24, October 12, 19, 1867; *Sioux City Times*, November 27, 1869; De Trobriand, *Military Life*, p. 21; Smith, "Twenty-second Regiment," pp. 680–81.

12. *Union and Dakotian*, September 30, 1865, August 11, 1866, July 6, 1867.

13. Orders No. 12, January 30, 1866, Orders No. 24, February 27, 1866, Orders No. 37, April 12, 1866, Orders No. 38, April 14, 1866, General Order No. 1, January 7, 1867, General Order No. 2, January 9, 1867, and General Order No. 9, March 29, 1867, all in Headquarters, Fort Randall, NA, RG 393, Part 5, Entry 8, Vol. 1, Fort Randall, S.D.; Post Order No. 152, Headquarters, Fort Randall, December 30, 1867, Ledger, "Special Orders. Hdqrs Fort Randall, D.T.," NA, RG 393, Part 5, Entry 9, Vol. 3, Fort Randall, S.D. Dryer's remains, along with his family, were escorted via Denison, Iowa, to Detroit. Special Order No. 24, Headquarters, Fort Randall, March 7, 1867, Ledger, "Special Orders. Hdqrs Fort Randall, D.T."; Medical History, p. 8. Six months after Dryer's death, another officer, Second Lieutenant Robert A. Gibson, died at Fort Randall. His funeral took place on September 23, 1867. *Union and Dakotian*, September 28, 1867. Dryer's obituary appeared in the *Army and Navy Journal* 4:542.

14. General Order No. 7, March 10, 1867, Headquarters, Fort Randall, NA, RG 393, Part 5, Entry 8, Vol. 1, Fort Randall, S.D.

15. General Order No. 12, April 4, 1867, ibid.

16. General Order No. 6, April 24, 1868, ibid.

17. Special Order No. 121, Headquarters, Fort Randall, April 1, 1864, NA, RG 393, Part 5, Entry 9, Vol. 2, Fort Randall, S.D.; Special Orders No. 18,

Headquarters, District of Iowa, February 6, 1865, NA, RG 393, Entry 6, Letters and Telegrams Received, Fort Randall, S.D., Box 1; Orders No. 18, February 16, 1866, and General Orders No. 38, October 30, 1870, Headquarters, Fort Randall, NA, RG 393, Part 5, Entry 8, Vol. 1, Fort Randall, S.D. An army engineer observed that "the channel runs close to Randall Point, and is obstructed by loose rocks, causing a very stiff current around the point. At 6.30 [P.M.] we attempted to cross the bar opposite Randall, and ran hard aground. The bar washed from under us very rapidly, and at 12 midnight, washed us across where we lay until morning. . . . This bar is a very troublesome one, and can only be remedied by clearing the channel at the point above, and throwing the water in bulk to the left shore. All the boats down within the last two weeks [early September 1867] have grounded here, and lain from 6 to 48 hours." Charles W. Howell, "An Army Engineer on the Missouri in 1867," ed. Leland R. Johnson, *Nebraska History* 53 (Summer 1972): 283–84.

18. *Independent*, December 27, 1865, January 20, 1866.

19. *Independent*, January 20, 1866.

20. *Independent*, March 29, 1866.

21. *Independent*, December 27, 1865. The issues of the *Independent* for which the South Dakota State Historical Society has copies are those dated November 29, December 20, 27, 1865, and January 20, March 29, 1866.

22. Post Orders No. 83, July 3, 1867, Headquarters, Fort Randall, December 30, 1867, Ledger, "Special Orders. Hdqrs Fort Randall, D.T."; General Orders No. 13, July 3, 1868, Special Order No. 28, August 10, 1866, and Special Order No. 22, March 8, 1867, all Headquarters, Fort Randall, NA, RG 393, Part 5, Entry 8, Vol. 1, Fort Randall, S.D.; *Sioux City Times*, August 28, 1869; *Fort Randall Independent* 5 (December 1996): 1–2.

23. Delos, *Peddlers and Post Traders*, p. 190. As evidence of the sutler store's attraction to nonmilitary personnel, a wayfarer arriving from Montana in September 1866 recorded the following: "Randall is reached at 10 A.M. and a grand stampede is made for the sutler and commissary [sic] department. Here we find a plenty of vegetables, eggs, butter &c. &c., and the miners throw their sacks and boxes over the counter at the clerks and call for eggs by the dozen regardless of the price—in fact they don't ask the price. They want such articles as they call for and will have them, cost what they may. After regaling ourselves in such luxuries as melons the steamer again starts down stream." Gurdon P. Lester, "A Round Trip to the Montana Mines: The 1866 Travel Journal of Gurdon P. Lester," ed. Charles W. Martin, *Nebraska History* 46 (December 1965): 311.

24. *Weekly Dakotian,* November 11, 1862; *Independent,* December 6, 1865, January 20, 1866; Special Orders No. 127, Headquarters, Department of Dakota, August 25, 1869, NA, RG 393, Entry 19, Letter and Telegrams Received, 1892, Fort Randall Orders Received, 1867–74, Miscellaneous Records, 1817–92; General Order No. 54, August 9, 1866, General Order No. 60, November 24, 1866, and General Order No. 9, March 29, 1867, all Headquarters, Fort Randall, NA, RG 393, Part 5, Entry 8, Vol. 1, Fort Randall, S.D.; Post Orders No. 108, September 17, 1867, Ledger, "Special Orders. Hdqrs Fort Randall, D.T."; General Orders No. 3, Headquarters, Middle District, Fort Sully, D.T., May 9, 1869, NA, RG 393, Entry 19, Letters and Telegrams Received, 1892, Fort Randall Orders Received, 1867–74, Miscellaneous Records, 1817–92.

25. *Union and Dakotian,* October 20, 27, November 24, 1866; Acting County Attorney George H. Hand to Major Joseph Whistler, October 1, 1869, NA, RG 393, Entry 6, Letters and Telegrams Received, Fort Randall, S.D., Box 2.

26. *Union and Dakotian,* December 8, 1866; AAG, Department of Dakota, to Commanding Officer, Fort Randall, June 18, 1867, and AAG, Headquarters, Division of the Missouri, to AAG, Headquarters, District of Southeastern Dakota, May 16, 1868, both in NA, RG 393, Entry 6, Letters and Telegrams Received, Fort Randall, S.D. Box 2; Athearn, *Forts of the Upper Missouri,* pp. 230–31.

27. William P. Dole to Secretary of the Interior, November 15, 1864, and Clark W. Thompson to Superintendent of Indian Affairs, St. Paul, October 1, 1864, in Robinson, "Digest of Reports," pp. 351–52, 371–73; Schell, *History of South Dakota,* p. 90; Kenyon, "History of Fort Randall," p. 44; Kappler, *Indian Treaties,* pp. 874–75. The "Peace Policy" was President Grant's initiative to remove the Indians to reservations and to effect their acculturation and assimilation into white society using agents appointed from various religious denominations, such as Catholic, Methodist, Baptist, Quaker, Episcopalian, Presbyterian, and Congregationalist. The policy enjoyed mixed success, at best, largely due to congressional negligence in legislating sufficient appropriations to enable change. Its best explication can be found in Henry E. Fritz, *The Movement for Indian Assimilation, 1860–1890* (Philadelphia: University of Pennsylvania Press, 1963), pp. 135–67.

28. Schell, *History of South Dakota,* pp. 86–88; Kenyon, "History of Fort Randall," p. 46; Athearn, *Forts of the Upper Missouri,* pp. 207–11; Sievers, "Westward by Indian Treaty," pp. 80–86. The Fort Sully treaties with the

Upper and Lower Yanktonais and the Minneconjous, Hunkpapas, Oglalas, Brulés, Blackfeet Sioux, Two Kettles, and Sans Arcs of October 10–
28, 1865, appear in Kappler, *Indian Treaties*, pp. 883–87, 896–908.

29. Schell, *History of South Dakota*, pp. 90–92; *Union and Dakotian*, December 8, 1866; Roy W. Meyer, "The Establishment of the Santee Reservation, 1866–1869," *Nebraska History* 45 (March 1964): 62–63; Ernest L.
Shusky, *The Forgotten Sioux: An Ethnohistory of the Lower Brulé Reservation* (Chicago: Nelson-Hall, 1975), pp. 74–75.

30. Red Cloud's War was named after the Oglala Lakota chief who resisted
U.S. Army presence in what is today northern Wyoming and southeastern Montana between 1866 and 1868. Several notable engagements occurred, including the so-called Fort Phil Kearny Massacre, in which the
Lakotas, Northern Cheyennes, and Northern Arapahos wiped out a command from that post. Utley, *Frontier Regulars*, pp. 93–110.

31. Letter from post surgeon Hackenburg, August 1, 1868, to *Hudson Daily
Star*, undated clipping in Medical History.

32. Adams, *General William S. Harney*, pp. 264–65; Report of Captain De-
Witt C. Poole, August 20, 1869, in Will G. Robinson, comp. "Digest of the
Reports of the Commissioner of Indian Affairs as Pertains to Dakota Indi-
ans, 1869–1872," *South Dakota Historical Collections* 28 (1956): 182–83;
letter from post surgeon Hackenburg, August 24, 1868, to *Hudson Daily
Star*, undated clipping in Medical History; Schell, *History of South Da-
kota*, pp. 91–92; *Union and Dakotian*, August 15, 1868; George E. Hyde,
Red Cloud's Folk: A History of the Oglala Sioux (Norman: University of
Oklahoma Press, 1937), pp. 168–75; James C. Olson, *Red Cloud and the
Sioux Problem* (Lincoln: University of Nebraska Press, 1965), pp. 78–79,
83; Athearn, *Forts of the Upper Missouri*, pp. 260–61; *Report of the Secre-
tary of War, 1868*, p. 34; George E. Hyde, *Spotted Tail's Folk: A History of the
Brule Sioux* (Norman: University of Oklahoma Press, 1961), pp. 130–53;
Harry H. Anderson, "A History of the Cheyenne River Indian Agency and
Its Military Post, Fort Bennett, 1865–1891," *South Dakota Historical Col-
lections* 28 (1956): 406; Robert W. Larson, *Red Cloud: Warrior-Statesman
of the Lakota Sioux* (Norman: University of Oklahoma Press, 1997), pp.
124–25, 144–45; Kenyon, "History of Fort Randall," p. 48; John E. Mills,
Historic Sites Archeology in the Fort Randall Reservoir South Dakota, River
Basin Surveys Papers, No. 16 (Washington, D.C.: Government Printing
Office, 1960), pp. 36–41, plate 3.

33. Letter from post surgeon Hackenburg, October 10, 1868, to the *Hudson
Daily Star*, October 20, 1868, clipping in Medical History.

34. Kenyon, "History of Fort Randall," pp. 53–55; Circular, Headquarters, Fort Randall, March 16, 1866, NA, RG 393, Part 5, Entry 8, Vol. 1, Fort Randall, S.D.

35. Post Returns, June 1867; Orders No. 29, Headquarters, Fort Randall, March 12, 1866, NA, RG 393, Part 5, Entry 8, Vol. 1, Fort Randall, S.D.; "Census of Indians and others entitled to draw rations at Fort Randall D.T. in obedience to Special Order No. 60 dated Head Quarters Fort Randall D.T. July 6, 1868," NA, RG 393, Entry 19, Letters and Telegrams Received, 1892, Fort Randall Orders Received, 1867–74, Miscellaneous Records, 1817–92; Special Orders No. 38, Headquarters, Fort Randall, April 18, 1869, NA, RG 393, Part 5, Entry 9, Vol. 3, "Special Orders."

36. William A. Thomas to parents, October 6, 1869. Larry Ness Collection, Yankton, S.D.

37. Post Returns, March 1869; Major General Winfield Scott Hancock to Sully, November 8, 1869, NA, RG 393, Entry 6, Letters and Telegrams Received, Fort Randall, S.D. Box 2; Kenyon, "History of Fort Randall," pp. 56–59, 60–61; DeWitt C. Poole, *Among the Sioux of Dakota: Eighteen Months Experience as an Indian Agent* (New York: D. Van Nostrand, 1881), chaps. 13 and 14, as cited in Kenyon, "History of Fort Randall," p. 59; Hyde, *Spotted Tail's Folk*, pp. 150–53; Special Orders No. 69, Headquarters, Fort Randall, May 25, 1870, NA, RG 393, Part 5, Entry 9, Vol. 3, "Special Orders"; Special Orders No. 12, Headquarters, Middle District, July 2, 1869, NA, RG 393, Entry 19, Letters and Telegrams Received, 1892, Fort Randall Orders Received, 1867–74, Miscellaneous Records, 1817–92; *Report of the Secretary of War, 1867*, pp. 48, 51–52; *Union and Dakotian*, June 8, 1867, May 2, 1868; Athearn, *Forts of the Upper Missouri*, pp. 237, 241.

38. Letter from post surgeon Hackenburg, January 8, 1869, to the *Hudson Daily Star*, January 20, 1869, clipping in Medical History. An enumeration of sixteen Indian crania forwarded to the Army Medical Museum appears in Hackenburg to Surgeon General, U.S. Army, January 18, 1869, in Medical History, pp. 104–5.

39. Brown and Irwin, "Ponca," pp. 424–25; Mulhair, *Ponca Agency*, pp. 31–40.

6. TURBULENT SEVENTIES

1. Athearn, *Forts of the Upper Missouri*, p. 261. Among vessels docking at Fort Randall during the 1870s were *Far West*, *Ida Stockdale*, *Esperanza*, *Key West*, *Durfee*, *Nellie Peck*, *Mary McDonald*, *Western*, *Miner*, *General Terry*, *Peninah*, *Black Hills*, *Mollie Moore*, *Katie Kuntz*, and *Hiram Wood*.

Medical History. For White Swan, see Adeline S. Gnirk, *Saga of the Missouri River Reveille* (Gregory, S.D.: Gregory Times-Advocate, 1981), pp. 48–49.

2. Post Returns, January 1867–December 1879, as appropriate; Regimental Returns of the Twenty-second Infantry, Return for June 1874, NA Microfilm Publications M665, Roll 230; Kenyon, "History of Fort Randall," pp. 59–61; "The First Regiment of Infantry," in *Army of the United States*, ed. Rodenbough and Haskin, p. 411; Smith, "Twenty-second Regiment," p. 685; Special Orders No. 125, Headquarters, Department of Dakota, June 16, 1874, NA, RG 393, Entry 19, Letters and Telegrams Received, 1892, Fort Randall Orders Received, 1867–74, Miscellaneous Records, 1817–92; *Sioux City Times*, February 22, April 26, 1870, March 2, 1871. See also *Report of the Secretary of War* (Washington, D.C.: Government Printing Office) for the following years: *1870*, pp. 25, 66–67; *1871*, pp. 25, 26, 88–89; *1872*, pp. 37, 38, 104–5; *1873*, pp. 37, 60–61; *1874*, pp. 10, 35, 72–73; *1875*, pp. 59, 60, 61, 62, 144–45; *1876*, pp. 44–45, 63, 455, 456, 457, 458; *1877*, pp. 18–19, 35, 482, 485; *1878*, pp. 16–17, 72, 77; *1879*, pp. 22–23, 47, 50.

3. *Sioux City Daily Journal*, November 4, 1871; Medical History, July, August, September, November 1871, January, March 1872; Kenyon, "History of Fort Randall," pp. 68–69. The cottonwood grove is also mentioned in Thomas P. Roberts, *Report of a Reconnaissance of the Missouri River in 1872* (Washington, D.C.: Government Printing Office, 1872), p. 7. It has been suggested that the rebuilt Fort Randall stood farther downstream and farther back from the river than the post erected in 1856. Kenyon, "History of Fort Randall," p. 69n.35; Mattes, "Historic Sites," pp. 482–84. However, comparison of plats executed in 1856, ca. 1860s, ca. 1867, and 1873 (reproduced in Kenyon, "History of Fort Randall"), especially as they regard the respective alignments of the commanding officer's quarters and post hospital and their juxtapositions relative to each other, does not bear this supposition out, and the seeming differences might better be accounted for by seasonal fluctuations in the river level producing commensurate changes in the channel and shoreline. Moreover, Billings, *Report on Hygiene of the United States Army*, p. 418, stated in 1873 that the log commanding officer's house is the same as that built in 1856–57, thoroughly renovated and with a frame addition raised in 1871. See plats, Fort Randall, Nebraska Territory, 1856, "Ground Plan of Buildings in Quartermaster Department Fort Randall D.T. [ca. 1865], and "Fort

Randall, Dacota Ty [ca. 1867]," all in NA, RG 77, Miscellaneous Forts File; "Fort Randall Dakota Territory, 1873" and details of post buildings as erected and/or modified in 1871–72, in Billings, *Report on Hygiene of the United States Army*, pp. 418–20. A description of the post before the renewal program of the early 1870s by post surgeons Hackenburg and A. I. Comfort is in Billings, *Report on Barracks and Hospitals*, pp. 386–87. A most detailed account of the buildings at Fort Randall as of 1873 appears in "Locality and history of Post" and "Description of Post," in Medical History, pp. 7–20. For specifications for military buildings, some of which conformed with those raised at Fort Randall, see "Report of the Quartermaster-General," October 10, 1872, in *Report of the Secretary of War, 1872*, following p. 280.

4. Circular, Headquarters, Fort Randall, D.T., November 26, 1876, NA, RG 393, Part 5, Entry 11, Vol. 1, Fort Randall, S.D.

5. Circular, Headquarters, Fort Randall, July 3, 1874, ibid.; "The Mystery Church," *South Dakota Historical Collections* 12 (1924): 187–88; *Sioux Falls Argus-Leader*, March 27, 1928; "The Old Church, I.O.O.F. Hall, and Library at Fort Randall," n.d., Vertical Files, South Dakota State Historical Society; *Army and Navy Journal*, December 6, 1879; *Fort Randall Independent* 1 (October 1992): 1–2, and 2 (March 1993): 6; J. P. Cox, "Old Fort Randall," *The Westerners Brand Book* (Chicago) 8 (July 1951): 35; Kenyon, "History of Fort Randall," pp. 91–92, 96; Gnirk, *Missouri River Reveille*, pp. 43–45.

6. Lieutenant Colonel Pinkney Lugenbeel, First Infantry, to AAG, Department of Dakota, October 1, 1877, in *Report of the Secretary of War, 1877*, pp. 564–65; Special Orders No. 16, Headquarters, Fort Sully, D.T., February 9, 1873, NA, RG 393, Entry 19, Letters and Telegrams Received, 1892, Fort Randall Orders Received, 1867–74, Miscellaneous Records, 1817–92; General Orders No. 24, War Department, Adjutant General's Office, March 17, 1871, in *Index of General Orders, Adjutant General's Office, 1871* (Washington, D.C.: Government Printing Office, 1872), p. 6; Billings, *Report on Hygiene of the United States Army*, p. 420; Gnirk, *Missouri River Reveille*, p. 37.

7. Information contained in various volumes of post special orders and post general orders for Fort Randall during the 1870s. NA, RG 393, Part 5, Entry 9.

8. General Orders No. 3, January 17, 1872, No. 5, February 29, 1872, and No. 24, August 6, 1872, all Headquarters, Fort Randall, D.T., NA, RG 393,

Part 5, Entry 8, Vol. 2, Fort Randall, S.D.; *Sioux City Daily Journal*, November 1, 1871; Kenyon, "History of Fort Randall," p. 93.

9. General Orders No. 13, Headquarters, Fort Randall, D.T., April 10, 1874, NA, RG 393, Part 5, Entry 8, Vol. 2, Fort Randall, S.D.

10. Special Order No. 78, Headquarters, Fort Randall, D.T., July 3, 1876, in "Post Special Orders from November 2nd 1875, to December 31st 1878," NA, RG 393, Part 5, Entry 9, Vol. 6, Fort Randall, S.D.

11. Special Orders No. 161, November 20, 1875, Special Orders No. 13, February 15, 1876, Special Order No. 78, July 3, 1876, and Special Orders No. 63, June 6, 1878, all Headquarters, Fort Randall, D.T., in "Post Special Orders from November 2nd 1875, to December 31st 1878"; General Orders No. 101, War Department, Adjutant General's Office, October 8, 1873, in *General Orders, War Department, Adjutant General's Office, 1873* (Washington, D.C.: Government Printing Office, 1873); Order, Headquarters, Fort Randall, D.T., September 6, 1874, and Circulars, Headquarters, Fort Randall, September 24, 1876, and November 12, 1879, all three in NA, RG 393, Part 5, Entry 11, Vol. 1, Fort Randall, S.D.; Medical History, July 1872; Kenyon, "History of Fort Randall," p. 95.

12. Biographical note on James Hervey Pratt, 1825–1910, in the calendar for MS501, Series 1, Box 1, "Pratt," Fort Randall, Manuscript Department, Nebraska State Historical Society Library, Lincoln (see also Thomas W. Dunlay, "James Hervey Pratt: Frontier Entrepreneur," *Nebraska History* 59 [Summer 1978]: 211–30); General Orders No. 2, January 21, 1873, and No. 23, October 6, 1879, Headquarters, Fort Randall, D.T., both in NA, RG 393, Part 5, Entry 8, Vol. 2, Fort Randall, S.D.; letter from John Cunningham, August 28, 1878, MS501, Fort Randall.

13. General Orders No. 23, Headquarters, Fort Randall, D.T., October 6, 1879, NA, RG 393, Part 5, Entry 8, Vol. 2, Fort Randall, S.D.

14. Delo, *Peddlers and Post Traders*, pp. 158–61, 174–75, 182–83; Kenyon, "History of Fort Randall," pp. 93–94. The other posts were Fort Benton, Fort Peck (both in Montana Territory), Fort Buford, Fort Stevenson, Fort Abraham Lincoln, Fort Rice, Standing Rock, Fort Sully, and Lower Brulé (all in Dakota). Ibid., pp. 159–60.

15. John E. Cox, *Five Years in the Army* (Owensville, Ind.: privately published, 1892; reprint, New York: Sol Lewis, 1973), pp. 16–17.

16. *Army and Navy Journal*, January 28, 1871; Cox, *Five Years in the Army*, pp. 16–17; *Yankton Press*, August 10, 1870, February 14, 25, July 3, 10, 1872, January 15, July 16, 1875, and *Union County Courier*, February 26, 1873,

cited in Kenyon, "History of Fort Randall," pp. 71–73; Kenyon, "History of Fort Randall," pp. 94, 96; Medical History, June 1872.

17. *Yankton Press*, July 3, 1872, cited in Kenyon, "History of Fort Randall," p. 72; William F. Cody, *The Life of Hon. William F. Cody Known as Buffalo Bill the Famous Hunter, Scout, and Guide: An Autobiography* (Hartford, Conn.: Frank Bliss, 1879), p. 315; Medical History, September 1872, May 1873; Custer letter, May 14, 1873, Fort Randall, Item 2080–73, NA Microfilm Publication M666, Roll 112; Post Returns, May 1873; Heitman, *Historical Register and Dictionary*, 1:329; Dan L. Thrapp, *Encyclopedia of Frontier Biography*, 3 vols. (Glendale, Calif.: Arthur H. Clark, 1988), 1:327–38; Michael J. Brodhead, *A Soldier-Scientist in the American Southwest* (Tucson: Arizona Historical Society, 1973); Elliot Coues, *Field Ornithology* (Salem, Mass.: Naturalists' Agency, 1874).

18. *Sioux Falls Argus-Leader*, March 3, 1963.

19. John E. Cox, "Soldiering in Dakota Territories in the Seventies: A Communication," *North Dakota History* 6, no. 1 (1931): 78; Ray H. Mattison, *The Army Post on the Northern Plains, 1865–1885* (Gering, Neb.: Oregon Trail Museum Association, 1956; reprinted from *Nebraska History* 35 [March 1954]), pp. 14, 20, 23; Stallard, *Glittering Misery*, p. 70; Medical History, December 1869–June 1873, February 1872 (smallpox); letter regarding pursuit of deserters, Second Lieutenant Benjamin C. Lockwood, August 6, 1871, eBay item #2119652868, July 2002; *Sioux City Daily Journal*, January 31, 1871; Don Rickey Jr., *Forty Miles a Day on Beans and Hay: The Enlisted Soldier Fighting the Indian Wars* (Norman: University of Oklahoma Press, 1963), p. 148. From May 1872 to June 1873, acting assistant surgeon George E. Lord served as post surgeon at Fort Randall. He would be killed with Custer's battalion at the Battle of the Little Big Horn River in Montana Territory in little more than three years. Medical History, May 1872, June 1873.

20. *Report of the Secretary of War, 1870*, p. 26; "Record of Events," in Post Returns, March, May, June, August 1870, May, September 1872, November 1873, July, August 1874, November 1875, April, May, August, September, November 1876, December 1877, December 1878, May, June, July, August 1879.

21. Smith, "Twenty-second Regiment," pp. 783–84; "Record of Events," in Post Returns, August 1871, July, October 1872; Special Orders No. 142, Headquarters, Department of Dakota, July 17, 1872, NA, RG 39, Entry 19, Letters and Telegrams Received 1892, Fort Randall Orders Received,

1867–74, Miscellaneous Records, 1817–92. The complete escort consisted of six companies of the Eighth Infantry, three companies of the Seventeenth Infantry, three companies of the Twenty-second Infantry, besides a detachment of mounted infantry, a detachment of Indian scouts, and a detachment sufficient to operate two Gatling guns.

22. "Record of Events," in Post Returns, May, October 1873; Smith, "Twenty-second Regiment," pp. 684–85; Special Orders No. 70, April 10, 1873, No. 73, April 13, 1873, and No. 189, August 25, 1873, all Headquarters, Department of Dakota, NA, RG 393, Entry 19, Letters and Telegrams Received, 1892, Fort Randall Orders Received, 1867–74, Miscellaneous Records, 1817–92. The Yellowstone Expedition of 1873 is treated in depth in Lawrence A. Frost, *Custer's 7th Cav and the Campaign of 1873* (El Segundo, Calif.: Upton and Sons, 1986).

23. Grant K. Anderson, "The Black Hills Exclusion Policy: Judicial Challenges," *Nebraska History* 58 (Spring 1977): 3–4.

24. Cox, *Five Years in the United States Army*, p. 17.

25. Paul A. Hutton, *Phil Sheridan and His Army* (Lincoln: University of Nebraska Press, 1985), pp. 290–92; Kenyon, "History of Fort Randall," pp. 77–81; A. Ivins Comfort, "From the Missouri River to the Black Hills in Mid-Winter of 1874," in *War Papers Read Before the Commandery of the State of Wisconsin, Military Order of the Loyal Legion of the United States* (Milwaukee: Burdick and Allen, 1903), pp. 249–58; Watson Parker, ed., "The Report of Captain John Mix of a Scout to the Black Hills, March-April 1875," *South Dakota History* 7 (Fall 1977): 385–401; Circular, Headquarters, Fort Randall, April 9, 1875, NA, RG 393, Part 5, Entry 11, Vol. 1, Fort Randall, S.D.; "Record of Events," in Post Returns, April, May, June, July, August 1875; "Report of Campaigns, Expeditions and Scouts in the Southern District Department of Dakota," 1875–79, NA, RG 393, Part 1, Entry 1203, Vol. 1; Cox, *Five Years in the United States Army*, pp. 17–36; Anson Mills, *My Story* (Washington, D.C.: Byron S. Adams, 1918), pp. 152–54; Watson Parker, *Gold in the Black Hills* (Pierre: South Dakota State Historical Society Press, 2003), pp. 29–36; Watson Parker, "The Majors and the Miners: The Role of the U.S. Army in the Black Hills Gold Rush," *Journal of the West* 11 (January 1972): 104–5; Anderson, "Black Hills Exclusion Policy," pp. 5–24; Schell, *History of South Dakota*, pp. 126–32; *Fort Randall Independent* 3 (January 1994): 1–2. Besides Benteen of Company H, the officers of the Seventh Cavalry who were stationed at Fort Randall in May–September 1875 were: Captain Myles Moylan, Com-

pany A; First Lieutenant Thomas M. McDougall, Company E; First Lieutenant Francis M. Gibson, Company H; Second Lieutenant William T. Craycroft, Company E; Second Lieutenant Charles C. DeRudio, Company A; and Second Lieutenant Charles A. Varnum, Company A. Post Returns, May 1875.

26. *Winners of the West,* November 30, 1926.

27. Jerome A. Greene, *Yellowstone Command: Colonel Nelson A. Miles and the Great Sioux War, 1876–1877* (Lincoln: University of Nebraska Press, 1991), pp. 14, 32, 184, 215, 221; Regimental Returns of the First Infantry, Return for June, August 1876, NA Microfilm Publication M665, Roll 7; *Yankton Daily Press and Dakotaian,* July 8, 9, 1876; *Report of the Secretary of War, 1877,* p. 564; General Orders No. 3, Headquarters, Military Division of the Missouri, April 5, 1877, NA, RG 393, Microfilm roll 17, Little Bighorn Battlefield National Monument; "Record of Events," in Post Returns, May, June, July, August, September, October, November 1878; *Fort Randall Independent* 2 (October 1993): 1, 7 (March 1998): 1–3; Robert Lee, *Fort Meade and the Black Hills* (Lincoln: University of Nebraska Press, 1991), pp. 22–24. The passage of Fort Randall by the *E. H. Durfee* is unspecifically referenced in Nelson A. Miles, *Personal Recollections and Observations of General Nelson A. Miles* (Chicago: Werner, 1896), p. 213. In Miles's *Serving the Republic: Memoirs of the Civil and Military Life of Nelson A. Miles, Lieutenant-General, United States Army* (New York: Harpers and Brothers, 1911), p. 138, the author noted that "as we passed the military installations along the Upper Missouri the small garrisons frequently gathered on the banks, waving their salutations, and signaling 'success' to those who were going to take the places of the ones who had fallen [with Custer]." The *Durfee's* passage of Fort Randall on July 17 is calculated from information in the *Yankton Daily Press and Dakotaian,* July 18, 1876. See also Greene, *Yellowstone Command,* p. 22.

28. *Report of the Secretary of War, 1877,* pp. 56, 486; Regimental Returns of the First Infantry for July and August 1877, NA Microfilm Publication M665, Roll 7; "Record of Events," in Post Returns, July, August 1877; Hutton, *Phil Sheridan,* p. 176.

29. General Orders No. 3, Headquarters, Fort Randall, January 17, 1872, NA, RG 393, Part 5, Entry 8, Vol. 2, Fort Randall, S.D.

30. DeMallie, "Yankton and Yanktonai," p. 780; Kingsbury and Smith, *History of Dakota Territory,* 1:657; *Sioux City Times,* April 26, 1870; *Sioux City Daily Journal,* October 23, 1870; General Orders No. 1, Headquar-

ters, Fort Randall, January 21, 1873, NA, RG 393, Part 5, Entry 8, Vol. 2, Fort Randall, S.D.; Special Orders No. 18, Headquarters, Fort Randall, February 1, 1878. NA, RG 393, Part 5, Entry 9, Vol. 6, Fort Randall, S.D.; Kenyon, "History of Fort Randall," p. 90.

31. Cox, *Five Years in the United States Army*, p. 36.

32. Ibid., pp. 38–39.

33. Brown and Irwin, "Ponca," p. 425; Kingsbury and Smith, *History of Dakota Territory*, 1:657; *Sioux City Daily Journal*, December 16, 28, 1870; *Report of the Secretary of War, 1872*, p. 39; Agent Henry E. Gregory to Commissioner of Indian Affairs, October 10, 1872, in Robinson, "Digest of the Reports," pp. 323–24; McGinnis, *Counting Coup*, pp. 127–28; "First Regiment of Infantry," p. 411; *Report of the Secretary of War, 1875*, p. 65; Reports of Danvers and Captain Kinzie Bates, First Infantry, reprinted in *Fort Randall Independent* 2 (January 1993): 2; Rickey, *Forty Miles a Day*, p. 295. For an overview of the Sioux raids on the Poncas from 1869 to 1876, see Mulhair, *Ponca Agency*, pp. 42–62. Warfare between the Brulés and the Poncas went back decades. See, for example, White, "Winning of the West," p. 326.

34. General Orders No. 15, Headquarters, Fort Randall, July 13, 1875, NA, RG 393, Part 5, Entry 8, Vol. 2, Fort Randall, S.D.

35. Lugenbeel to AAG, Department of Dakota, April 26, 1876, quoted in Mulhair, *Ponca Agency*, pp. 70–71.

36. Mulhair, *Ponca Agency*, pp. 63–77; Brown and Irwin, "Ponca," pp. 426–27; Kenyon, "History of Fort Randall," pp. 86–87; Lugenbeel to AAG, Department of Dakota, October 1, 1877, in *Report of the Secretary of War, 1877*, p. 564; "Record of Events," in Post Returns, May, June 1877.

37. Lugenbeel to AAG, Department of Dakota, October 1, 1877, in *Report of the Secretary of War, 1877*, pp. 564–65; "Record of Events," in Post Returns, December 1878; Regimental Returns of the First Infantry, May 1879; *Fort Randall Independent* 2 (October 1993): 1. The standard treatment of the Ponca removal and succeeding events is chronicled in Thomas Henry Tibbles (Zylyff), *The Ponca Chiefs: An Indian's Attempt to Appeal from the Tomahawk to the Courts, a Full History of the Robbery of the Ponca Tribe of Indians* (Boston: Lockwood, Brooks, 1880; reprinted as *The Ponca Chiefs: An Account of the Trial of Standing Bear*, Lincoln: University of Nebraska Press, 1972). See also James T. King, "'A Better Way': General George Crook and the Ponca Indians," in *The Western American Indian: Case Studies in Tribal History*, ed. Richard N. Ellis (Lincoln: University of Nebraska Press, 1972), pp. 76–87.

38. *Sioux City Daily Times*, September 5, 1869, quoted in Athearn, *Forts of the Upper Missouri*, p. 270.

39. *Sioux City Daily Times*, September 5, 22, December 22, 1869, quoted in Athearn, *Forts of the Upper Missouri*, p. 270; Jackson, "Holding Down the Fort," pp. 14, 19.

40. Federal Writers' Project, *Nebraska: A Guide to the Cornhusker State* (New York: The Viking Press, 1939), pp. 101–2; Special Orders No. 25, Headquarters, Fort Randall, February 18, 1871, NA, RG 393, Part 5, Entry 9, Vol. 4, Fort Randall, S.D.; Special Orders No. 203, December 19, 1871, No. 10, January 16, 1872, No. 76, June 13, 1873, No. 89, July 9, 1873, No. 124, September 12, 1873, No. 125, September 15, 1873, and Special Order No. 133, September 25, 1875, all seven Headquarters, Fort Randall, in NA, RG 393, Part 5, Entry 9, Vol. 5, Fort Randall, S.D.; Special Orders No. 71, Headquarters, Fort Randall, June 23, 1879, NA, RG 393, Entry 9, Vol. 7, Fort Randall, S.D.; letter, August 30, 1873, Fort Randall, regarding Lakota raid on Bohemian settlement, Item 3892–73, NA Microfilm Publication M666, Roll 125; *Report of the Secretary of War, 1875*, p. 65; petition of settlers, February 1878, to Commanding Officer, Fort Randall, Item 600–78, NA Microfilm Publication M666, Roll 391; "Record of Events," in Post Returns, July 1875, June 1879.

41. Notice signed by Lieutenant Colonel Elwell S. Otis, Headquarters, Fort Randall, December 4, 1870, NA, RG 393, Entry 19, Letters and Telegrams Received, 1892, Fort Randall Orders Received, 1867–74, Miscellaneous Records, 1817–92.

42. *Sioux City Daily Journal*, December 29, 1870, January 24, 1871; Otis to Kerwin Wilson, December 28, 1870, Captain John Hartley, Twenty-second Infantry, to Joseph Ellis, December 28, 1870, and "Proceedings of a Board of Officers," March 8, 1871, all three in NA, RG 393, Entry 19, Letters and Telegrams Received, 1892, Fort Randall Orders Received, 1867–74, Miscellaneous Records, 1817–92; U.S., Congress, *Claims of Settlers on Fort Randall Reservation*, 42nd Cong., 3rd sess., H. Ex. Doc. No. 32, December 10, 1872; General Orders No. 47, War Department, Adjutant General's Office, May 25, 1874, in *Index of General Orders, Adjutant General's Office, 1874* (Washington, D.C.: Government Printing Office, 1875); Special Orders No. 124, War Department, Adjutant General's Office, June 5, 1874, NA, RG 393, Entry 19, Letters and Telegrams Received, 1892, Fort Randall Orders Received, 1867–74, Miscellaneous Records, 1817–92; Special Orders No. 92, Headquarters, Fort Randall, August 18, 1879, NA, RG 393, Part 5, Entry 9, Vol. 7, Fort Randall, S.D.; Athearn, *Forts*

of the Upper Missouri, pp. 286–87; Green, "Administration of the Public Domain," pp. 247–48. A list of settlers with claims on the military reservation appears in Gnirk, *Missouri River Reveille,* pp. 41–42.

7. WANING YEARS

1. Letter regarding potential abandonment of posts, May 7, 1879, including remarks by Brigadier General Alfred H. Terry, Letters Received, Adjutant General's Office, Item 2908-79, NA Microfilm Publication M666, Roll 490; Schell, *History of South Dakota,* p. 163; Kenyon, "History of Fort Randall," p. 116; "Estimates for Buildings at Military Posts," in "Report of the General of the Army," November 6, 1882, in *Report of the Secretary of War, 1882* (Washington, D.C.: Government Printing Office, 1882), pp. 10, 12, 16. Regarding Sherman's visit, post surgeon John D. Hall noted that "he showed his usual practical sense, with a quick eye for the chief things about a building, or about the lay of the land." Medical History, July 1880.

2. Post Returns, June, July, August, September 1880, November, December 1882, January, November, December 1883, May, July, September 1884, September, October 1886, September 1888, May 1889; Regimental Returns of the First Infantry, May, July 1880, NA Microfilm Publication M665, Roll 7; *Report of the Secretary of War, 1880,* pp. 14–15, *1881,* pp. 54–55, *1882,* pp. 36–37, 81, 83, *1883,* p. 106, *1884,* pp. 60–61, 106, *1885,* pp. 82–83, 135, *1886,* pp. 86–87, 132, *1887,* pp. 88–89, 148, *1888,* pp. 78–79, 157, *1889,* pp. 98–99, 162; Henry R. Brinkerhoff, "The Fifteenth Regiment of Infantry," and George L. Andrews, "Twenty-fifth Regiment of Infantry," both in *Army of the United States,* ed. Rodenbough and Haskin, pp. 627–28; John H. Nankivell, comp., ed., *The History of the Twenty-fifth Regiment United States Infantry, 1869–1926* (reprint, Fort Collins, Colo.: Old Army Press, 1972), pp. 36–37; Arlen L. Fowler, *The Black Infantry in the West, 1869–1891* (Norman: University of Oklahoma Press, 1996), pp. 49–50. The other all-black regiments were the Twenty-fourth Infantry, the Ninth Cavalry, and the Tenth Cavalry, all organized in 1869. The cavalry troopers were purportedly nicknamed "Buffalo Soldiers" by Indians, probably because their hair approximated in texture and appearance the fur of buffaloes. In more recent years, the term has been popularly applied to infantry as well as cavalry, and today it is commonly used in reference to all black soldiers from the time of its proper historical application until well into the twentieth century.

3. This description of Fort Randall's physical condition and upgrading, including quoted material unless otherwise specified, is drawn from the

following reports: Colonel William R. Shafter to U.S. Indian Agent, Rosebud Agency, D.T., February 11, 1880, NA, RG 75, Records of the Bureau of Indian Affairs, General Correspondence, Rosebud Agency, Box A-354, January–February 1880; Inspection Report, Fort Randall, September 5, 1880, NA, RG 159, Records of the Office of the Inspector General, Entry 15, Letters Received 1207, 1880, Box 15; Inspection Report, Fort Randall, October 29, 1881, NA, RG 159, Entry 15, Letters Received 1262, 1881, Box 21; Inspection Report, Fort Randall, December 3, 1881, NA, RG 393, Entry 6, Letters and Telegrams Received, Fort Randall, S.D., Box 6; Inspection Report, Fort Randall, September 5, 1881, NA, RG 159, Entry 15, Letters Received 1178, 1881, Box 20; Inspection Report, Fort Randall, August 5, 1882, NA, RG 159, Entry 15, Letters Received 947, 1882, Box 24; Inspection Report, Fort Randall, September 5, 1882, NA, RG 159, Entry 15, Letters Received 950, 1882, Box 24; Post Returns, December 1884; Medical History, January 1881; *Report of the Secretary of War, 1882*, p. 450, *1885*, pp. 457, 471, *1886*, pp. 416, 426, *1887*, p. 430; Inspection Report, Fort Randall, September 1, 1883, NA, RG 159, Entry 15, Letters Received, 1883, Box 29; Inspection Report, Fort Randall, October 9, 1883, NA, RG 159, Entry 15, Letters Received, 1884, Box 30; Inspection Report, Fort Randall, letter of February 2, 1884, NA, RG 393, Entry 6, Letters and Telegrams Received, Fort Randall, S.D., Box 7; Inspection Report, Fort Randall, September 1, 1884, NA, RG 159, Entry 15, Letters Received, 1884, Box 33; Inspection Report, Fort Randall, September 5, 1885, NA, RG 159, Entry 15, Letters Received, 1885, Box 37; Inspection Report, Fort Randall, August 1, 1887, NA, RG 159, Entry 15, Letters Received, 1887, Box 50; Inspection Report, Fort Randall, June 30, 1889, NA, RG 159, Entry 15, Letters Received, 1889, Box 62; Inspection Report, Fort Randall, June 27, 28, 1889, NA, RG 159, Entry 15, Letters Received, 1889, Box 66.

4. Inspection Report, Fort Randall, September 23, 24, 1886, NA, RG 159, Entry 15, Letters Received, 1886, Box 39.

5. Inspection Report, Fort Randall, June 27, 28, 1889, NA, RG 159, Entry 15, Letters Received, 1889, Box 66; *Report of the Secretary of War, 1889*, pp. 409, 509–10; Kenyon, "History of Fort Randall," p. 115; unidentified newspaper clipping, ca. 1891–92, in photograph album entitled, on its leather cover, "Photographs," with an impression of an insignia of the Twenty-first Infantry and, on the inside page, "Views of Fort Randall," Larry Ness Collection, Yankton, S.D.; Captain H. Baxter Quimby to Post Adjutant, Fort Randall, June 24, 1881, NA, RG 393, Entry 6, Letters and Telegrams Received, Fort Randall, S.D., Box 6; General Orders No. 102,

Headquarters of the Army, Adjutant General's Office, August 22, 1882, in *Index of General Orders, Adjutant General's Office, 1882* (Washington, D.C.: Government Printing Office, 1883), pp. 1–8; Gnirk, *Missouri River Reveille*, p. 37.

6. Denny Moran, "Denny Moran's Reminiscences of Fort Randall," *South Dakota Historical Collections* 23 (1947): pp. 277–78.

7. Post Returns, June 1883; U.S. Congress, *Report to Accompany Senate Bill 1814*, 47th Cong., 1st sess. S. Report No. 628, May 23, 1882; U.S. Congress, *Fort Randall Military Reservation, Dakota*, 48th Cong., 1st sess. H. Report No. 201, February 5, 1884; AAG, Department of Dakota, to Commanding Officer, Fort Randall, July 5, 1884, NA, RG 393, Entry 6, Letters and Telegrams Received, Fort Randall, S.D., Box 7; General Orders No. 80, Headquarters of the Army, July 28, 1884, in *Index of General Orders and Circulars, Adjutant General's Office, 1884* (Washington, D.C.: Government Printing Office, 1885); *Report of the Secretary of War, 1889*, pp. 738, 744; Green, "Administration of the Public Domain," pp. 248–49.

8. Medical History, March 1881, March 1884; "Report of the Surgeon-General," September 26, 1888, in *Report of the Secretary of War, 1888*, p. 683; *Army and Navy Journal*, January 14, 1888. Gorgas went on to become an internationally known army doctor and scientist because of his work in the treatment of yellow fever in Cuba (1898–99) and the Panama Canal Zone (1904). He became surgeon general of the army in 1914 and headed the Army Medical Service during World War I. Richard B. Morris and Jeffrey B. Morris, eds., *Encyclopedia of American History: Bicentennial Edition* (New York: Harper and Row, 1976), p. 1043.

9. Andrews to AAG, Department of Texas, March 22, 1880, reprinted in Frank N. Schubert, comp., *Voices of the Buffalo Soldier: Records, Reports, and Recollections of Military Life and Service in the West* (Albuquerque: University of New Mexico Press, 2003), pp. 109–10; *Army and Navy Journal*, February 5, 1881.

10. *Army and Navy Journal*, January 8, 1881.

11. *Army and Navy Journal*, May 15, 1881.

12. *Army and Navy Journal*, February 2, 1881; quotation of anonymous complainant, Fort Randall, August 16, 1881, with endorsements, NA, RG 393, Entry 6, Letters and Telegrams Received, Fort Randall, S.D., Box 6. On the matter of prejudice against the soldiers of the Twenty-fifth Infantry while at Fort Randall, see Fowler, *Black Infantry in the West*, p. 129.

13. For particulars of the sensational Geddes case, see Louise Barnett, *Un-*

gentlemanly Acts: The Army's Notorious Incest Trial (New York: Hill and Wang, 2000), especially pp. 194–201.

14. Inspection Report, Fort Randall, September 1, 1884, NA, RG 159, Entry 15, Letters Received, 1884, Box 33; *Report of the Secretary of War, 1889*, p. 77.

15. Invoice of Company K, May 10, 1881, Folder 5, and "Ordnance and Ordnance Stores pertaining to Company F, 25th Infantry for the quarter ending June 30, 1882," Folder 1, both in H7734, Fort Randall Quartermaster Papers, State Archives, South Dakota State Historical Society. For details of the appearance of all this equipment, see Douglas C. McChristian, *The U.S. Army in the West, 1870–1880: Uniforms, Weapons, and Equipment* (Norman: University of Oklahoma Press, 1995). Changes to uniforms and equipment introduced in the 1880s are reflected in *U.S. Army Uniforms and Equipment, 1889, by the Quartermaster General* (Lincoln: University of Nebraska Press, 1986).

16. Adapted from General Orders No. 55, Headquarters, Fort Randall, August 8, 1880, NA, RG 393, Part 5, Entry 8, Vol. 3, Fort Randall, S.D.

17. Ibid.; Orders No. 17 and No. 94, both in Headquarters, Fort Randall, May 21, 1881, NA, RG 393, Part 5, Entry 8, Vol. 3, Fort Randall, S.D.; Inspection Report, Fort Randall, September 1, 1884, and September 5, 1885. For details of the target practice in 1888, see Orders No. 9, Headquarters, Fort Randall, May 14, 1888, NA, RG 393, Part 5, Entry 10, Vol. 3, Fort Randall, S.D.

18. Orders No. 29, Headquarters, Fort Randall, September 31, 1888, NA, RG 393, Part 5, Entry 10, Vol. 3, Fort Randall, S.D.; Circular, Fort Randall, October 29, 1886, and Circular, Headquarters, Fort Randall, January 30, 1886, both in NA, RG 393, Part 5, Entry 10, Vol. 2, Fort Randall, S.D.

19. Inspection Report, Fort Randall, September 1, 1884; AAG, Department of Dakota, to Commanding Officer, Fort Randall, April 13, 1881, and Depot Quartermaster, Yankton, D.T., to Commanding Officer, Fort Randall, April 13, 1881, both in NA, RG 393, Entry 6, Letters and Telegrams Received, Fort Randall, S.D., Box 6; Petitions to Commanding Officer, Fort Randall, from Sunnyside, Nebraska, June 24, 1882, and Keya Paha, Nebraska, June 26, 1882, NA, RG 393, Entry 6, Letters and Telegrams Received, Fort Randall, S.D., Box 7; *Report of the Secretary of War, 1881*, pp. 111–12; Inspection Report, Fort Randall, September 5, 1882; Kenyon, "History of Fort Randall," pp. 116–17; Fowler, *Black Infantry*, pp. 52–53; Nankivel, *History of the Twenty-fifth Regiment*, p. 37.

20. Winfred W. Barton, *John P. Williamson: A Brother to the Sioux* (New York: Fleming H. Revell, 1919), pp. 156–58, as cited in Kenyon, "History of Fort Randall," p. 112; Jerome A. Greene, "The Sioux Land Commission of 1889: Prelude to Wounded Knee," *South Dakota History* 1 (Winter 1970): 44, 66.

21. Moran, "Reminiscences," p. 268; Sara L. Bernson and Robert J. Eggers, "Black People in South Dakota History," *South Dakota History* 7 (Summer 1977): 247; Kenyon, "History of Fort Randall," p. 120; Herbert Martin, interview, August 1954, in "Indian Wars Veterans—Information on the United States Army and the Indian Wars," Don Rickey Jr. Collection, Manuscript Division, U.S. Military History Institute, Carlisle, Pa.

22. *Army and Navy Journal*, July 22, 1882.

23. Marie D. Gorgas and Burton J. Hendrick, *William Crawford Gorgas: His Life and Work* (New York: Doubleday, Page, 1924), pp. 53, 56, cited in Athearn, *Forts of the Upper Missouri*, pp. 287–88; "Circular letter to the Officers of the Post," Headquarters, Fort Randall, January 4, 1889, NA, RG 393, Entry 10, Vol. 3, Fort Randall, S.D.; *Army and Navy Journal*, February 28, 1885.

24. Kenyon, "History of Fort Randall," p. 120; *Army and Navy Journal*, February 21, 1880; Circular No. 7, Headquarters, Fort Randall, February 22, 1887, NA, RG 393, Entry 10, Vol. 2, Fort Randall, S.D.

25. *Army and Navy Journal*, September 7, 1889.

26. Telegrams, AAG, Division of the Missouri, to Brigadier General Alfred H. Terry, August 22, 1881, AAG, Department of Dakota, to Commanding Officer, Fort Randall, August 26, 1881, AAG, Department of Dakota, to Commanding Officer, Fort Yates, August 26, 1881, and Gilbert to Commanding Officer, Fort Randall, September 10, 1881, all four in NA, RG 393, Entry 6, Letters and Telegrams Received, Fort Randall, S.D., Box 6; *Report of the Secretary of War, 1881*, pp. 81, 107–8; Robert M. Utley, *The Lance and the Shield: The Life and Times of Sitting Bull* (New York: Henry Holt, 1993), pp. 240–41; Stanley Vestal, *New Sources of Indian History, 1850–1891* (Norman: University of Oklahoma Press, 1934), pp. 266–68. The events surrounding the submission of the Hunkpapas are detailed in Paul L. Hedren, *Sitting Bull's Surrender at Fort Buford: An Episode of American History* (Williston, N.D.: Fort Union Association, 1997). The number of Lakotas sent to Fort Randall decreased between September 7, when 198 men, women, and children were earmarked to leave Fort Yates, and September 10, when, according to Gilbert's missive, 172 actually departed. (On September 7, there were 47 males aged sixteen years and

over, 44 males under sixteen, 66 females sixteen and over, and 41 females under age sixteen, for a total of 198 persons.) Orders No. 162, Headquarters, Fort Yates, September 7, 1881, NA, RG 393, Entry 6, Letters and Telegrams Received, Fort Randall, S.D., Box 6.

27. Orders No. 191, Headquarters, Fort Yates, September 6, 1881, and AAG, Department of Dakota, to Commanding Officer, Fort Randall, September 12, 1881, both in NA, RG 393, Entry 6, Letters and Telegrams Received, Fort Randall, S.D., Box 6; Medical History, September 1881. Allison remained until early November. AAG, Department of Dakota, to Commanding Officer, Fort Randall, November 3, 1881, and "List of Indian Prisoners of War (Sitting Bull's Band) turned over by Captain W. S. Howe, 17th Infantry, to Colonel G. L. Andrews, 25th Infantry, on the 18th day of September 1881," both in NA, RG 393, Entry 6, Letters and Telegrams Received, Fort Randall, S.D., Box 6.

28. Chief, Commissary of Subsistence, Department of Dakota, to Chief Quartermaster, Department of Dakota, September 21, 1881, W. S. Andrews, Indian Agent, Yankton, to Colonel George L. Andrews, Fort Randall, September 28, 1881, and Andrews to AAG, Department of Dakota, September 28, 1881, all in NA, RG 393, Entry 6, Letters and Telegrams Received, Fort Randall, S.D., Box 6.

29. "List of Indian Prisoners of War"; "List of Indians (Sitting Bull's Party) Turned Over at Fort Randall (D.T.) Sept. 18, 1881," stamped received, June 13, 1883, NA, RG 393, Entry 7, Letters Received, Fort Yates, N.D. Each of these lists contains discrepancies in their bottom line totals—the first contains 167 souls, the latter 165—although an enumeration of the contents of both, to include names missed on either, netted a likely proper total of 172. A complete list of names derived from information appearing on both lists is in appendix C. (I am indebted to Ephriam Dickson of the Utah Museum of Natural History, Salt Lake City, for providing data to help clarify figures and transcriptions of the original documents.) An unofficial tally of the people in May 1882 gave the number of males as 68 and the number of females as 93, for a total of 161. Photo No. 18, Bailey, Dix, and Mead photograph series, 1882, Sitting Bull Collection, State Archives, South Dakota State Historical Society, Pierre.

30. Post Returns, October 1881, as cited in Kenyon, "History of Fort Randall," p. 108; Medical History, October, November 1881; Major William W. Sanders to AAG, Department of Dakota, October 29, 1881, NA, RG 159, Records of the Office of the Inspector General, Entry 15, Letters Received 1262, 1881, Box 21. General Terry approved the use of the overshoes for

the Indians. Inspection Report, December 3, 1881, NA, RG 393, Entry 6, Letters and Telegrams Received, Fort Randall, S.D., Box 6. The German artist Rudolf Cronau, who visited Sitting Bull and his people in October at Fort Randall, perhaps exaggeratedly wrote that "preparations had been made to confine them on a very small area, enclosed by heavy palisades. There was also an ugly looking watch-tower, with loop-holes, through which the prisoners could be shot down in a few seconds. But to the great embarrassment of the officers of Fort Randall, Sitting Bull angrily protested against these attempts to treat him and his followers like criminals. As a result of these strong protests, the chief and his companions were permitted to make their camps outside of the fort and to walk around its neighborhood." Rudolf Cronau, "My Visit among the Hostile Dakota Indians and How They Became My Friends," *South Dakota Historical Collections* 22 (1946): 415.

31. Rev. Martin Marty to Commanding Officer, Fort Randall, November 1881, NA, RG 393, Entry 6, Letters and Telegrams Received, Fort Randall, S.D., Box 6.

32. Indian Agent W. S. Andrews to Colonel George L. Andrews, September 23, 28, 1881, NA, RG 393, Entry 6, Letters and Telegrams Received, Fort Randall, S.D., Box 6; Utley, *Lance and the Shield*, pp. 242, 244. The five children were: Small Soldier, age 13, son of Sitting Bull; Charge the House, 13, son of Fur Coat; Rock, 11, son of Looking Back Bear; Yellow, 14, daughter of Man Who Takes the Gun Away; and Bread, 14, daughter of Big Legs. Orders No. 2, Headquarters, Fort Randall, January 3, 1882, NA, RG 393, Part 5, Entry 8, Vol. 3, Fort Randall, S.D. One of the girls suffered from tuberculosis and curvature of the spine and died at Yankton Agency on June 30, 1882. Amelia Ives to Commanding Officer, Fort Randall, July 1, 1882, NA, RG 393, Entry 6, Letters and Telegrams Received, Fort Randall, S.D., Box 7.

33. Andrews to AAG, Department of Dakota, September 26, 1881, in Mark Diedrich, comp., ed. *Sitting Bull: The Collected Speeches* (Rochester, Minn.: Coyote Books, 1998), p. 145.

34. Walking Elk to Andrews, Fort Randall, December 3, 1881, NA, RG 393, Entry 6, Letters and Telegrams Received, Fort Randall, S.D., Box 6.

35. Diedrich, *Sitting Bull*, p. 146; Williamson to Andrews, December 12, 1881, Colonel C. C. Gilbert to Andrews, November 17, 1881, and Williamson to Andrews, December 12, 1881, all three in NA, RG 393, Entry 6, Letters and Telegrams Received, Fort Randall, S.D., Box 6; Utley, *Lance and the Shield*, pp. 243–44; Vestal, *New Sources*, pp. 269–70. The Boyton visit is

described in "The Boyton Odyssey," *Holiday* 6 (October 1949): 12–14, as cited in Kenyon, "History of Fort Randall," p. 121.

36. Cronau, "My Visit," pp. 416–19; Utley, *Lance and the Shield*, pp. 242–43; Vestal, *New Sources*, pp. 270–71.

37. Utley, *Lance and the Shield*, p. 245; Circular Nos. 1 and 2, Headquarters, Fort Randall, April 8, 14, 1882, NA, RG 393, Part 5, Entry 8, Vol. 3, Fort Randall, S.D. See also "Mem. Orders," Fort Randall, January 22, 1883, which decreed: "All Indians held at the post as prisoners will keep away from the vicinity of the garrison. They will be allowed to come to the Traders store daily (Sundays excepted) between 3 & 5 P.M." NA, RG 393, Part 5, Entry 10, "Post Orders and Circulars," Vol. 1, Fort Randall, S.D.

38. Medical History, February, March, June, August 1882; Photo No. 17, "Issuing Supplies," Bailey, Dix, and Mead photograph series; Depot Quartermaster, St. Paul, Minnesota, to Commanding Officer, Fort Randall, March 18, September 11, 1882, NA, RG 393, Entry 6, Letters and Telegrams Received, Fort Randall, S.D., Box 7.

39. AAG, Department of Dakota, to Commanding Officer, Fort Randall, August 9, 1882, NA, RG 393, Entry 6, Letters and Telegrams Received, Fort Randall, S.D., Box 7.

40. First Lieutenant Richard H. Pratt to Commanding Officer, Fort Randall, August 7, 1882, and Pratt to Andrews, August 7, 1882, both ibid.; Utley, *Lance and the Shield*, pp. 244–45; Vestal, *New Sources*, pp. 272–73; Inspection Report, Fort Randall, August 5, 1882, NA, RG 159, Entry 15, Letters Received 947, 1882, Box 24. Lieutenant Pratt, who operated the United States Indian Service Training School for Indian Youth at Carlisle Barracks, Pennsylvania, wrote the commanding officer on October 30, 1882: "If . . . Sitting Bull still prefers not to send his children we must let the matter drop as the Department does not want any children here except with the full consent of their people and parents." NA, RG 393, Entry 6, Letters and Telegrams Received, Fort Randall, S.D., Box 7.

41. Enclosed in Major William W. Sanders, Eighth Infantry, to AAG, Department of Dakota, August 5, 1882, NA, RG 159, Entry 15, Letters Received 947, 1882, Box 24.

42. Vestal, *New Sources*, pp. 272, 281. For more on the Ahern–Sitting Bull relationship, see ibid., pp. 271–73, 280–82, and Stanley Vestal, *Sitting Bull: Champion of the Sioux* (Norman: University of Oklahoma Press, 1957), pp. 237–38.

43. See, for example, Sitting Bull to the Indian Agent, Rosebud Agency, November 24, 1882, requesting visitation from several relatives and friends,

ostensibly to help him haul wood. NA (Central Plains Region), Kansas City, Mo., RG 75, Records of the Bureau of Indian Affairs, General Correspondence Rosebud Agency, Box A-356, file Oct.–Dec. 1882.

44. One of the photographs, all of which are reproduced here, depicts the Twenty-fifth Infantry band. The entire set of twenty-four Bailey, Dix, and Mead photographs reposes in the Sitting Bull Collection of the South Dakota State Historical Society. The photographs (not as stereopticons) also appear in the Stanley J. Morrow Collection of the society, and there is conjecture that they might have been taken by Morrow and sold to Bailey, Dix, and Mead. "The Sitting Bull Collection," *South Dakota History* 5 (Summer 1975): 245–65. Twenty of the images are also in the collections of the Nebraska State Historical Society, Lincoln, while others are in the W. H. Over Museum, Vermillion, S.D. Paula Richardson Fleming and Judith Luskey, *The North American Indian in Early Photographs* (New York: Harper and Row, 1986), state that pictures of Sitting Bull were taken by A. G. Johnson at the same time (p. 47). See also Frank Goodyear, "The Narratives of Sitting Bull's Surrender: Bailey, Dix, and Mead's Photographic Western," in *Dressing in Feathers: The Construction of the Indian in American Popular Culture*, ed. S. Elizabeth Bird (Boulder, Colo.: Westview Press, 1996), pp. 29–43.

45. Strike the Ree to Secretary of War Lincoln, December 11, 1882, quoted in Diedrich, *Sitting Bull*, p. 149.

46. McLaughlin to Commissioner of Indian Affairs, February 15, 1883, Adjutant General, Department of Dakota, March 22, 1883, transmitting correspondence "on subject of 'Sitting Bull's' removal from Ft. Randall to Standing Rock Agency, D.T.," NA, RG 33, Entry 6, Letters and Telegrams Received, Fort Randall, S.D., Box 7.

47. Secretary of the Interior Henry M. Teller to Secretary of War, February 23, 1883, and Adjutant General Richard C. Drum to Commanding Officer, Military Division of the Missouri, March 17, 1883, both in NA, RG 393, Entry 6, Letters and Telegrams Received, Fort Randall, S.D., Box 7; Utley, *Lance and the Shield*, pp. 245–46.

48. Special Orders No. 54, Headquarters, Department of Dakota, March 29, 1883 (copy provided by James May, Little Rock, Ark.); Medical History, April 1883; Post Returns, April, May 1883 (that of April indicates that the number of Indians totaled 152); "List of Chiefs, Headmen, etc., of 'Sitting Bull's' tribe, en-route from Fort Randall to Standing Rock Agency, D.T.," NA, RG 393, Entry 19, Letters and Telegrams Received, 1892, Fort Randall Orders Received, 1867–74, Miscellaneous Records, 1817–92 (com-

pare this list with that contained in Vestal, *New Sources*, pp. 293–94, to note several minor discrepancies); *Report of the Secretary of War, 1883*, p. 113; Utley, *Lance and the Shield*, pp. 246–47.

49. Marie Louise Lotze, "How South Dakota Became a State," *South Dakota Historical Collections* 14 (1928): 483; Schell, *History of South Dakota*, pp. 219–22.

8. LAST DAYS AND AFTER

1. Schell, *History of South Dakota*, pp. 158–68, 252–53, 299; Green, "Administration of the Public Domain," pp. 246–47.

2. General Orders No. 9, Headquarters, Department of the Army, January 27, 1891, and Orders No. 2, Headquarters, Department of the Platte, February 6, 1891, both in Post Returns, February 1891; Post Returns, May, August 1891; Medical History, May, August, November 1891, April 1892; Brinkerhoff, "Fifteenth Regiment," pp. 627–28; Frederick H. E. Ebstein, "Twenty-first Regiment of Infantry," in *Army of the United States*, ed. Rodenbough and Haskins, p. 679; *Report of the Secretary of War, 1890* (Washington, D.C.: Government Printing Office, 1890), pp. 72, 192, 755, *1891*, pp. 110–11, 172–73, 253, and *1892*, pp. 82, 89, 435.

3. *Report of the Secretary of War, 1890*, pp. 668, 681, 701, *1891*, pp. 510–11, and *1892*, pp. 304, 409.

4. Medical History, March 1889, July 1890. The March reference contains plans, specifications, and estimates for the construction, along with copies of correspondence to and from department headquarters regarding the proposed work.

5. Medical History, March, August, December 1891. Post surgeon Junius L. Powell's comments regarding the ventilation problem appear in "Report of the Surgeon-General," September 30, 1892, in *Report of the Secretary of War, 1892*, pp. 509, 513. The water problem was not addressed "on account of the probable abandonment of the post." Ibid., p. 522.

6. AAG, Department of Dakota, to Commanding Officer, Fort Randall, July 15, 1890, NA, RG 393, Entry 6, Letters and Telegrams Received, Fort Randall, S.D., Box 9.

7. U.S. Congress, *Report to Accompany Senate Bill 3206*, 52nd Cong., 1st sess. S. Report No. 912, July 13, 1892; U.S. Congress, *Report to Accompany Senate Bill 2931*, 52nd Cong., 1st sess. S. Report No. 950.

8. Circular No. 1, Headquarters, Fort Randall, February 20, 1891, NA, RG 393, Entry 10, Vol. 4, Fort Randall, S.D.

9. Orders No. 4, February 27, 1891, Orders No. 6, March 3, 1891, Orders

No. 70, September 6, 1891, all Headquarters, Fort Randall, NA, RG 393, Entry 10, Vol. 4, Fort Randall, S.D.; Ebstein, "Twenty-first Regiment," p. 679.

10. Medical History, April 1891.

11. Circular No. 7, May 29, 1891, and Orders No. 75, June 23, 1892, both Headquarters, Fort Randall, NA, RG 393, Part 5, Entry 10, Vol. 4, Fort Randall, S.D.; Adjutant General to Superintendent, Recruiting Service, June 15, 1892, NA, RG 393, Entry 19, Letters and Telegrams Received, 1892, Fort Randall Orders Received, 1867–74, Miscellaneous Records, 1817–92 (teacher).

12. Commanding Officer, Fort Randall, to AAG, Department of the Platte, with endorsements, October 4, 1892, NA, RG 393, Entry 19, Letters and Telegrams Received, 1892, Fort Randall Orders Received, 1867–74, Miscellaneous Records, 1817–92.

13. AAG, Department of the Platte, to Commanding Officer, Fort Randall, January 9, 1892, and Commanding Officer, Fort Randall, to AAG, Department of the Platte, February 27, 1892, both ibid.

14. Delo, *Peddlers and Post Traders*, pp. 189–92.

15. D. L. Pratt Jr. to Commanding Officer, Fort Randall, April 16, 1892, with endorsements, NA, RG 393, Entry 19, Letters and Telegrams Received, 1892, Fort Randall Orders Received, 1867–74, Miscellaneous Records, 1817–92.

16. *Report of the Secretary of War, 1892*, p. 58; Kenyon, "History of Fort Randall," pp. 118–19.

17. Captain William H. Boyle to AAG, Department of the Platte, January 2, 1892, NA, RG 393, Entry 19, Letters and Telegrams Received, 1892, Fort Randall Orders Received, 1867–74, Miscellaneous Records, 1817–92.

18. *Report of the Secretary of War, 1890*, p. 191; Medical History, February 1890; "Report of Scouts by 1st Lieut. A. R. Paxton, 2nd Lieut. W. N. Blow, and 2nd Lieut. R. C. Williams, 15th Infantry," n.d., NA, RG 393, Entry 19, Letters and Telegrams Received 1892, Fort Randall Orders Received, 1867–74, Miscellaneous Records, 1817–92; Mattison, "Report on Historic Sites," p. 94.

19. "Memorandum of the views of the Division Commander in regard to operations in the field against hostiles," November 24, 1890, NA, RG 393, Entry 6, Letters and Telegrams Received, Fort Randall, S.D., Box 9; Utley, *Frontier Regulars*, p. 403.

20. AAG, Department of Dakota, to Commanding Officer, Fort Randall, December 9, 1890, and Indian Agent J. George Wright to Conrad, Decem-

ber 19, 1890, both in NA, RG 393, Entry 6, Letters and Telegrams Received, Fort Randall, S.D., Box 9; *Army and Navy Journal*, December 27, 1890. Between December 3 and 11, 1890, six soldiers from Company C, Fifteenth Infantry, at Fort Randall, escorted seventeen Indian prisoners from Chamberlain, South Dakota, to Fort Snelling, Minnesota. Post Returns, December 1890.

21. Orders No. 69, September 5, 1891, citing Special Order No. 102, Headquarters, Department of the Platte, September 1, 1892, Orders No. 74, June 17, 1892, and No. 106, October 9, 1892, all three Headquarters, Fort Randall, NA, RG 393, Part 5, Entry 10, Vol. 4, Fort Randall, S.D.; Boyle to AAG, Department of the Platte, March 5, 1892, NA, RG 393, Entry 19, Letters and Telegrams Received, 1892, Fort Randall Orders Received, 1867–74, Miscellaneous Records, 1817–92; Medical History, September 1891; Moran, "Reminiscences," p. 287. General Order No. 28 is reproduced in *The Indian as a Soldier at Fort Custer, Montana, 1890–1895*, comp., ed. Richard Upton (El Segundo, Calif.: Upton and Sons, 1983), pp. 121–22. The most thorough exposition of the enlistment of Indians appears in Robert Lee, "Warriors in Ranks: American Indian Units in the Regular Army, 1891–1897," *South Dakota History* 21 (Fall 1991): 263–316, but see also Byron Price, "The Utopian Experiment: The U.S. Army and the Indian, 1890–1897," *By Valor & Arms: The Journal of American Military History* 3, no. 1: 15–35; Jack D. Foner, *The United States Soldier between Two Wars: Army Life and Reform, 1865–1898* (New York: Humanities Press, 1970), pp. 129–31; William H. Powell, "The Indian as a Soldier," *United Service* 3 (March 1890): 229–38; and Edward M. Coffman, *The Old Army: A Portrait of the American Army in Peacetime, 1784–1898* (New York: Oxford University Press, 1986), pp. 259–61. There were twenty-one Yanktons, fourteen Brulés, one Sisseton Santee, and one Oglala in the unit. Lee, "Warriors in Ranks," p. 306 (a roster of individuals appears on pp. 307–8). One of the Indian enlistees, Private Charles Ree, accidentally shot himself while hunting on the Yankton Indian Reservation and died on August 22, 1892. Indian Agent E. W. Fortes to Seay, August 23, 1892, and Seay to Post Adjutant, August 25, 1892, both in NA, RG 393, Entry 19, Letters and Telegrams Received 1892, Fort Randall Orders Received, 1867–74, Miscellaneous Records, 1817–92. On the closing of Fort Randall in November 1892, Company I transferred to Fort Sidney, Nebraska, and in 1894 transferred to Fort Omaha, where in December its members were discharged. Lee, "Warriors in Ranks," pp. 306–7.

22. Gary S. Freedom, "'Forticide' Policies on the Northern Great Plains," *Periodical: Journal of America's Military Past* 19 (Fall 1992): 122–23; Orders No. 114, December 5, 1892, and No. 112, November 14, 1892, both Headquarters, Fort Randall, NA, RG 393, Part 5, Entry 10, Vol. 4. Fort Randall, S.D.; Medical History, October 1892; *Report of the Secretary of War, 1893* (Washington, D.C.: Government Printing Office, 1893), p. 131; Kenyon, "History of Fort Randall," p. 123, citing post return of November 1892.

23. General Orders No. 84, Headquarters of the Army, October 27, 1893, in *General Orders and Circulars, Adjutant General's Office, 1893* (Washington, D.C.: Government Printing Office, 1894); *Report of the Secretary of War, 1893*, p. 371, *1894*, pp. 63–64, 133, 254, *1895*, pp. 109, 111–12, *1898*, pp. 128–29, 150, 153, and *1899*, pp. 156, 158–59; U.S. Congress, *Fort Randall Military Reservation*, 52d Cong., 2nd sess., H. Report No. 2283; Green, "Administration of the Public Domain," p. 249. See especially the documentation in Kenyon, "History of Fort Randall," pp. 124–25, notes 44–47. The boundary realignment had occurred in 1882 when the forty-third parallel, comprising the southern boundary of Dakota Territory, was projected east from the Keya Paha River, its former terminus, to the Missouri River, thereby placing the southeastern corner of the Fort Randall Military Reservation in Nebraska. Stephen Sargent Visher, "The Boundaries of South Dakota," *South Dakota Historical Collections* 9 (1918): 383; Will G. Robinson, "South Dakota Boundaries," *South Dakota Historical Collections* 32 (1964): 248.

24. Schusky, *Forgotten Sioux*, pp. 147–48.

25. Moran, "Reminiscences," p. 290. Despite these Indians' belief to the contrary, there was no provision for turning over the abandoned fort to the Sioux.

26. Clipping, "Fort Randall's Decay," unidentified newspaper, 1895, Vertical Files, South Dakota State Historical Society.

27. *Report of the Secretary of War, 1893*, p. 382; Moran, "Reminiscences," p. 287–88; clipping, "Old Fort Randall," unidentified newspaper, ca. 1900, Vertical Files, South Dakota State Historical Society. Eight mostly civilian burials remained at the cemetery site as of 1946–48. See Mattes, "Report on Historic Sites," pp. 486–87, and Gnirk, *Missouri River Reveille*, pp. 46–47.

28. Clipping, "Fort Randall's Decay."

29. Clipping, "Old Fort Randall."

30. Moran, "Reminiscences," p. 291; Gnirk, *Missouri River Reveille*, p. 42.

31. *Tripp Ledger* (South Dakota), September 1922.

32. Clipping, "Aged Mayor of Gregory Pleads for the Preservation of Old Fort Randall Site," unidentified newspaper, ca. November 1925, Vertical Files, South Dakota State Historical Society. Reider's background is recounted in Gnirk, *Missouri River Reveille*, pp. 36–37.

33. Clipping, "Aged Mayor of Gregory Pleads for the Preservation of Old Fort Randall Site."

34. For the chapel, see ibid.; clipping, "Fort Randall's Decay"; clipping, "Missionary Tells History of Old 'Mystery Church' at Fort Randall," unidentified newspaper, Vertical Files, South Dakota State Historical Society; *Sioux Falls Argus-Leader*, March 28, 1928; *Mitchell (S.D.) Daily Republic*, November 21, 1939; Moran, "Reminiscences," p. 306; Robinson to U.S. Engineer, Omaha District, Corps of Engineers, September 10, 1955 (concerning post commissary sergeant quarters), Robinson to South Dakota State Historical Society Executive Committee, September 10, 1955, and Robinson to Governor Sigurd Anderson, all three in Vertical Files, South Dakota State Historical Society; Schell, *History of South Dakota*, pp. 324–6; Mills, *Historic Sites Archeology*, p. 33. Historic American Buildings Survey drawings of the chapel were prepared in 1947, and the Fort Randall Historic District was listed on the National Register of Historic Places in 1976. Condition monitoring of the Fort Randall chapel has been a continuing process. See Les Siroky, "Fort Randall Chapel Stabilization," November 1989, National Park Service, Denver, Colorado; Glenn H. Mannes, "Condition Report of the Fort Randall Chapel, Lake Francis Case, Pickstown, South Dakota," architect's report, November 1989, Yankton, South Dakota; and Mark A. Chavez, *Condition Assessment Report: Fort Randall Chapel Ruins* (Omaha, Neb.: National Park Service, 2003).

35. For additional archaeology related to Fort Randall, see Paul L. Cooper, "Preliminary Appraisal of the Archeological and Paleontological Resources of the Fort Randall Reservoir, South Dakota" (Washington, D.C.: Smithsonian Institution, River Basin Surveys, Missouri Valley Project, 1947); Robert B. Cumming Jr., "Appraisal of the Archeological and Paleontological Resources of the Fort Randall Reservoir, South Dakota: Supplement" (Washington, D.C.: Smithsonian Institution, River Basin Surveys, Missouri Valley Project, 1953); "Site Analysis of the Fort Randall Reservoir, South Dakota" (Lincoln, Neb.: National Park Service Midwest Archeological Center, 1953); Oscar L. Mallory, "Reappraisal of the Archeological Sites in the Fort Randall Reservoir, South Dakota: Supplement to the Appraisals of September 1947 and July 1953" (Wash-

ington, D.C.: Smithsonian Institution, River Basin Surveys, Missouri Valley Project, 1965); Adrien Hannus, Edward J. Lueck, and R. Peter Winham, *Cultural Resource Investigation of the Historic Fort Randall Post Cemetery, Gregory County, South Dakota*, Archeological Contract Series No. 20 (Sioux Falls, S.D.: Archeology Laboratory of the Center of Western Studies, Augustana College, 1986); "Evaluation and Reconstruction of the Fort Randall Post Cemetery in Gregory County, South Dakota," *South Dakota Archaeology* 12 (1988): 22–37; William B. Lees, "Archeology of the Subaltern's Quarters, Fort Randall (39GR15), South Dakota: Final Report on the 1987 Investigations," *South Dakota Archaeology* 15 (1991): 1–71; Holmes A. Semken, Cary Miller, and John Cordell, "Inventory of Identified Vertebrates Recovered from Fort Randall Historic Site, South Dakota (39GR15)," n.d., and "Fort Randall Military Post Historic Site Archeological Data Recovery Program," n.d., both in Fort Randall Project Office, Omaha District, U.S. Army Corps of Engineers, Pickstown, S.D.

Bibliography

MANUSCRIPT MATERIALS AND COLLECTIONS

Larry Ness Collection, private collection, Yankton, South Dakota

National Archives, Central Plains Region, Kansas City, Missouri
>   Record Group 75, Records of the Bureau of Indian Affairs

National Archives, Washington, D.C.
>   Record Group 75, Records of the Bureau of Indian Affairs
>   Record Group 77, Records of the Office of the Chief of Engineers
>   Record Group 92, Records of the Office of the Quartermaster General
>   Record Group 94, Records of the Adjutant General's Office
>   >   Microfilm Publication M617 (Post Returns)
>   >   Regimental Returns of the First Infantry, Microfilm Publication M665
>   >   Regimental Returns of the Twenty-second Infantry, Microfilm Publication M665
>   Record Group 159, Records of the Office of the Inspector General
>   Record Group 393, Records of United States Army Continental Commands

Nebraska State Historical Society, Manuscript Department, Lincoln
>   James Hervey Pratt Materials

Sioux City Public Museum, Sioux City, Iowa
>   O. B. Talley Collection

South Dakota State Historical Society, State Archives, Pierre
>   Fort Randall Quartermaster Papers
>   Sitting Bull Collection
>   Stanley J. Morrow Collection
>   Vertical Files

University of South Dakota, I. D. Weeks Library, Vermillion
>   Horace Austin Collection

U.S. Army Military History Institute, Manuscript Division, Carlisle Barracks, Pennsylvania
>   Civil War Miscellaneous Collection
>   Don Rickey Jr. Collection

Yale University, Yale University Library, Beinecke Rare Book and Manuscript Library, New Haven, Connecticut
>   Martin Lambert Collection

GOVERNMENT PUBLICATIONS AND REPORTS

Billings, John S. *Report on Barracks and Hospitals with Descriptions of Military Posts.* Circular No. 4, War Department, Surgeon General's Office, December 5, 1870. Reprint, New York: Sol Lewis, 1974.

————. *Report on Hygiene of the United States Army with Descriptions of Military Posts.* Circular No. 8, War Department, Surgeon General's Office, May 1, 1875. Reprint, New York: Sol Lewis, 1974.

Chavez, Mark A. *Condition Assessment Report: Fort Randall Chapel Ruins.* Omaha, Neb.: National Park Service, 2003.

Cooper, Paul L. "Preliminary Appraisal of the Archeological and Paleontological Resources of the Fort Randall Reservoir, South Dakota." Washington, D.C.: Smithsonian Institution, River Basin Surveys, Missouri Valley Project, 1947.

Cumming, Robert B., Jr. "Appraisal of the Archeological and Paleontological Resources of the Fort Randall Reservoir, South Dakota: Supplement." Washington, D.C.: Smithsonian Institution, River Basin Surveys, Missouri Valley Project, 1953.

"Fort Randall Military Post Historic Site Archeological Data Recovery Program." Omaha District, U.S. Army Corps of Engineers, n.d.

General Orders, War Department, Adjutant General's Office, 1873. Washington, D.C.: Government Printing Office, 1873.

General Orders and Circulars, Adjutant General's Office, 1893. Washington, D.C.: Government Printing Office, 1894.

Greene, Jerome A. *Reconnaissance Survey of Indian-U.S. Army Battlefields of the Northern Plains.* Denver: National Park Service, 1998.

Heitman, Francis B., comp. *Historical Register and Dictionary of the United States Army, from Its Organization, September 29, 1789, to March 2, 1903.* 2 vols. Washington, D.C.: Government Printing Office, 1903.

Hodge, Frederick W., ed. *Handbook of American Indians North of Mexico.* 2 parts. Washington, D.C.: Government Printing Office, 1910.

Index of General Orders, Adjutant General's Office, 1871. Washington, D.C.: Government Printing Office, 1872.

Index of General Orders, Adjutant General's Office, 1874. Washington, D.C.: Government Printing Office, 1875.

Index of General Orders, Adjutant General's Office, 1882. Washington, D.C.: Government Printing Office, 1883.

Index of General Orders and Circulars, Adjutant General's Office, 1884. Washington, D.C.: Government Printing Office, 1885.

Kappler, Charles J., comp., ed. *Indian Treaties, 1778–1883.* New York:

Interland, 1972. Reprint of vol. 2 of *Indian Affairs: Laws and Treaties*.
Washington, D.C.: Government Printing Office, 1904.

Mallory, Oscar L. "Reappraisal of the Archeological Sites in the Fort Randall
Reservoir, South Dakota: Supplement to the Appraisals of September
1947 and July 1953." Washington, D.C.: Smithsonian Institution, River
Basin Surveys, Missouri Valley Project, 1965.

Miller, Carl F. *The Excavation and Investigation of Fort Lookout Trading Post
(39LM57) in the Fort Randall Reservoir, South Dakota*. River Basin Survey
Papers, No. 17, Bureau of American Ethnology Bulletin 176.
Washington, D.C.: Government Printing Office, 1960.

Mills, John E. *Historic Sites Archeology in the Fort Randall Reservoir South
Dakota*. River Basin Survey Papers, No. 16. Washington, D.C.:
Government Printing Office, 1960.

Outline Descriptions of the Posts in the Military Division of the Missouri.
Chicago: Headquarters, Military Division of the Missouri, 1876. Reprint,
Fort Collins, Colo.: Old Army Press, 1972.

Regulations for the Army of the United States, 1857. New York: Harper and
Brothers, 1857.

Report of the Commissioner of Indian Affairs, 1878. Washington, D.C.:
Government Printing Office, 1878.

Report of the Secretary of the Interior, 1895. Washington, D.C.: Government
Printing Office, 1895.

Report of the Secretary of the Interior, 1898. Washington, D.C.: Government
Printing Office, 1898.

Report of the Secretary of the Interior, 1899. Washington, D.C.: Government
Printing Office, 1899.

Report of the Secretary of War, 1856. Washington, D.C.: A. O. P. Nicholson,
1857.

Report of the Secretary of War, 1857. Washington, D.C.: William A. Harris,
1857.

Report of the Secretary of War, 1858. Washington, D.C.: William A. Harris,
1859.

Report of the Secretary of War, 1860. Washington, D.C.: Government Printing
Office, 1860.

Report of the Secretary of War, 1861. Washington, D.C.: Government Printing
Office, 1861.

Report of the Secretary of War, 1863. Washington, D.C.: Government Printing
Office, 1863.

Report of the Secretary of War, 1867. Washington, D.C.: Government Printing Office, 1867.

Report of the Secretary of War, 1868. Washington, D.C.: Government Printing Office, 1868.

Report of the Secretary of War, 1869. Washington, D.C.: Government Printing Office, 1869.

Report of the Secretary of War, 1870. Washington, D.C.: Government Printing Office, 1870.

Report of the Secretary of War, 1871. Washington, D.C.: Government Printing Office, 1871.

Report of the Secretary of War, 1872. Washington, D.C.: Government Printing Office, 1872.

Report of the Secretary of War, 1873. Washington, D.C.: Government Printing Office, 1873.

Report of the Secretary of War, 1874. Washington, D.C.: Government Printing Office, 1874.

Report of the Secretary of War, 1875. Washington, D.C.: Government Printing Office, 1875.

Report of the Secretary of War, 1876. Washington, D.C.: Government Printing Office, 1876.

Report of the Secretary of War, 1877. Washington, D.C.: Government Printing Office, 1877.

Report of the Secretary of War, 1878. Washington, D.C.: Government Printing Office, 1878.

Report of the Secretary of War, 1879. Washington, D.C.: Government Printing Office, 1879.

Report of the Secretary of War, 1880. Washington, D.C.: Government Printing Office, 1880.

Report of the Secretary of War, 1881. Washington, D.C.: Government Printing Office, 1881.

Report of the Secretary of War, 1882. Washington, D.C.: Government Printing Office, 1882.

Report of the Secretary of War, 1883. Washington, D.C.: Government Printing Office, 1884.

Report of the Secretary of War, 1884. Washington, D.C.: Government Printing Office, 1884.

Report of the Secretary of War, 1885. Washington, D.C.: Government Printing Office, 1885.

Report of the Secretary of War, 1886. Washington, D.C.: Government Printing Office, 1886.

Report of the Secretary of War, 1887. Washington, D.C.: Government Printing Office, 1887.

Report of the Secretary of War, 1888. Washington, D.C.: Government Printing Office, 1888.

Report of the Secretary of War, 1889. Washington, D.C.: Government Printing Office, 1889.

Report of the Secretary of War, 1890. Washington, D.C.: Government Printing Office, 1890.

Report of the Secretary of War, 1891. Washington, D.C.: Government Printing Office, 1891.

Report of the Secretary of War, 1892. Washington, D.C.: Government Printing Office, 1892.

Report of the Secretary of War, 1893. Washington, D.C.: Government Printing Office, 1893.

Report of the Secretary of War, 1894. Washington, D.C.: Government Printing Office, 1894.

Report of the Secretary of War, 1895. Washington, D.C.: Government Printing Office, 1895.

Report of the Secretary of War, 1899. Washington, D.C.: Government Printing Office, 1899.

Revised Regulations for the Army of the United States, 1861. Philadelphia: J. B. Lippincott, 1861.

Roberts, Thomas P. *Report of a Reconnaissance of the Missouri River in 1872.* Washington, D.C.: Government Printing Office, 1872.

Semken, Holmes A., Cary Miller, and John Cordell. "Inventory of Identified Vertebrates Recovered from Fort Randall Historic Site, South Dakota (39GR15)," n.d. Fort Randall Project Office, Omaha District, U.S. Army Corps of Engineers, Pickstown, S.D.

Siroky, Les. "Fort Randall Chapel Stabilization," ca. 1980. National Park Service, Denver, Colo.

"Site Analysis of the Fort Randall Reservoir, South Dakota," 1953, National Park Service Midwest Archeological Center, Lincoln, Neb.

Sturtevant, William C., gen. ed. *Handbook of North American Indians.* Vol. 13, *Plains,* 2 Parts, ed. Raymond J. DeMallie. Washington, D.C.: Smithsonian Institution, 2001.

Thian, Raphael P., comp. *Notes Illustrating the Military Geography of the*

United States, 1813–1880. Washington, D.C.: Adjutant General's Office,
　　1881. Reprint, Austin: University of Texas Press, 1979.

U.S. Congress. House. *Claims of Settlers on Fort Randall Reservation.* 42nd
　　Cong., 3rd sess. H. Ex. Doc. No. 32, December 10, 1872.

U.S. Congress. House. *Fort Randall Military Reservation.* 47th Cong., 1st
　　sess. H. Report No. 846, March 24, 1882.

U.S. Congress. House. *Fort Randall Military Reservation, Dakota.* 48th
　　Cong., 1st sess. H. Report No. 201, February 5, 1884.

U.S. Congress. Senate. *In the Senate of the United States.* 47th Cong., 1st
　　sess. S. Report No. 628, May 23, 1882.

U.S. Congress. Senate. *Minutes of a council held at Fort Pierre, Nebraska
　　Territory, on the 1st day of March 1856, by Brevet Brigadier General
　　William S. Harney, United States army, commanding the Sioux expedition,
　　with the delegations from nine of the bands of Sioux.* 34th Cong., 1st sess. S.
　　Ex. Doc. No. 94., 1856.

U.S. Congress. Senate. *Report to Accompany Senate Bill 2931.* 52nd Cong., 1st
　　sess. S. Report No. 950.

U.S. Congress. Senate. *Report to Accompany Senate Bill 3206.* 52nd Cong., 1st
　　sess. S. Report No. 912, July 13, 1892.

*The War of the Rebellion: A Compilation of the Official Records of the Union
　　and Confederate Armies.* 70 vols. Washington, D.C.: Government
　　Printing Office, 1880–1902.

BOOKS

Adams, George Rollie. *General William S. Harney: Prince of Dragoons.*
　　Lincoln: University of Nebraska Press, 2001.

Armstrong, Moses K. *The Early Empire Builders of the Great West.* St. Paul,
　　Minn.: E. W. Porter, 1901.

Athearn, Robert G. *Forts of the Upper Missouri.* Englewood Cliffs, N.J.:
　　Prentice-Hall, 1967.

————. *William Tecumseh Sherman and the Settlement of the West.* Norman:
　　University of Oklahoma Press, 1956.

Barbour, Barton H. *Fort Union and the Upper Missouri Fur Trade.* Norman:
　　University of Oklahoma Press, 2001.

Barnett, Louise. *Ungentlemanly Acts: The Army's Notorious Incest Trial.* New
　　York: Hill and Wang, 2000.

Barton, Winifred W. *John P. Williamson: A Brother to the Sioux.* New York:
　　Fleming H. Revell, 1919.

Brodhead, Michael J. *A Soldier-Scientist in the American Southwest*. Tucson: Arizona Historical Society, 1973.

Butts, Michele Tucker. *Galvanized Yankees on the Upper Missouri: The Face of Loyalty*. Boulder: University Press of Colorado, 2003.

Cody, William F. *The Life of Hon. William F. Cody Known as Buffalo Bill the Famous Hunter, Scout, and Guide: An Autobiography*. Hartford, Conn.: Frank Bliss, 1879.

Coffman, Edward M. *The Old Army: A Portrait of the American Army in Peacetime, 1784–1898*. New York: Oxford University Press, 1986.

Coues, Elliott. *Field Ornithology*. Salem, Mass.: Naturalists' Agency, 1874.

Cox, John E. *Five Years in the Army*. Owensville, Ind.: privately published, 1892. Reprint, New York: Sol Lewis, 1973.

Delo, David M. *Peddlers and Post Traders: The Army Sutler on the Frontier*. Helena, Mont.: Kingfisher Books, 1998.

De Trobriand, Philippe Regis Denis de Keredern. *Military Life in Dakota: The Journal of Philippe Regis de Trobriand*. Trans., ed. Lucile M. Kane. St. Paul, Minn.: Alvord Memorial Association, 1951.

Diedrich, Mark, comp., ed. *Sitting Bull: The Collected Speeches*. Rochester, Minn.: Coyote Books, 1998.

Eales, Anne Bruner. *Army Wives on the American Frontier: Living by the Bugle*. Boulder, Colo.: Johnson Books, 1996.

Ellis, Richard N. *General Pope and U.S. Indian Policy*. Albuquerque: University of New Mexico Press, 1970.

————, ed. *The Western American Indian: Case Studies in Tribal History*. Lincoln: University of Nebraska Press, 1972.

Federal Writers' Project. *Nebraska: A Guide to the Cornhusker State*. New York: Viking Press, 1939.

Fleming, Paula Richardson, and Judith Luskey. *The North American Indian in Early Photographs*. New York: Harper and Row, 1986.

Foner, Jack. *The United States Soldier between Two Wars: Army Life and Reform, 1865–1898*. New York: Humanities Press, 1970.

Fowler, Arlen L. *The Black Infantry in the West, 1869–1891*. Norman: University of Oklahoma Press, 1996.

Frazer, Robert W. *Forts of the West*. Norman: University of Oklahoma Press, 1965.

Fritz, Henry E. *The Movement for Indian Assimilation, 1860–1890*. Philadelphia: University of Pennsylvania Press, 1963.

Frost, Lawrence A. *Custer's 7th Cav and the Campaign of 1873*. El Segundo, Calif.: Upton and Sons, 1986.

Gnirk, Adeline S. *Saga of the Missouri River Reveille*. Gregory, S.D.: Gregory Times-Advocate, 1981.

Goetzmann, William H. *Army Exploration in the American West, 1803–1863*. New Haven, Conn.: Yale University Press, 1959.

Gorgas, Marie D., and Burton J. Hendrick. *William Crawford Gorgas: His Life and Work*. New York: Doubleday, Page, 1924.

Greene, Jerome A. *Yellowstone Command: Colonel Nelson A. Miles and the Great Sioux War, 1876–1877*. Lincoln: University of Nebraska Press, 1991.

Hafen, LeRoy R., and Ann W. Hafen, comps. *Powder River Campaigns and Sawyers Expedition of 1865*. Glendale, Calif.: Arthur H. Clark, 1961.

Hassrick, Royal B. *The Sioux: Life and Customs of a Warrior Society*. Norman: University of Oklahoma Press, 1964.

Hedren, Paul L. *Sitting Bull's Surrender at Fort Buford: An Episode of American History*. Williston, N.D.: Fort Union Association, 1997.

Hutton, Paul A. *Phil Sheridan and His Army*. Lincoln: University of Nebraska Press, 1985.

Hyde, George E. *Red Cloud's Folk: A History of the Oglala Sioux*. Norman: University of Oklahoma Press, 1937.

———. *Spotted Tail's Folk: A History of the Brule Sioux*. Norman: University of Oklahoma Press, 1961.

Jennewein, J. Leonard, and Jane Boorman, eds. *Dakota Panorama*. Pierre, S.D.: Dakota Territory Centennial Commission, 1961.

Josephy, Alvin M., Jr. *The Civil War in the American West*. New York: Alfred A. Knopf, 1991.

Kingsbury, George W. *History of Dakota Territory*, with George Martin Smith, *South Dakota: Its History and Its People*. 5 vols. Chicago: S. J. Clarke, 1950.

Lamar, Howard Roberts. *Dakota Territory, 1861–1889: A Study of Frontier Politics*. New Haven, Conn.: Yale University Press, 1956.

Langellier, John P., and Bill Younghusband. *U.S. Dragoons, 1833–55*. London: Osprey Military, 1995.

Larson, Robert W. *Red Cloud: Warrior-Statesman of the Lakota Sioux*. Norman: University of Oklahoma Press, 1997.

Lee, Robert. *Fort Meade and the Black Hills*. Lincoln: University of Nebraska Press, 1991.

Mattison, Ray H. *The Army Post on the Northern Plains, 1865–1885*. Gering, Neb.: Oregon Trail Museum Association, 1956. Reprinted from *Nebraska History* 35 (March 1954).

McChristian, Douglas C. *The U.S. Army in the West, 1870–1880: Uniforms, Weapons, and Equipment*. Norman: University of Oklahoma Press, 1995.

McGinnis, Anthony. *Counting Coup and Cutting Horses: Intertribal Warfare on the Northern Plains, 1738–1889*. Evergreen, Colo.: Cordillera Press, 1990.

Meyer, Roy W. *History of the Santee Sioux: United States Indian Policy on Trial*. Lincoln: University of Nebraska Press, 1967.

Miles, Nelson A. *Personal Recollections of General Nelson A. Miles*. Chicago: Werner, 1896.

———. *Serving the Republic: Memoirs of the Civil and Military Life of Nelson A. Miles, Lieutenant-General, United States Army*. New York: Harper and Brothers, 1911.

Mills, Anson. *My Story*. Washington, D.C.: Byron S. Adams, 1918.

Moore, John H. *The Cheyenne Nation: A Social and Demographic History*. Lincoln: University of Nebraska Press, 1987.

Morris, Richard B., and Jeffrey B. Morris, eds. *Encyclopedia of American History: Bicentennial Edition*. New York: Harper and Row, 1976.

Mulhair, Charles. *Ponca Agency*. Niobrara, Neb.: privately published, 1992.

Myers, Frank. *Soldiering in Dakota, Among the Indians, in 1863–4–5*. Huron, D.T.: Huronite Printing House, 1888. Reprint, Pierre, S.D.: South Dakota State Historical Society, 1936.

Nankivell, John H., comp., ed. *The History of the Twenty-fifth Regiment United States Infantry, 1869–1926*. Reprint, Fort Collins, Colo.: Old Army Press, 1972.

Nester, William R. *The Arikara War: The First Plains Indian War*. Missoula, Mont.: Mountain Press, 2001.

Olson, James C. *Red Cloud and the Sioux Problem*. Lincoln: University of Nebraska Press, 1965.

Parker, Watson. *Gold in the Black Hills*. Norman: University of Oklahoma Press, 1966. Reprint, Pierre: South Dakota State Historical Society Press, 2003.

Paul, R. Eli. *Blue Water Creek and the First Sioux War*. Norman: University of Oklahoma Press, 2004.

Poole, DeWitt C. *Among the Sioux of Dakota: Eighteen Months Experience as an Indian Agent*. New York: D. Van Nostrand, 1881.

Rickey, Don, Jr. *Forty Miles a Day on Beans and Hay: The Enlisted Soldier Fighting the Indian Wars*. Norman: University of Oklahoma Press, 1963.

Robinson, Doane, comp. *Doane Robinson's Encyclopedia of South Dakota*. Pierre, S.D.: by the author, 1925.

Robinson, Willard B. *American Forts: Architectural Form and Function.* Urbana: University of Illinois Press, 1977.

Rodenbough, Theophilus F., and William L. Haskin, eds. *The Army of the United States: Historical Sketches of Staff and Line, with Portraits of Generals-in-Chief.* New York: Maynard, Merrill, 1896.

Schell, Herbert S. *History of South Dakota,* 4th ed., rev. John E. Miller. Pierre: South Dakota State Historical Society Press, 2004.

Schubert, Frank N., comp. *Voices of the Buffalo Soldier: Records, Reports, and Recollections of Military Life and Service in the West.* Albuquerque: University of New Mexico Press, 2003.

Shusky, Ernest L. *The Forgotten Sioux: An Ethnohistory of the Lower Brule Reservation.* Chicago: Nelson-Hall, 1975.

Stallard, Patricia Y. *Glittering Misery: Dependents of the Indian Fighting Army.* Fort Collins, Colo.: Old Army Press, 1978.

Steffen, Randy. *The Horse Soldier, 1776–1943.* 4 vols. Norman: University of Oklahoma Press, 1978.

Tate, Michael L. *The Frontier Army in the Settlement of the West.* Norman: University of Oklahoma Press, 1999.

Thrapp, Dan L. *Encyclopedia of Frontier Biography.* 3 vols. Glendale, Calif.: Arthur H. Clark, 1988.

Tibbles, Thomas Henry. *The Ponca Chiefs: An Indian's Attempt to Appeal from the Tomahawk to the Courts, a Full History of the Robbery of the Ponca Tribe of Indians.* Boston: Lockwood, Brooks. Reprinted as *The Ponca Chiefs: An Account of the Trial of Standing Bear.* Lincoln: University of Nebraska Press, 1972.

Turnley, Parmenas Taylor. *Reminiscences of Parmenas Taylor Turnley, from the Cradle to Three-Score and Ten.* Chicago: Donohue and Henneberry, 1893.

Upton, Richard, comp., ed. *The Indian as a Soldier at Fort Custer, Montana, 1890–1895.* El Segundo, Calif.: Upton and Sons, 1983.

Urwin, Gregory J. W. *The United States Infantry: An Illustrated History, 1775–1918.* London: Blandford Press, 1988.

U.S. Army Uniforms and Equipment, 1889, by the Quartermaster General. Lincoln: University of Nebraska Press, 1986.

Utley, Robert M. *Frontier Regulars: The United States Army and the Indian, 1866–1891.* New York: Macmillan, 1973.

———. *Frontiersmen in Blue: The United States Army and the Indian, 1848–1865.* New York: Macmillan, 1967.

———. *The Lance and the Shield: The Life and Times of Sitting Bull.* New York: Henry Holt, 1993.

Vestal, Stanley. *New Sources of Indian History, 1850–1891.* Norman: University of Oklahoma Press, 1934.

———. *Sitting Bull: Champion of the Sioux.* Norman: University of Oklahoma Press, 1957.

Wishart, David J. *An Unspeakable Sadness: The Dispossession of the Nebraska Indians.* Lincoln: University of Nebraska Press, 1994.

ARTICLES, THESES, AND REPORTS

Anderson, Grant K. "The Black Hills Exclusion Policy: Judicial Challenges." *Nebraska History* 58 (Spring 1977): 1–24.

Anderson, Harry H. "A History of the Cheyenne River Indian Agency and Its Military Post, Fort Bennett, 1865–1891." *South Dakota Historical Collections* 28 (1956): 300–551.

Armstrong, Moses K. "History of Dakota, Montana and Idaho." *South Dakota Historical Collections* 14 (1928): 9–70.

Arnold, Joseph Warren. "Joseph Warren Arnold's Journal of His Trip to and from Montana, 1864–1866." Ed. Charles W. Martin. *Nebraska History* 55 (Winter 1974): 273–314.

Bernson, Sara L., and Robert J. Eggers. "Black People in South Dakota History." *South Dakota History* 7 (Summer 1977): 241–70.

Blackburn, William Maxwell. "A History of Dakota." Ed. DeLorme W. Robinson. *South Dakota Historical Collections* 1 (1902): 41–83.

Briggs, Harold Edward. "Early History of Clay County." *South Dakota Historical Collections* 13 (1926): 69–157.

"The Census of 1860." *South Dakota Historical Collections* 10 (1920): 396–439.

Clow, Richmond L. "General William S. Harney on the Northern Plains." *South Dakota History* 16 (Fall 1986): 229–48.

Comfort, A. Ivins. "From the Missouri River to the Black Hills in Mid-Winter of 1874." In *War Papers Read before the Commandery of the State of Wisconsin, Military Order of the Loyal Legion of the United States,* pp. 249–58. Milwaukee: Burdick and Allen, 1903.

Cox, J. P. "Old Fort Randall." *The Westerners Brand Book* (Chicago), 8 (July 1951): 35.

Cox, John E. "Soldiering in Dakota Territory in the Seventies: A Communication." *North Dakota History* 6, no. 1 (1931): 63–81.

Cronau, Rudolf. "My Visit among the Hostile Dakota Indians and How They Became My Friends." *South Dakota Historical Collections* 22 (1946): 410–25.

Dunlay, Thomas W. "James Hervey Pratt: Frontier Entrepreneur." *Nebraska History* 59 (Summer 1978): 211–30.

English, A. M. "Dakota's First Soldiers: History of the First Dakota Cavalry, 1862–1865." *South Dakota Historical Collections* 9 (1918): 241–307.

"Evaluation and Reconstruction of the Fort Randall Post Cemetery in Gregory County, South Dakota." *South Dakota Archaeology* 12 (1988): 22–37.

Flanagan, Vincent J. "Gouverneur Kemble Warren, Explorer of the Nebraska Territory." *Nebraska History* 51 (Summer 1970): 171–98.

Fort Randall Independent (reenactor/hobbyist newsletter). 1992, 1993, 1994, 1996, 1998.

Freedom, Gary S. "'Forticide' Policies on the Northern Great Plains." *Periodical: Journal of America's Military Past* 19 (Fall 1992): 118–27.

"General Warren in South Dakota." *South Dakota Historical Collections* 11 (1922): 58–139.

Gilchrist, Leonard W. "The Missouri River Journal of Leonard W. Gilchrist, 1866." Ed. James E. Potter. *Nebraska History* 58 (Fall 1977): 267–300.

Goodyear, Frank. "The Narratives of Sitting Bull's Surrender: Bailey, Dix, and Mead's Photographic Western." In *Dressing in Feathers: The Construction of the Indian in American Popular Culture*, ed. S. Elizabeth Bird, pp. 29–43. Boulder, Colo.: Westview Press, 1996.

Green, Charles L. "The Administration of the Public Domain in South Dakota." *South Dakota Historical Collections* 20 (1940): 7–280.

Greene, Jerome A. "The Sioux Land Commission of 1889: Prelude to Wounded Knee." *South Dakota History* 1 (Winter 1970): 41–72.

Hannus, L. Adrien, Edward J. Lueck, and R. Peter Winham. *Cultural Resource Investigation of the Historic Fort Randall Post Cemetery, Gregory County, South Dakota*. Archeological Contract Series No. 20. Sioux Falls, S.D.: Archeology Laboratory of the Center for Western Studies, Augustana College, 1986.

Hanson, Charles E. "The Fort Pierre–Fort Laramie Trail." *Museum of the Fur Trade Quarterly* 1 (Summer 1965): 3–7.

Hanson, James A. "A Forgotten Fur Trade Trail." *Nebraska History* 68 (Spring 1987): 2–9.

Howell, Charles W. "An Army Engineer on the Missouri in 1867." Ed. Leland R. Johnson. *Nebraska History* 53 (Summer 1972): 253–91.

Jackson, Brenda. "Holding Down the Fort: A History of Dakota Territory's Fort Randall." *South Dakota History* 32 (Spring 2002): 1–27.

"Journal of Dr. Elias J. Marsh: Account of a Steamboat Trip on the Missouri River, May–August 1859." *South Dakota Historical Review* 1 (January 1936): 79–123.

Kenyon, Carlton W. "History of Fort Randall." Master's thesis, University of South Dakota, 1947.

Lee, Robert. "Warriors in Ranks: American Indian Units in the Regular Army, 1891–97." *South Dakota History* 21 (Fall 1991): 263–316.

Lees, William B. "Archeology of the Subaltern's Quarters, Fort Randall (39GR15), South Dakota: Final Report of the 1987 Investigations." *South Dakota Archaeology* 15 (1991): 1–71.

Lester, Gurdon P. "A Round Trip to the Montana Mines: The 1866 Travel Journal of Gurdon P. Lester." Ed. Charles W. Martin. *Nebraska History*, 46 (December 1965): 273–313.

Lotze, Marie Louise. "How South Dakota Became a State." *South Dakota Historical Collections* 14 (1928): 467–84.

"Lyman County." *South Dakota Historical Collections* 12 (1924): 249–57.

Mannes, Glenn H. "Condition Report of the Fort Randall Chapel, Lake Francis Case, Pickstown, South Dakota." Architect's report, November 1989, Yankton, S.D.

Mattes, Merrill J. "Report on Historic Sites in the Fort Randall Reservoir Area, Missouri River, South Dakota." *South Dakota Historical Collections* 24 (1949): 470–577.

Mattison, Ray H., ed. "The Harney Expedition against the Sioux: The Journal of Capt. John B. S. Todd." *Nebraska History* 43 (June 1962): 89–130.

———. "Report on Historic Sites Adjacent to the Missouri River, between the Big Sioux River and Fort Randall Dam, Including Those in the Gavins Point Reservoir Area." *South Dakota Historical Collections* 28 (1956): 22–98.

———. "Report on the Historic Sites in the Big Bend Reservoir Area, Missouri River, South Dakota." *South Dakota Historical Collections* 31 (1962): 243–86.

McLaird, James D., and Lesta V. Turchen. "Exploring the Black Hills, 1855–1875: Reports of the Government Expeditions." *South Dakota History* 3 (Fall 1973): 359–89.

Meyer, Roy W. "The Establishment of the Santee Reservation, 1866–1869." *Nebraska History* 45 (March 1964): 59–98.

Meyers, Augustus. "Dakota in the Fifties." *South Dakota Historical Collections* 10 (1920): 130–94.

Moran, Denny. "Denny Moran's Reminiscences of Ft. Randall." *South Dakota Historical Collections* 23 (1947): 266–306.

"The Mystery Church." *South Dakota Historical Collections* 12 (1924): 187–88.

Nichols, Roger. "Backdrop for Disaster: Causes of the Arikara War of 1823." *South Dakota History* 14 (Summer 1984): 93–113.

Nowak, Timothy R. "From Fort Pierre to Fort Randall: The Army's First Use of Portable Cottages." *South Dakota History* 32 (Summer 2002): 95–116.

"Official Correspondence Pertaining to the War of the Outbreak, 1862–1865." *South Dakota Historical Collections* 31 (1962): 469–563.

"Official Correspondence Pertaining to the War of the Outbreak, 1862–1865." *South Dakota Historical Collections* 8 (1916): 100–588.

"Official Correspondence Relating to Fort Pierre." *South Dakota Historical Collections* 1 (1902): 381–440.

"Old South Dakota Trails." *South Dakota Historical Collections* 14 (1924): 149–55.

Palais, Hyman. "South Dakota Stage and Wagon Roads." *South Dakota Historical Collections* 25 (1950): 212–64.

Parker, Watson. "The Majors and the Miners: The Role of the U.S. Army in the Black Hills Gold Rush." *Journal of the West* 11 (January 1972): 99–113.

———, ed. "The Report of Captain John Mix of a Scout to the Black Hills, March–April 1875." *South Dakota History* 7 (Fall 1977): 385–401.

Pattee, John. "Dakota Campaigns." *South Dakota Historical Collections* 5 (1910): 275–329.

Poriss, Ralph G. "Lambert's Letters from the Dakota Territory." *McKeel's Weekly Stamp Newspaper*, August 16, 1996, pp. 5, 27.

Powell, William H. "The Indian as a Soldier." *United Service* 3 (March 1890): 229–38.

Price, Byron. "The Utopian Experiment: The U.S. Army and the Indian, 1890–1897." *By Valor & Arms: The Journal of American Military History* 3, no. 1: 15–35.

Roberts, R. Jay. "History of Agate Springs." *Nebraska History* 47 (September 1966): 265–94.

Robinson, Doane. "Before the Settlers Came." *South Dakota Historical Collections* 12 (1924): 189–97.

Robinson, Will G., comp. "Digest of Reports of the Commissioners of Indian Affairs—1853–1869." *South Dakota Historical Collections* 27 (1954): 160–515.

———, comp. "Digest of the Reports of the Commissioners of Indian Affairs as Pertains to Dakota Indians, 1869–1872." *South Dakota Report and Historical Collections* 28 (1956): 179–344.

———. "South Dakota Boundaries." *South Dakota Historical Collections* 32 (1964): 232–59.

Rowen, Richard D., ed. "The Second Nebraska's Campaign against the Sioux." *Nebraska History* 44 (March 1963): 3–52.

Sievers, Michael A. "Westward by Indian Treaty: The Upper Missouri Example." *Nebraska History* 56 (Spring 1975): 7–108.

"The Sitting Bull Collection." *South Dakota History* 5 (Summer 1975): 245–65.

Taft, Robert. "The Pictorial Record of the Old West: II. W. J. Hays." *Kansas Historical Quarterly* 14 (May 1946): 144–65.

Visher, Stephen Sargent. "The Boundaries of South Dakota." *South Dakota Historical Collections* 9 (1918): 380–85.

White, Richard. "The Winning of the West: The Expansion of the Western Sioux in the Eighteenth and Nineteenth Centuries." *Journal of American History* 65 (September 1978): 319–43.

Wilson, Frederick T. "Fort Pierre and Its Neighbors." *South Dakota Historical Collections* 1 (1902): 261–379.

NEWSPAPERS

Army and Navy Journal, 1867, 1871, 1879, 1880, 1881, 1882, 1885, 1888, 1889, 1890

Daily Press and Dakotaian (Yankton), 1876

Daily Republic (Mitchell, S.D.), 1939

Dakota Union (Yankton), 1864

Dakotian (Yankton), 1863, 1864

Independent (Fort Randall), 1865, 1866

Sioux City Daily Journal, 1870, 1871

Sioux City Daily Times, 1869

Sioux City Eagle, 1857, 1858, 1859

Sioux City Register, 1859, 1861

Sioux City Times, 1860, 1869, 1870, 1871

Sioux Falls Argus-Leader, 1928, 1963

Union and Dakotian (Yankton), 1864, 1865, 1866, 1867, 1868, 1869
Weekly Dakotian (Yankton), 1861, 1862, 1863, 1864, 1866
Winners of the West, 1926
Yankton Press, 1870, 1872

Index

[page numbers in italics indicate illustrations]

Northern Pacific Railroad, 114
Northwestern Indian Commission, 97–98

O'Beirne, Richard F., 127, 130, 166
O'Fallon, Benjamin, 5
O'Fallon's Creek, 114
O'Hara, James, 110
Oglala Indians, 22. *See also* Lakota Indians; Pine Ridge Agency
Omaha, 35
Omaha Indians, 2, 25–26, 97, 122, 143
Omnibus Bill, 148
One Bull (Sioux Indian), 141, *153*, *158*
Order of Good Templars. *See* Independent Order of Good Templars
Orders: General No. 15, 121; General No. 28, 171, Special No. 54, 147
Oregon Trail, 7–8
Otis, Elwell S., 90–92, 106, 120

Pague, Samuel S., 72
Paige, George H., 12
Pattee, John, 35–37, 39–40, 46, 48, 81–82
Pawnee Indians, 2, 25–26
Paxton, Alexis R., 170
Peace Policy, 5, 97, 104, 119, 213n.27
Picotte, Charles, 24
Pierre Choteau Jr. and Company, 4
Pine Ridge Agency, 122, 143, 146
Pine Ridge Indian Reservation, 170
Pinney, George M., 40
Pitcher, Thomas G., 106
Platte Creek, 40, 42
Platte River, 30, 80
Pollock, Samuel N., 41, 42–43, 47–50, 209n.23
Ponca Agency, 109, 114, 121–22
Ponca Creek, 32, 171
Ponca Indians, 2, 28, 45, 102, 119–

20; move to Oklahoma, 121–22, 125; reservation of, 26, 32, 36, 87, 97, 103, 120–22; and Santee Outbreak, 38–39; and Yankton Indians, 17, 22, 25–27
Poole, DeWitt C., 102
Pope, John, 34, 38, 43, 51, 82
Portable cottages, 9, 11, 12
Post Council of Administration, 17–18, 36, 47, 91, 95, 109, 167
Powder River, 114
Powell, Junius L., 168
Pratt Creek, 96
Pratt, D. L., Jr., 169
Pratt, James H., 110
Presbyterian church, 119
Proctor, Redfield, 171
Prostitution, 28, 36, 105–6, 113, 137
Punishments, military, 18

Quartermaster's office, 9, 12, 15–16, 65, *66*, 130, 141, 172
Quimby, H. Baxter, 136

Railroads, 165; and army posts, 2, 125–26. *See also* individual railroads by name
Randall, Daniel, 11, 195n.15
Raynolds, William F., 20
Red Cloud (Sioux Indian), 98, 100, 122, 214n.30
Red Cloud Agency, 100, 114, 116
Redfield, Alexander H., 27–29
Reider, Gustave, 175
Reunion Creek, 116
Roads: 16, 29–32, 87–88, 109; "dug way," 31–32; to Fort Laramie, 20, 29, 31, 89; Fort Randall Military, 29–30; Great Platte River, 7; to gold fields; 31, 96, 99, 119; military, 30, 130; Sioux City and Big Cheyenne, 31, 96

Sutler, 14, 17, 95–96, 169. *See also* Todd, John B. S.; trader, post
Swaine, Peter T., 72, 126–27
Swift Bear (Sioux Indian), 171
Swimming pool, 130, 168, 174

Tackett, G. L., 47
Tackett Station, 42
Tannat, Thomas R., 35
Telegraph lines, 109, 125, 127
Terry, Alfred H., 87, 96, 112, 115, 118, 133
Teton River, 9
Theaker, Hugh A., 127, 138
Thompson, Clark W., 41
Thompson, Mrs. T. J., 175
Todd, John B. S., 18, 24, 30, 32, 35, 40, 196n.28, 203n.8; as sutler, 15, 17, 36, 95
Took Their Guns (Sioux Indian), 141
Topographical engineers, 9, 20
Trader, post, 110–11, 169. *See also* Sutler
Trask, Eugene F., 42, 85
Treaties, 5–6, 11, 23, 26, 97; Fort Laramie, 8, 23, 97, 99, 103, 105, 115, 121; Fort Sully, 98; Yankton, 24
Truteau, Jean Baptiste, 2–3
Turnley, Parmenas, 9, 12, 88
Twenty-second U.S. Infantry Temperance Association, 111
Twilight, 27
Two Kettle Indians. *See* Lakota Indians

Uniforms, army, 17, 75, 134, 136, 169, 198n.37
United States Army departments: Atlantic, Division of the, 106; Dakota, 87, 91, 148, 167; East, 165; First Military district of the Northwest, 42; Gulf, 117; Kansas, 34; Lakes, 106; Missouri, Military Division of the, 88, 119, 170; Northwest, 34, 49, 149; Platte, 88, 166, 169; Southeastern Dakota, District of, 90; Southern District of the Department of the Dakotas, 106; West, 34
United States Army regiments: Dakota Volunteer Cavalry, 35, 47, 203n.5; Eleventh Infantry, 119; Fifteenth Infantry, 71, 72, 126–28, 131, 135–36, 137, 147, 165–66, 170; Fifth Infantry, 118; First Dakota Cavalry, 36, 37, 40, 42, 45, 48, 50, 79; First Infantry, 106, 116, 118–19, 122–23, 126, 139; First U.S. Volunteers, 49; Forty-First Iowa Battalion Infantry, 79, Forty-First Iowa Volunteer Infantry, 39, 40, 42, 43; Fourteenth Infantry, 106; Fourteenth Iowa Volunteer Infantry, 35, 39, 79; Fourth Artillery, 9, 10, 19–20, 30, 34–35, 37; Fourth Infantry, 106; Fourth U.S. Volunteer Infantry, 90; Ninth Infantry, 115; Second Dragoons, 9, 10–12, 14, 19; Second Infantry, 9–12, 14, 19–20, 43; Second Nebraska Cavalry, 43, 47; Seventeenth Infantry, 115, 140; Seventh Cavalry, 106, 112, 114–15, 117, 119, 123; Seventh Iowa Volunteer Cavalry, 43, 45–46, 48–49, 90; Sixth Infantry, 9–10, 15, 115; Sixth Iowa Cavalry, 41, 43, 45–47, 49–51, 90; Sixth Iowa Infantry, 48; Tenth Cavalry, 133; Tenth Infantry, 9, 10, 19; Third Cavalry, 112, 116; Thirteenth Infantry, 90; Thirtieth Wisconsin Volunteer Infantry, 43–45, 49; Thirty-first

Infantry, 88; Twentieth Infantry, 114; Twenty-fifth Infantry, 70, 126, 132–33, 136–37, 144, 159; Twenty-First Infantry, 166, 169, 172; Twenty-second Infantry, 88, 90, 99, 102, 106, 112, 114–15, 118
Upper Missouri Land Company, 27
Upton's Infantry Tactics, 109, 129

Vermillion, D.T., 27, 29, 47, 50, 136
Vermillion River, 29

W. J. Behan, 147
Wahpekute Sioux, 22. *See also* Santee Indians
Wahpeton Indians, 22. *See also* Santee Indians
Walker, Fergus, 116–17
Walking Elk (Sioux Indian), 142
War of 1812, 3, 4, 23
Warren, Gouverneur K., 9, 20–21, 29, 30
Wau-kam-how-kah (Winnebago Indian), 47
Weapons, 81, 134–35. *See also* Arms and ammunition
Webb, Charles A., 90, 102–3
Weekly Dakotian, 42
Wekuthke (Winnebago Indian), 47
Well, artesian, 130
Wessels, Henry W., 9, 20, 27
Westward migration. *See* Settlers
Whetstone Agency, 99–100, 102, 114
Whisky, 123. *See also* Alcoholic beverages
Whistler, Joseph N. G., 90, 114, 127
White Clay Creek, 122
White Dog (Sioux Indian), 141

White River, 29
White Swan (Sioux Indian), 144
White Swan (town), 31, 42, 105, 111, 120, 136
Whitestone Hill, N.Dak., 45
Williams, Joseph L., 46
Williams, Robert C., 170
Williamson, John, 143, 146
Winnebago Indians, 41, 47, 84, 97
Wittich, Willis, 166
Women and children: at Fort Randall, 18–19, 44, 47, 75, 81; as captives, 40, 82–84, 138–39, 205n.31, 208n.22. *See also* Sitting Bull, band of
Wood Lake, Minn., 38, 81
Wounded Knee, 171

Yankton, D.T., 27, 29, 31, 40, 136, 165
Yankton Agency, 42, 47, 50, 105, 142, 143, 171; annuities, 36–37, 136, 140
Yankton Home Guards, 35
Yankton Indians, 2, 6, 7, 27, 28, 119–20, 125, 170; and Ponca Indians, 17, 22–25; and Santee Outbreak, 38–39, 81; and Sitting Bull, 141
Yankton Indian Reservation, 32, 87, 97, 131, 137, 165
Yanktonai Indians, 6, 48, 98
Yellow Breast (Sioux Indian), 172
Yellow Dog (Sioux Indian), 141
Yellow Medicine Creek, 122
Yellowstone Expeditions, 105, 114, 115
Yellowstone River, 49, 87, 114, 143